Presented to

_____

By

_____

Date

_____

Grace
for the Moment™
365 Devotions for Kids

MAX
LUCADO

ADAPTED BY TAMA FORTNER

A Division of Thomas Nelson Publishers

NASHVILLE   DALLAS   MEXICO CITY   RIO DE JANEIRO

Published in Nashville, Tennessee, by Tommy Nelson®. Tommy Nelson is a registered trademark of Thomas Nelson, Inc.

Tommy Nelson, Inc., titles may be purchased in bulk for educational, business, fund-raising, or sales promotional use. For information, please e-mail SpecialMarkets@ThomasNelson.com.

Cover design by Bruce DeRoos.

Library of Congress Cataloging-in-Publication Data

Fortner, Tama, 1969-
  Grace for the moment : 365 devotions for kids / Max Lucado ; adapted by Tama Fortner.
    p. cm.
  ISBN 978-1-4003-2034-9 (hardcover)
  1. Devotional calendars--Juvenile literature. I. Lucado, Max. Grace for the moment. II. Title.
  BV4870.F67 2012
  242'.62--dc23
                    2012008683

Printed in Italy
20 21 RTLO 15 14

For Valerie Taylor
You love kids, and we love you because you do!

Acknowledgments

This book has been carefully shepherded by Michelle Burke and Laura Minchew. My special appreciation goes to our student editors: Gibson Burke, Gabrielle Burke, Nicholas Burgess, Miranda Carpenter, Owen Di Giosia, Josiah Fredrickson, Phoebe Lovins, Kendalyn Lytle, Keaton Patrick, Shaeffer Quinn, Sheldon Quinn, Kendra Robinson, Skyler Russell, Arielle Sancinc, and their teacher, Mrs. Jo Fredrickson.

A Note from Max

Parents take care of their children. That's their job. They provide a home and food and clothes. They also give love and comfort. They teach right from wrong. That's what parents do.

And that's what God does too. He gives us what we need: hope and forgiveness and joy. He comforts our sadness. And, most important, He gives us grace.

Grace is God saying, "I know you've messed up, but I still love you anyway." Grace is when you tell God you're sorry and He says, "You're forgiven." One of my favorite Bible verses explains it like this: "Let us, then, feel free to come before God's throne. Here there is grace. And we can receive mercy and grace to help us when we need it" (Hebrews 4:16).

Did you see those last few words? "When we need it." Not too soon, not too late. Exactly when we need it.

Just as parents make sure their children have what they need, God will make sure you have what you need. From His own hand, your heavenly Father will give you exactly what you need.

And who knows? He just may use this book to do it.

MAX LUCADO

It's Up to You

A lot of things will happen today. Some good. Some not so good. You can't always choose what happens in your day. But you can choose how you think about it and what you do about it.

So before you even get out of bed, before all the busyness of the world barges in on you . . . *choose*. Choose to follow God this day. What does that mean? It means . . .

Choose love . . .
Love God—and love everything and everyone God loves.

Choose joy . . .
Smile. Look for things to be happy about. See a problem as a chance to let God help you.

Choose peace . . .
Forgive others because God forgives you.

Choose patience . . .
Instead of being angry at having to wait, thank God for a time to pray.

Choose kindness . . .
Be kind to everyone around you because God is kind to you.

Choose goodness . . .
Do the right thing—even when it isn't easy,
and even when no one else is.

Choose faithfulness . . .
Keep your promises. Be a true friend.

Choose gentleness . . .
Let the things you do and say build
others up, not tear them down.

Choose self-control . . .
When things don't go your way, remem-
ber God has a perfect plan for your life.

My Prayer for Today
Love, joy, peace, patience, kindness, goodness,
faithfulness, gentleness, and self-control—
that is what I will try to show today.
I pray, Lord, that You will help me.
When I mess up, please forgive my mistakes,
and cover me with Your grace.
And then, when this day is all done,
I will lay my head on my pillow
and rest.
Amen.

January

The Lord is kind and shows mercy.
He does not become angry quickly but is full of love.

—PSALM 145:8

God Listens

I pour out my problems to him.
I tell him my troubles.

—PSALM 142:2

You can talk to God because God listens. *Always.* What you have to say matters in heaven. He takes you very seriously. When you speak to God, He turns to hear your voice. No need to worry about being ignored. God never says, "Not right now."

Even if your words come out wrong . . . even if what you have to say doesn't seem important to anyone else, it's important to God, and He listens.

He listens in the morning and in the night . . . and even in math class. He listens to the joy of the ballplayer who makes the game-winning play . . . and to the tears of the one who didn't. He listens to the sadness of someone who is sick . . . and to the fears of someone facing the first day in a new school. When the lonely ask for a friend and the frightened ask for courage, God listens.

Very carefully.

Growing in Grace

Just as God listens to you, families and friends should listen to each other. When you take time to listen, you make others feel important. When someone wants to talk, don't say, "In a minute." Say, "I'm listening!"

God Chooses You

You are chosen people.

—1 PETER 2:9

Do you ever feel invisible? As if nobody even notices you? *Maybe some new clothes will get me noticed,* you think. And maybe they do. For a little while. But then the latest craze is yesterday's news, and you're back to . . . invisible. Want a change that lasts? Learn to see yourself as God sees you—covered with the "clothes of salvation" and wrapped in "a coat of goodness" (Isaiah 61:10).

Do you ever feel like a nobody? When you do, remember what you are really worth. Remember what—or rather who—God gave to save you: "You were bought with the precious blood of the death of Christ, who was like a pure and perfect lamb" (1 Peter 1:19).

If you ever start to feel invisible or left out, remember this: God *chooses* you to be His child. That can be hard to remember sometimes. So pray about it. Think about it. Let the way God sees you change the way you see yourself.

Growing in Grace

God chooses to see you as His wonderful creation. How do you choose to see your family and friends? They are each a wonderful creation of God. Your mom. Your dad. Even your sister and brother. Find something you love about each of your family members and friends—then tell them what it is.

Worry Doesn't Work

I was young, and now I am old.
But I have never seen the Lord leave good people helpless.

—PSALM 37:25

Do you ever worry? We all do. Maybe you worry about things such as *How will I do on the math test? Why is my best friend acting that way? Will my mom and dad be angry with me if I mess up?*

Some worries can be fixed with a little studying or even a heart-to-heart talk. But what about those worries that are too big for you—like thunderstorms, or sickness, or the terrible things you see on the news? You could spend your whole life worrying!

Honestly, do you think that's what God wants? God didn't send Jesus to save you just so you could worry. Jesus wasn't nailed to the cross just so He could ignore your prayers. Worrying can't fix anything, but God can. Trust Him with all those things you worry about. God has even "put his angels in charge of you" to "watch over you wherever you go" (Psalm 91:11).

Worry? I don't think so.

Growing in Grace

Got worries? Try this: Imagine putting your worries in a box. Wrap it up tight with string, and tie it with a big knot. Say a prayer and hand that box of worry over to God. Then relax—and trust God to take care of you!

God Lives Here

You know the Father. . . . The word of God lives in you.

—1 JOHN 2:14

Have you ever done any decorating in your room? Maybe you added a poster here. Put out a favorite collection there. Maybe you even got to pick the color for the walls. You added this and changed that until it looked like *you* lived there.

Well, God loves to decorate too. Actually, God *has* to decorate. Let Him live long enough in a heart, and that heart will begin to change. He'll move some forgiveness into that corner. He'll add some shelves and fill them up with His Word. It's not always pleasant though. You might feel a little uncomfortable when He knocks down that wall of jealousy or anger, but that new spirit of kindness He puts in will look and feel great. Then He'll paint your whole heart with love—love for Him and love for others.

God wants to give your heart a complete makeover. So He won't stop working until He's completely finished—until it looks just like *He* lives there.

Growing in Grace

Decorate your room with God's Word. Write favorite Bible verses on sticky notes. Then stick them by your light switch, above your pillow, or anywhere else you're sure to see them. God loves it when you make "room" for Him!

Don't Give Up

Is anything too hard for the Lord? No!

—GENESIS 18:14

Surprise! God does it again!

What did He do? He answered a prayer. That's what He does for those who believe in Him. But sometimes it's in the most surprising way! Look at what He did for these faithful folks....

Just when everyone said it was impossible, ninety-year-old Sarah had a baby (Genesis 17:17; 21:2). Just when no one else had the courage to even try, David took down a giant with just a stone (1 Samuel 17:50). And even though it didn't make sense, Joshua marched around Jericho, and the walls came tumbling down (Joshua 6).

What's the lesson for you? Just three words: Don't give up!

Do you think you've got a problem too big for God? A test too hard? A fear too scary? A friendship too broken? Keep praying! God is watching. And the God who surprised Sarah, David, and Joshua is already working on an answer to your prayers.

So don't give up. For if you do, you may miss the surprise!

Growing in Grace

To see God's surprising answers in your life, try this: Write your prayers on pieces of paper and tuck them in a special box. Every week or so, read over your prayers. Which ones has God already taken care of? Did any of His answers surprise you?

At Home with God

"If anyone loves me, then he will obey my teaching. My Father will love him, and we will come to him and make our home with him."

—JOHN 14:23

God wants to be your home. He doesn't just want to be the friend's house you visit or the clubhouse you hang out in sometimes. He doesn't want to be your vacation spot or even the place you hope to live someday when you're older.

He wants to be the place where you live all the time—starting right now. He wants to be the place that you come to for answers, for help, and for comfort. He wants to be your home.

For many people this is a new way of thinking. They only think of God as Someone to talk about or to pray to. He is just Someone they visit on Sundays or holidays. He is a miracle worker, not a *place* to live. But your Father wants to be much more. Your Father wants you to live with Him all the time (Acts 17:28). God wants to be the home that you carry with you wherever you go.

Growing in Grace

A snail takes his home with him wherever he goes. No matter where trouble strikes, he always has a safe house to climb inside. The next time you see a snail, think about how God wants to be the home that goes wherever you go. Be like the snail—just without the slime!

Be Brave!

I will not remember their sins anymore.

—HEBREWS 8:12

The Bible says that "those who are in Christ Jesus are not judged guilty" (Romans 8:1). It also says that God will "make right any person who has faith in Jesus" (3:26).

That is great news for God's children! Because sometimes, even when you *want* to do right, you do wrong. We all do. That's why God's promises are so wonderful! If you believe in Jesus and obey Him, God promises that your sins will all be taken away and that they will be hidden by Jesus. So when God looks at you, He doesn't see your sin; He sees the One who saves you—Jesus.

That means that you don't have to worry about messing up. You've already won because Jesus saves you. Trusting in that promise gives you the courage to try to do the right thing—even when you know you might mess up. Trusting in that promise lets you be brave.

Growing in Grace

Grab some friends and play a game of hide-and-seek. As you hide, remember how Jesus hides your sins and mistakes. And as you seek, remember how God promises never to seek for your forgiven sins!

Washed Clean

Then [Jesus] poured water into a bowl and
began to wash the followers' feet.

—JOHN 13:5

In Bible times, the roads were often made of dirt, so people's feet were caked with mud and dirt. Washing those feet was the yuckiest job around. It was a servant's job. But at the Last Supper, Jesus became the servant. He washed His followers' feet, the dirtiest part of them. And He will wash the dirtiest part of you . . . if you let Him.

Sin makes your heart even dirtier than those followers' feet. Jesus will wash away that dirt, but only if you *confess*—or tell Him—that you are dirty. Tell Him about that bad thought, that bad word, that thing you wish you hadn't done.

If you pretend your heart is clean—that you never mess up or sin—Jesus cannot wash you. You will never be clean until you first tell Him you are dirty. But if you just tell Him, He will wash all those sins away. He will wash you "whiter than snow" (Psalm 51:7).

Growing in Grace

The next time it rains, ask your parents if you can go outside and splash in the mud. Go ahead. Get dirty. Thank God for the rain that washes the earth. Then, as you clean off your feet to go inside, thank Him for Jesus, who washes away the dirt of sin.

Jesus Knows

When [Jesus] lived on earth, he was tempted in every way that we are, but he did not sin.

—HEBREWS 4:15

Some people might think, *Jesus, it's easy for You up there. You're in heaven. You just don't know how hard it is down here.* But those people would be wrong. The Bible says He "is able to understand" (Hebrews 4:15).

Jesus knows. He knows because He *Himself* left heaven and came to earth. He didn't send an angel or a messenger. And He didn't come as God. He made Himself completely human.

Do you ever feel angry, scared, or left out? Jesus did. Did you know that Jesus was once your age? He had parents to obey and brothers and sisters to get along with. He fell down, and He fell asleep. He went to school and played with friends. He was laughed at, and He was hurt.

Jesus knows everything you're going through. It's one of the reasons He came to earth—so He would know what it feels like. And so He could help you get through it.

Growing in Grace

Jesus can help you because He's "been there and done that." Is there someone you can help because you've been there and done that? Teach a younger child to catch a ball. Walk with a frightened preschooler to Bible class. Help your brother or sister study for a test.

Made for Heaven

"My kingdom is from another place."

—JOHN 18:36

Being unhappy here on earth makes you wish for heaven. You see, God uses your unhappiness to get your attention, to help you remember that heaven is waiting for you. How sad it would be if you settled for earth when the joy of heaven is waiting.

You won't ever feel completely happy and at home here on earth. You're not supposed to. It is not your home. First Peter 2:11 says, "You are like visitors and strangers in this world."

You see, God didn't make you for earth. He made you for heaven. Oh yes, you will have some happy times on earth. You will have times of joy. You will catch glimpses of God's light. You will laugh and love and be loved. But those happy times are just a taste of what heaven will be like. For in heaven, you will finally be home.

Growing in Grace

The best way to cheer yourself up is to cheer someone else up. High-five a friend who's having a bad day. Take out the trash for your tired teacher. Or just smile at the people you meet. They'll feel better and—before you know it—you will too.

God with You

"The Son of Man came to find lost people and save them."

—LUKE 19:10

Have you ever felt God with you? Because God is always with you. Oh, you won't be able to see Him standing right next to you in line or sitting behind you on the bus. But He is there—just in a different way.

God is there in the kindness of a stranger. In the beauty of the sunset. In the gentle word and the hug just when you need it. Do you see Him now?

God even gives us Himself. Through Jesus, He came to seek and to save *you*. Even when you choose your selfishness over His love, He still stays with you. He never forces you to believe in Him, but He also never leaves you. He goes with you wherever you go. And He will use all His power to help you see that He really is God, that He loves you, and that you can trust Him to lead you home to heaven.

Growing in Grace

God goes wherever you go. He shows Himself to you in both big ways and small ways. Be on the lookout for God today. Make a list of all the different ways you see Him in your world. And then thank Him for every one.

Serving Jesus

Martha became angry because she had so much work to do. . . . But the Lord answered her, . . . "Mary has chosen the right thing, and it will never be taken away from her."

—LUKE 10:40-42

Martha was a dear friend of Jesus. But the Bible tells us about a time when she was worried. She was having Jesus over for dinner. She was *really* going to be serving God! She wanted everything to be just right for Jesus. But she made one very big mistake. She was working so hard for Jesus that she let her work become more important than her Lord.

You see, Martha wanted Jesus to praise *her* for all her work. She forgot that she was supposed to be praising *Him* with her work. She forgot that the meal was to honor Jesus. What began as a way to serve Jesus turned into a way to serve herself.

It is important to serve Jesus. But don't serve Him just so that others will see you. Don't serve Him so that others will be pleased with you or say nice things about you. Remember—you are the servant, and He is the One to be served.

Growing in Grace

Want to make sure you are serving Jesus and not yourself? Serve in secret. Find something you can do—take out the trash, feed the dog, water the plants—but don't let anyone know you did it. Secret servants make God smile.

God Thinks of You

Pray and ask God for everything you need.
And when you pray, always give thanks.

—PHILIPPIANS 4:6

I n heaven, there is no difference between Sunday morning and Tuesday afternoon.

God wants to speak to you on the playground just as much as He does in the church. He wants your praise in the lunch-room as well as in the Sunday-school room. He listens to you just as hard in math class as He does in Bible class. You may go days without thinking of Him, but there's never a moment when He's not thinking of you.

Paul's goal was to "capture every thought and make it give up and obey Christ" (2 Corinthians 10:5). Make that your goal too. Tell yourself what to think. Think about good things, about God and His gifts.

"Never stop praying" (1 Thessalonians 5:17) and "let heaven fill your thoughts" (Colossians 3:2 TLB).

Growing in Grace

How can you worship God on Tuesdays, Thursdays, and every day in between? Thank Him for the first thing you see each morning. Praise Him for the last thing you see each night. Sing praises in the car. Pray for each friend on the playground. Make God a habit every day.

Just the Way You Are

In your lives you must think and act like Christ Jesus.

—PHILIPPIANS 2:5

One of the greatest truths about God is this: God loves you just the way you are . . . but He's still working on you. He wants you to be just like Jesus.

God cannot love you any more than He already does. If you think God would love you more if you never messed up, you're wrong. If you think He would love you more if you never had any bad thoughts, you're wrong. If you think He would love you more if you made straight As . . . if you were taller, shorter, faster, smarter . . . you're wrong.

Don't think God's love is like the love of people. Some people may love you more if you are good or love you less if you mess up. But not God. He loves you just the way you are. And because He loves you, He is still working on you. He wants to make you better. He wants you to be *just like Jesus.*

Growing in Grace

Want to be more like Jesus? Do what He would do. If a friend snaps at you, shrug it off. Dad have a bad day? Give him a hug and a "Thanks, Dad!" for his hard work. If your brother or sister says something mean, say something nice back. It's what Jesus would do.

God's Good Gifts

Every good action and every perfect gift is from God.

—JAMES 1:17

Do you ever look around and see all the things you wish you had? All the things you don't have but your friends do? If you find yourself doing this, stop and just look at all the gifts God has given you:

- God sent His angels to take care of you, His Holy Spirit to live inside you, His church to help you, and His Word to guide you.
- Every time you speak, He listens. Every time you pray, He answers.
- He will give you the strength to do the right thing even when it is hard.
- He will always be there to comfort you and help wipe away your tears.
- He always wants to see you.

But the very best gift of all? You have been chosen by Christ. You are a beloved child of God!

Growing in Grace

Some of God's greatest gifts are the special people He has placed in your life. Make a card for one of those people. Fill it with your best artwork. Then write this note inside:

You are a gift from God!

Waiting on God

"God's people cry to him night and day. God will always give them what is right, and he will not be slow to answer them."

—LUKE 18:7

God always answers your prayers. *Always.* Every single time. Sometimes He says yes. Sometimes He says no. And sometimes He says . . . wait.

Waiting is a hard thing to do. It's hard to wait for your turn. It's hard to wait for Christmas, and sometimes it's hard to wait for God. You may even start to think that He's not doing anything. But God is always working in your life. You may hear nothing, but He is speaking. You may see nothing, but He is there working. With God there are no accidents. He uses everything that happens to bring you closer to Him.

Why does God ask you to wait? That's a tough question to answer, but God's timing *is* always perfect. And He will *always* do what is right for you.

So keep praying. God will give you just the right answer at just the right time. That's a promise!

Growing in Grace

Everyone has to wait. In line. In traffic. In school. The next time you have to wait, give that time to God. Sing a song of praise. Practice saying a verse from His Word. Or count how many blessings you can see around you at that very moment.

A Coat of Goodness

You were all baptized into Christ, and so you were all clothed with Christ. This shows that you are all children of God.

—GALATIANS 3:26–27

Does Jesus care what clothes you wear?

Yes, He does! In fact, the Bible tells us exactly what kind of clothes God wants you to wear: "Clothe yourselves with the Lord Jesus Christ" (Romans 13:14).

God's kind of clothing has nothing to do with jeans or shirts or dresses. It is your spiritual clothing that He cares about. Listen to what Isaiah says about God's special clothing: "The Lord makes me very happy. . . . The Lord has covered me with clothes of salvation. He has covered me with a coat of goodness" (Isaiah 61:10).

When you believe in God, He gives you a heavenly "coat of goodness." You can only get this coat from God, and it is only for His children. Unlike your winter coat, you will never outgrow it, and it will never wear out.

God's "coat of goodness" is always a perfect fit.

Growing in Grace

Getting dressed isn't just about jeans and a shirt. Get your spiritual clothes on too. Pull on socks and ask God to help you walk in His way. Slip on your shirt and ask God to fill your heart with His love for others. Pop on a hat and ask God to fill your mind with good thoughts.

Planting Seeds of Kindness

Plant what is right. Then you will harvest
good things from your loyalty to me.

—HOSEA 10:12

Want to see a miracle? Plant a kind word in the heart of someone who is sad and hurting. Water it with a prayer and add a sunny smile—and then watch what happens.

Want to see some more miracles? Fix a snack for your mom or dad without being asked. Smile at your teacher just because. Give a friend a pat on the back when she's had a tough day. Draw something special for a person who is sick. Bring in the mail or the newspaper for an older neighbor. Offer to clean up even when it's not your turn.

Sowing seeds of kindness is like sowing beans. You don't know how they grow or why; you just know they do. And somehow that one little seed of kindness that you plant will grow into a whole garden of good deeds.

Never doubt the power of a seed.

Growing in Grace

Sow some flower seeds. Fill each cup of an egg carton with dirt. Poke a seed—like petunias or snapdragons—into each cup. Add a little water and sunshine. As they grow, think about how they started from tiny seeds. What do you think will grow from a seed of kindness?

The Lord's House

"I will be with you always."

—MATTHEW 28:20

David wasn't a perfect man, but he did try his best to do the things that would please God. That is why David was called a man after God's own heart (Acts 13:22 NKJV). In Psalm 27:4, David said, "I ask only one thing from the Lord. . . . Let me live in the Lord's house all my life."

What is this "Lord's house" that David is talking about? Is David talking about a real house? Is he wishing for a building with four walls and a door to come and go through? No. The Bible says that God "does not live in temples that men build" (Acts 17:24).

When David says, "I will live in the house of the Lord forever" (Psalm 23:6), he's not talking about a house like the one you live in. David is saying that he wants to live in the presence of God, wherever he goes.

The wonderful news is that when you love Jesus, He promises to be with you wherever you go!

Growing in Grace

Make a bracelet to remind you that Jesus goes wherever you go. Take three eighteen-inch pieces of yarn or colored string and knot them together at one end. Braid the strings together and tie the bracelet around your wrist. Then—just like Jesus—it will go wherever you go.

A World Without Sin

Then wolves will live in peace with lambs.
And leopards will lie down to rest with goats.

—ISAIAH 11:6

Can you imagine a world without any sin? Without bad guys? Without bad news? It would be so much easier to be good! Why? Because the sin that is in the world all around you can sometimes cause you to sin.

If someone pushes you, you might push back. Hearing other people grumble can lead you to grumble. Listening to the terrible stories on the news can make you worry. The selfishness in others can make you be selfish instead of sharing. It can make you walk away instead of stopping to help.

Because of sin, you've snapped at your best friend, argued with your brother or sister, and sassed your mom and dad. Sin breaks promises and breaks hearts. But in heaven all of this will end.

Can you imagine a world without sin? If so, then you can imagine heaven.

Growing in Grace

Pretend you are a reporter for the evening news. Sin has left the world. What will the world look like? What stories will you tell? What's the weather like? Any news from the hospitals or prisons? Record your newscast and share it with a friend.

God's Still Working on You!

We are like clay, and you are the potter.
Your hands made us all.
—ISAIAH 64:8

God wants you to be just like Jesus. He knows that you aren't like Him right now—but God's still working on you!

Isn't that good news? You aren't stuck being the way you are today. You may be grumpy right now. But you don't have to live in "Grumpsville" forever. You are fixable. And just because you're selfish today, that doesn't mean you have to be selfish for your whole life.

Who said you can't change your heart? And why do people say things like "I have a bad temper. That's just the way I am"? Would you say that if something were wrong with your body? "I have a broken leg. That's just the way I am." Of course not! You would get help.

So can you get help for your selfishness or your grumpiness? Of course you can! Jesus can change your heart. He will help you have a heart just like His.

Growing in Grace

Grab some Play-Doh and shape it into your favorite animal. Look carefully at your creation. Your fingerprints are all over it because you made it. Now look closely at yourself. Whose fingerprints do you see? God's! His fingerprints of love, kindness, and gentleness are all over you!

A Real Person

He remembered us when we were in trouble.
His love continues forever.

—PSALM 136:23

Jesus chose to come to earth in a human body . . . just like yours.

The mouth that called Lazarus out of the grave was human . . . just like your mouth. The hand that touched the leper had dirt under its nails. The feet that the woman washed with her tears were dusty. And His tears—yes, He had tears too—they came from a heart that was as broken as yours or mine has ever been.

Because Jesus was so human, people came to Him. My, how they came to Him. They came at night as Nicodemus did. They touched Him as He walked down the street. They followed Him around the sea. They invited Him into their homes and sat their children at His feet. Why? Because He refused to be an "I'm-better-than-you" superstar on a stage. Instead, He chose to be a real person who could be touched and known by people . . . just like you.

Growing in Grace

Jesus was a real person. He didn't pretend to be better than everyone else. Instead, He served everyone else. He talked to people no one else would talk to. He ate with and walked with people rejected by others. Think of a way you can be "real" like Jesus today.

Blessings at God's Table

You prepare a meal for me in front of my enemies.

—PSALM 23:5

Close your eyes and imagine God's royal dining room. What will it look like? How big will the table be? Who will be sitting there with you?

You are invited to sit at God's table. Not because of how good you are, but because you believe God's promises to take His children home to heaven. And you'll enjoy your special place forever, not just for a day. You'll take your seat next to all the other sinners who've obeyed God and been washed clean of their sins—people like Moses and David and Ruth. And you will all share in God's glory and His blessings.

Here are just some of the blessings that will be waiting for you at His table: All your sins will be forgotten (Romans 8:1). You will be a part of God's kingdom (Colossians 1:13). You will be a child of God (Romans 8:15). You can go to God at any time (Ephesians 2:18). God will never leave you (Hebrews 13:5). And . . . *these blessings will last forever* (1 Peter 1:4)!

Growing in Grace

As you sit down at your own table, thank God for the people sitting with you. Talk with them about the blessings you will find at God's table in heaven. Are there some people from the Bible you can't wait to meet?

Jesus Cares . . . Anyway

When he landed, he saw a great crowd waiting. Jesus felt
sorry for them. . . . So he taught them many things.

—MARK 6:34

Jesus had been teaching people for hours. He needed to get away from the crowds. He needed to rest and to relax with His friends. So He got in a boat and crossed over the Sea of Galilee.

But the people followed Him. When Jesus stepped out of the boat, He stepped into a sea of people. And Jesus felt sorry for them. His love for the people was greater than His need for rest.

Many of those He healed would never say, "Thank You," but He healed them anyway. Most just wanted to be healthy, not holy, but He healed them anyway. Some of those who asked for bread would cry for Him to be killed just a few months later, but He healed them anyway.

Jesus cared for them . . . anyway.

Growing in Grace

Choose to love and be kind . . . anyway. If someone cuts in line, let him go first anyway. If your friends want to play a game you don't like, play it anyway. When you don't want to obey your parents, do it anyway. Do the right thing . . . anyway.

Adopted by God

The Spirit himself joins with our spirits to
say that we are God's children.

—ROMANS 8:16

When you believe in Jesus, God not only forgives your sins, but He also adopts you. Through an amazing series of events, you go from being a hopeless sinner to a beloved child of God.

What does that mean? It means that when you mess up, when you do something that you know is wrong (and we all do sometimes!), you deserve to be punished. But God loves you so much that He created a plan to forgive you. That plan meant sending His own Son, Jesus, to die on the cross. Jesus was punished for your sins so that you don't have to be. You are forgiven! But the story doesn't end with God's forgiveness.

It would be enough if God just forgave your sins, but He does more. He adopts you and gives you *His* name.

Growing in Grace

Pick out someone you admire for the way he or she loves God. Ask if you can interview him or her about what it's like to be a child of God. What advice does that person have for you as you start your life as a child of God?

Guard Your Attitude

We pray that the Lord Jesus Christ himself and
God our Father will comfort you and strengthen
you in every good thing you do and say.

—2 THESSALONIANS 2:16

L ord, don't you care that my sister has left me alone to do all
the work?" (Luke 10:40).

Martha's life was busy. She needed a break.

"Martha, Martha, you are getting worried and upset about
too many things," Jesus said to her. "Only one thing is important. Mary has chosen the right thing, and it will never be taken
away from her" (Luke 10:41–42).

What had Mary chosen? She had chosen to sit at the feet of
Christ. You see, God is more pleased with your quiet attention
than with your whiny work.

The heart behind your work—why you do it—matters more
than what type of work you do. A bad attitude spoils the gift of
your work for God. But a good attitude makes heaven smile.

Growing in Grace

*Chores aren't always fun, but they are important. Yes, even taking
out the trash. Next time you find yourself whining about your work,
talk to God. Ask Him to help you get rid of your grumpiness and
serve the way Jesus did—with love in His heart.*

You're Something Special

Nothing . . . in the whole world will ever be able
to separate us from the love of God.

—ROMANS 8:39

How long will God love you?
Not just on Easter Sunday when your shoes are shined and your hair is fixed. Not just when you're happy and kind. Not just then. Everybody loves you then.

But how will God feel about you when you snap at everyone around you? When you have hateful thoughts? When you sass your parents? How does God feel about you then?

Can anything separate you from the love Jesus has for you?

God answered that question long before you even asked it. He answered it by lighting up the sky with a star. He answered it by waking the shepherds with the song of angels. He answered it by sending His one and only Son to be born in a stable in Bethlehem—to save you.

By sending Jesus to live and die on earth, God said to all people, "You're something special. Nothing can keep Me from loving you."

Growing in Grace

Bad days happen. They just do. Next time you're feeling rotten—or when you've been rotten—ask your mom if you can use a dry erase marker on the mirror. Look at yourself in the mirror and draw a big heart around your face. Then write "Jesus loves me—even today."

A Hunch and a Hope

"Dear woman, you are made well because you believed.
Go in peace. You will have no more suffering."

—MARK 5:34

Everyone messes up and makes mistakes. When you do, it can sometimes be hard to confess your sins—even to God. Maybe you're embarrassed. Maybe you're ashamed. Maybe you look at the people around you and think that they're all perfect. That their faith is perfect. That they never mess up. So you're afraid to tell God that you've messed up.

If that sounds like you, look carefully at one person Jesus praised for her faith. It wasn't the perfect person. It wasn't the never-messes-up person. It was a poor, sick outcast—a woman who had been bleeding for twelve years. But she had faith. She had a hunch that Jesus *could* help her and a hope that He *would* help her.

Which, by the way, is a pretty good definition of faith. *A belief that He can help and a hope that He will.*

Growing in Grace

What you think is a mess can be beautiful. It's all in how you look at it. Look at the back of a wool rug. What a mess! But look at the front. Just as the creator made something beautiful of the mess, your Creator—God—will make something beautiful out of even your biggest messes.

The Heart of Jesus

The wisdom that comes from God is . . . pure . . .
peaceful, gentle, and easy to please.

—JAMES 3:17

The heart of Jesus was pure. The Savior was adored by thousands, yet He was happy to live a simple life. He was surrounded by sinners and servants, yet He never looked down on them. The people He created wanted to kill Him, but He forgave them before they even asked.

Listen to those who knew Him best. Peter traveled with Jesus for three and a half years. He described Jesus as a "pure and perfect lamb" (1 Peter 1:19). John spent the same amount of time with Jesus. He said, "There is no sin in Christ" (1 John 3:5).

Jesus' heart was peaceful. The disciples worried over how to feed the thousands of people, but not Jesus. He thanked God for the problem. The disciples shouted with fear in the storm, but not Jesus. He slept through it. Peter drew his sword to fight the soldiers, but not Jesus. He lifted His hand to heal. Jesus' heart was at peace.

Growing in Grace

Is your heart filled with love and peace? Or worry and fear? Imagine your heart is hardened with worry and fear, like a giant rock. How would it feel to carry that rock around all the time? Exhausting! Now imagine your heart filled with love and peace—like air in a balloon. You'll "float" through your day!

Jesus Feels Our Hurts

He felt sorry for them.

—MATTHEW 14:14

The book of Matthew was first written in Greek. The Greek word for "felt sorry" is *splanchnizomai*. Since you probably haven't studied *splanchnizomai* in school, this word won't mean much to you. But what it means is "in the gut."

So when Matthew wrote that Jesus felt sorry for the people, he didn't mean that Jesus just felt a little sad for them. No, it is far more powerful. Matthew was saying that Jesus felt their hurt like a punch in the gut:

He felt the limp of the crippled.
He felt the hurt of the sick.
He felt the loneliness of the leper.
He felt the shame of the sinful.

And once Jesus felt their hurts, He couldn't help but heal their hurts.

Growing in Grace

Whom do you feel sorry for? Is it someone in your class who is always being teased? Is it the orphan from another country you see on TV? Is it someone who doesn't know Jesus? Don't just feel sorry for them. Ask Jesus to show you how you can help.

The Lord Is Peace

The peace that God gives is so great
that we cannot understand it.

—PHILIPPIANS 4:7

Gideon was hiding when the Lord came to him and told him to lead His people to defeat the mighty forces of the Midianites. That's like God telling the smallest kid in school to stand up to the biggest bully. Or a grandmother to take on a bank robber. Or to use a flyswatter on a rattlesnake! "Y-y-ou b-b-better get somebody else," we would say.

That's when God reminds us that He knows *we* can't do it. But He can. And to prove it, He gives us a wonderful gift—a spirit of peace. It's a peace that we can't understand. A peace that helps us do the right thing. God gave it to David after He showed him Goliath. God gave it to Saul after the road to Damascus. And God gave it to Jesus after He showed Him the cross.

God also gave it to Gideon. So Gideon gave the name to God. He built an altar and named it *Jehovah-shalom*, which means "The Lord Is Peace" (Judges 6:24).

Growing in Grace

Can you see the wind? Do you understand how it works? No, but you can know it is real by the way it moves the trees. God's peace is the same way. You can't see it or understand it, but you can know it is real by the way it moves people.

February

The Lord is close to everyone who prays to him,
to all who truly pray to him.

—PSALM 145:18

Garden of the Heart

A person harvests only what he plants.

—GALATIANS 6:7

For just a moment, think of your heart as a garden. Like any garden, your heart has to be planted with seeds and cared for. Think of your thoughts as the seeds. Some thoughts grow into flowers. Others grow into weeds. If you plant seeds of hope, you will grow love and joy. But if you plant seeds of fear and anger, you will grow worry, jealousy, and even hate.

The proof is everywhere you look. Ever wonder how some people seem to see the good in everything and everyone? Nothing bad ever sticks to them. They are always so patient, so cheerful, so forgiving. Could it be that they carefully planted seeds of hope in their hearts, and now they are enjoying the harvest of goodness?

Ever wonder why other people always have such a sour attitude? Why they always seem so grumpy or so sad? You would, too, if your heart were a garden of weeds and thorns.

Growing in Grace

Want to see the difference between a sunny attitude and a dark, gloomy one? Take two small plants. Place one in a sunny spot and the other in a dark closet. Watch what happens over the next couple of weeks. Is it better to live in a garden of light or in darkness?

God Among Us

"Shout and be glad, Jerusalem. I am coming,
and I will live among you," says the Lord.

—ZECHARIAH 2:10

God became a baby. As Jesus, He came into a world filled with problems and sadness. "The Word became a man and lived among us. . . . The Word was full of grace and truth" (John 1:14).

The important word in this verse is *among*. He lived "*among* us." Jesus stepped down out of heaven and into the body of a tiny baby. He made His throne out of a manger and His royal court out of some cows. He took a common name—*Jesus* (which back then was as ordinary as the name *John* today)—and made it holy. He took common people and gave them His holiness. He became a friend of the sinner and a brother of the poor.

He could have lived over us or away from us. But He didn't. He chose to live *among* us.

Growing in Grace

Offer to help in your church's nursery. As you play with the babies and help take care of them, notice how helpless they are. Then imagine—the God of all creation became one of these helpless babies. And He did it because He loves you!

Your Turn Is Coming

Continue the way you are now. Then no
one will take away your crown.

—REVELATION 3:11

Some of you have never won a prize in your life. Oh, maybe you got a ribbon at field day for participation. Maybe you even won a cheap toy at the balloon-pop game at the fair. But you've never won anything really big. You've watched the stars of this world carry home the trophies and the blue ribbons. All you have are "almosts" and "could-have-beens."

If that sounds like you, then you'll love this promise: "When Christ, the Head Shepherd, comes, you will get a crown. This crown will be glorious, and it will never lose its beauty" (1 Peter 5:4).

Your turn is coming! The world may not see how great you are, but your Father does. And sooner than you can imagine, you will be blessed by Him!

Growing in Grace

Make your own crown from poster board. Cut a piece long enough to wrap around your head. Decorate with markers and plastic gems; then staple the ends together. Remember that although this crown may not last, Jesus has promised you a crown that will last forever.

God's Help Is Near

The Lord is close to everyone who prays to
him, to all who truly pray to him.

—PSALM 145:18

When you are hurt, you need healing. And healing begins
when you *do* something. You tell your mom. You get a
Band-Aid. You go to the doctor.

When you sin, your heart is hurt and needs healing. And just
as you have to do something when your body is hurt, when your
heart is hurt, you also have to do something. Healing begins
when you reach out to God, when you tell Him how sorry you
are, and when you ask Him to forgive you.

God's help is always near, but He only gives it to those who
ask for it. Nothing comes from doing nothing. God helps those
who bravely reach out to Him and ask for help.

When Noah built the ark, lives were saved. When the soldiers marched, the walls of Jericho tumbled down. When Moses
raised his staff, the sea parted. It was true then, and it is true
now. God always stops to help those who call on Him.

Growing in Grace

*Sometimes God uses other people to help you. Who is always near
and waiting to help you? Parents? Friends? Teachers? Make a thank-
you card for someone who is always there to help you. Write in it:
"Thank you for letting God use you!"*

One Purpose

"The Son of Man did not come for other people
to serve him. He came to serve others. The Son of
Man came to give his life to save many people."

—MATTHEW 20:28

Jesus refused to let anything turn Him away from what He came to do. His heart was full of purpose—one purpose. Jesus' goal was to save people from their sins. His whole life could be described with one sentence: "The Son of Man came to find lost people and save them" (Luke 19:10). But He was not so busy working toward His goal that He was unpleasant to be around.

Just the opposite! Children couldn't resist Jesus. He found beauty in the lilies and joy in worshiping God. When His followers saw problems, Jesus saw possibilities. He would spend days with crowds of sick people and still feel sorry for them. He spent more than thirty years on this earth. He lived in a world full of sin and anger and hatred. Yet He still saw enough beauty in people to die for their mistakes and for ours.

Growing in Grace

Jesus was on a mission to save mankind. Many people today have joined Him in that mission. We call them missionaries. They go out into the world to teach people about Jesus. Pray for a missionary today. Then write a letter telling him or her that you did!

Questions

"God can do all things."

—MARK 10:27

The questions that we ask show the things that we do not understand. Maybe you have questions such as these:

How can God be everywhere at one time? *God does not live in a body like yours, so He can do things that your body cannot do.*

How can God hear all the prayers of all the people? *Maybe His ears are different from yours.*

How can God be the Father, the Son, *and* the Holy Spirit—all at once? *Could it be that the natural laws of heaven are different from those of earth?*

If people down here on earth won't forgive me, how could God ever forgive me? *God is always able to forgive—to give you His grace—even when people can't or won't. He can always give you His grace because He invented it.*

Growing in Grace

Do you have a question about God? Take it to your mom or dad, a teacher, preacher, or youth minister. Ask them to help you look through the Bible for an answer. God's Word is always the best place to look for answers!

Living with God

Lord, I love the Temple where you live.
It is where your greatness is.

—PSALM 26:8

If you could ask God for just one thing, what would it be? David told us what he would ask: "I ask only one thing from the Lord. This is what I want: Let me live in the Lord's house all my life. Let me see the Lord's beauty. Let me look around in his Temple. During danger he will keep me safe in his shelter. He will hide me in his Holy Tent. Or he will keep me safe on a high mountain" (Psalm 27:4–5).

David asked to live in "the Lord's house." Was he talking about a real house or about heaven? Neither. David was talking about living in the *presence* of God. David wanted to be so close to God that His presence covered and protected him just like the walls of a house.

David wasn't just asking for a visit with God. He didn't want to stop by for a chat or a glass of lemonade on the back porch. He didn't ask to spend an evening with God. He wanted to *live* with God, to move in with Him and have his own room ... forever.

Growing in Grace

Wish lists can be fun to make ... for Christmas or birthdays. But what would you wish for from God? Wisdom? Patience? Kindness? Gentleness? A home with Him? Make a list of blessings you would like, and pray about them. Now what do you think God would want from you?

Jesus Understands

He took our suffering on him and felt our pain for us.

—ISAIAH 53:4

Jesus knows how you feel.

Do you ever feel worried about your schoolwork? Jesus knows how you feel. Does it seem that you've got more stuff to do than one child could ever possibly do? So did He. Do people seem to want you to do more and more? Jesus understands.

Have your feelings been hurt? Are you ever sad or frightened? Jesus knows all about that. Does it sometimes seem that even your family isn't paying attention to you? That your friends have turned against you? Jesus knows how you feel.

You are precious to Him. So precious that He became a human just like you so that you would come to Him.

When you have problems, He listens. When you hurt, He answers. When you question, He hears. He has been there.

Growing In Grace

When you have a problem, it's always helpful to talk to a friend or parent who's faced that same problem before. They can show you answers you hadn't thought of. But even before you talk to them, talk to Jesus. He's faced that problem before too. And He, too, can show you answers you hadn't thought of.

A Letter of Joy

Be full of joy in the Lord always. I will say again, be full of joy.

—PHILIPPIANS 4:4

L et's go back in history a couple of thousand years. Let's go to Rome, to a shabby little room surrounded by high walls. Inside there is a man seated on the floor. He's an older fellow. His shoulders droop down, and his head is balding. Chains are on his hands and feet.

This is the apostle Paul. He once followed the will of God wherever it would take him. Now he is stuck in a run-down house and chained to a Roman soldier.

He is writing a letter. Is he writing to God to tell Him how badly he has been treated? Is he making a list of everything that is wrong? Paul has every reason to whine and complain. But he isn't. Instead, Paul is writing a letter to the Philippians that—even some two thousand years later—is known as the letter of joy.

What did Paul have to be so joyful about? It's simple. Paul knew that the sufferings he had were "nothing compared to the great glory" that would be his in heaven (Romans 8:18).

Growing in Grace

Pretend that you are like Paul and are writing a letter about your life. Will you complain about everything that is not going your way? Or will you write about all your blessings? Can you make your letter be a "letter of joy"?

Ready for Planting

He has taken our sins away from us as
far as the east is from west.

—PSALM 103:12

Before the farmer plants the seed, he gets the land ready. He removes the rocks and pulls out the stumps. He knows that seed grows better if the land is prepared.

Confession does for your soul what preparing the land does for the field. *Confession* is when you invite God to walk through your heart to make it ready for planting His fruit.

Your confession to God might sound something like this: "There is a big rock of selfishness over here, Father. I can't budge it. And over there is a stump of jealousy. Its roots are long and deep. And may I show you this soil that's too dry and crusty for seeds." God's seed grows better if the soil of the heart is cleared.

And so the Father and the Son walk the field of your heart together. They dig and pull, preparing your heart for God's holy fruit. Confession invites God to plant His love and grace in your heart.

Growing in Grace

When you confess, God removes your sins as far as east is from west. But how far is that? Grab a compass and ask a grown-up to go for a walk. Start walking east. Keep walking! Do you ever start going west? No! East never touches west! And confessed sins never touch you again!

A Feast of Kindness

Suppose a believer is rich enough to have all that he needs. He sees his brother in Christ who is poor and does not have what he needs. What if the believer does not help the poor brother? Then the believer does not have God's love in his heart.

—1 JOHN 3:17

Leo Tolstoy was a great Russian writer. He told a story of a time when he was walking down the street and passed a beggar. Tolstoy reached into his pocket to give the beggar some money, but his pocket was empty! Tolstoy turned to the man and said, "I'm sorry, my brother, but I have nothing to give you."

The beggar smiled and said, "You have given me more than I asked for. You have called me *brother*."

When you are surrounded by loving family and friends, a kind word may be just a crumb to you. But to those who are lonely and needing love, a kind word is like a feast.

Growing in Grace

Are there people you pretend not to see? The kid who is different? The new girl? The boy no one sits with at lunch? Share a little of your time and a few kind words with that person. Give a feast of kindness to someone today.

See What God Has Done!

The heavens tell the glory of God.

—PSALM 19:1

It is important to pray. But it's just as important to believe that God is in heaven and answers your prayers. To pray without believing makes your prayers weak. If you're having trouble believing, spend some time looking up at the sun, moon, and stars. They show the power and majesty of God. Just look and see the great things that He has done!

Think about the sun. Every square yard of it gives off the power of more than 450 car engines. And yet our sun—as powerful as it is—is just one small star out of the 100 billion stars that make up our Milky Way galaxy. Hold a dime in your fingers and stretch your arm toward the night sky. That small dime blocks over 15 million stars from your view!

By showing us the heavens, Jesus is showing us His Father's awesomeness. It's as if Jesus is tapping you on the shoulder and saying, "Your Father made all of that, so you can believe that He can take care of you."

Growing in Grace

Check out a book on constellations at the library. Then, on a clear night, take a blanket and lie out under the stars. Can you find the Big Dipper? The Little Dipper? The North Star? How many stars can you count? Remember, the God who knows each of those stars also knows you!

A Life of Adventure

"Whoever tries to keep his life will give up true life.
But whoever gives up his life will have true life."

—LUKE 17:33

Life is filled with excitement and wonder. Chase after it. Hunt for it. Give it all you've got. Don't tell yourself you're too young to make a difference. David didn't start out as a king—he was a shepherd and the youngest in his family. Samuel was just a boy when the Lord first spoke to him.

Jesus doesn't set an age limit on His workers. He never says, "When you're all grown up, come and follow Me." He says, "Follow me" (Matthew 9:9).

God has a plan for each and every day of your life—including this day. Ask Him to show you what it is. Take a chance. Dare to be different. Make a new friend. Try out for the team. Lead a song in Bible class. Run for class president. Volunteer to help. Sure, it could be risky. You might get laughed at. Or you might just make a difference!

Growing in Grace

Just because you are young doesn't mean you can't make a difference. Is there a problem in your school, town, or church that you could help fix? Collect socks for homeless kids. Sweep the snow from your church's sidewalks. Be a friend to someone who needs it.

Your Very Own Blessing

God will give everyone the praise he should get.

—1 CORINTHIANS 4:5

Wow! What an incredible sentence! *God will give everyone the praise he should get.*

God won't just praise "the best of them" or just "a few of them." God will praise *everyone!*

You won't be left out. God will see to that. In fact, God Himself will give the praise. When it comes to giving out praise, God doesn't give the job to someone else. Gabriel doesn't speak for God. Michael doesn't hand out the crowns. God Himself does the job. God Himself will praise His children.

And what's more, His praise is personal! Awards aren't given for a whole nation at a time, a church at a time, or a family at a time. The crowns of praise are given out one at a time. God Himself will look you in the eye and bless you with the words, "You did well. You are a good servant" (Matthew 25:23).

Nothing could be more amazing than that!

Growing in Grace

Tell God you love Him in an extra-special way. Ask your mom for permission to fill a spray bottle with water and some food coloring. Then spray a message of love in the snow. (No snow? Use sidewalk chalk to make an extra big and bright message of praise.)

Led by God

"The Son does whatever the Father does."

—JOHN 5:19

The greatest thing about Jesus was this: His heart was led by God. That means that His thoughts were always on God and how best to serve Him. This shows us how close He was to His Father. Jesus said, "I am in the Father and the Father is in me" (John 14:11).

Jesus took His instructions from God. It was His habit to go to worship (Luke 4:16) and to memorize Scripture (v. 4). Luke said that Jesus "often slipped away to other places to be alone so that he could pray" (5:16). His times of prayer allowed Him to hear God speaking to Him and leading Him. Jesus once returned from prayer and chose His disciples (6:12–13). After another time of prayer, Jesus told the disciples it was time to move to another city (Mark 1:38).

Jesus let Himself be led by God.

Growing in Grace

Practice being led by someone else with a "trust walk." Let yourself be blindfolded, and then have a friend lead you around the room. You must trust your friend to lead you—even though you can't see him. In the same way, you must trust God to lead you—even though you can't see Him.

A Holy Joy

"Those people who know they have great spiritual needs
are happy. The kingdom of heaven belongs to them."

—MATTHEW 5:3

God promises to give *holy joy* to His children. Not just everyday joy, but holy and everlasting joy. And He doesn't promise it just to the rich or the famous or the superstars. He promises it to the most unlikely people: those who know they have messed up and who beg for His forgiveness; those whose hearts are broken because of their sin; those who forgive others—even the people who have hurt them deeply; those who keep their thoughts always on God and His love; those who reach out to hurting people with the love of Jesus; and those who are treated badly, laughed at, and made fun of for doing the good work of Jesus.

It is to these people that God promises a special blessing. A heavenly blessing. A holy joy.

Growing in Grace

The verses from Matthew 5:3–12 are known as the Beatitudes or "Bee-Attitudes." Draw and cut out eight bees (a circle with two wings). Write one of the "Bee-Attitudes" on each—spiritually needy, sad for sins, humble, wanting to do right, merciful, pure, peacemaking, and treated badly for doing good. Tape them to your mirror or door to help you "bee" right with God!

Imitating Jesus

"I did this as an example for you. So you
should do as I have done for you."

—JOHN 13:15

I t's a fact that you can write down: *you are what you see.* If you
only see yourself—and what you want—then you will be just
like the people Paul described in Philippians 3:19: "The way
they live is leading them to destruction. Instead of serving God,
they do whatever their bodies want. They do shameful things,
and they are proud of it. They think only about earthly things."

God doesn't want you only to see yourself. He wants you to
see Jesus and to imitate Him. That means He wants you to do
what Jesus would do.

Seeing Jesus—and doing what He would do—is what
Christianity is all about. Christian service—like helping the
poor and being a friend to the friendless—is imitating Jesus. To
see His love and power and kindness, and then to imitate Him,
is the greatest kind of faith.

Growing in Grace

*Take a good look at every person you meet today—from your
parents to your teacher to the lunchroom lady. Did you know that
each and every one of them is a child of God—specially made by
God? Ask yourself, How would Jesus treat them? Then ask God to
help you treat them just as Jesus would.*

God Cares About You

"Look at the birds in the air. They don't plant or harvest or store food in barns. But your heavenly Father feeds the birds."

—MATTHEW 6:26

Think about the earth. Scientists believe that the earth weighs about six sextillion tons. That's a six with *twenty-one zeros* after it!

The earth is tilted exactly twenty-one degrees. If it were tilted any more or less, the North and South Poles would melt and our seasons would change dramatically. And even though the earth spins at the rate of one thousand miles per hour, not one of us tumbles off into outer space!

As you look up at the sky, think about these questions: If God can place the stars and hold up the sky like a curtain, do you think He can lead you through your life? If God is mighty enough to set the sun on fire, could it be that He is mighty enough to light your path? If He cares enough about Saturn to give it rings or Venus to make it sparkle, do you think He cares enough about you to meet all your needs? Yes!

Growing in Grace

The God who placed and named each star (Psalm 147:4) is watching over you. As a reminder, cut star shapes from heavy paper and add some glitter. Hang them from pieces of string (six to twelve inches long) over your bed. Watch the stars twinkle and sway as you go to sleep, and thank God for watching over you.

Good Habits

So let us go on to grown-up teaching. Let us not go back
over the beginning lessons we learned about Christ.

—HEBREWS 6:1

I like the story of the little boy who fell out of bed. When his
mom asked him what happened, he answered, "I don't know.
I guess I stayed too close to where I got in."

It's easy to do the same thing with your faith. It's easy to
just stay where you are. But just as you are growing taller and
learning more in school, this is also the time to grow and learn
in Christ. Start some habits of faith such as these:

- Pray every day—not just a quick word at mealtime, but
  really talk to God and tell Him about your day.
- Read at least one verse of Scripture every day.
- Memorize a verse each week.
- Go to church and Bible study.
- Decide to do one good thing for someone else each day.

Don't make the mistake of the little boy. Don't stay too close
to where you got in. Jump right in, and start growing your faith!

Growing in Grace

*As you grow up, keep track of your growing faith. On a growth chart,
as you mark your physical growth, also note your spiritual growth.
Memorize a verse? Write it on the chart with a date. Help someone
learn about Jesus? Write it down. See how "tall" your faith can grow.*

Walking Like Jesus

Live like children who belong to the light.
—EPHESIANS 5:8

There's an old saying that goes, "Don't just talk the talk; walk the walk." But what does that mean? For Christians, it means walking—or living—like Jesus.

A lot of people can tell you what Jesus said. They know the verses by heart. They can say all the right words and sing all the right songs. They can "talk the talk." But not nearly as many people can *do* what Jesus said. They have trouble when it comes time to "walk the walk"—to live like Jesus said they should.

It's very easy to say, "Obey your parents." It's not so easy to stop playing and clean up your room. It's easy to say, "Forgive others." It's not so easy to forgive that friend who called you names. It's easy to say, "Love your enemies." It's not so easy to be kind to someone who has been unkind to you.

No, it's not easy at all. But it is "walking the walk"—and it's what Jesus wants you to do.

Growing in Grace

Read some of Jesus' very own words in Matthew 5:3–12. Reading Jesus' "talk" will help you learn to "walk the walk."

More Than You Can Imagine

"There are many rooms in my Father's house. . . .
I am going there to prepare a place for you."

—JOHN 14:2

Happiness on this earth is not real happiness. So beware of people who tell you that you can find perfect happiness here on earth. You won't find it. And don't listen to people who promise that happiness is in having the right friends, the right clothes, or the right house. Happiness is not just a puppy away.

Try this. Imagine a perfect world. Whatever that means to you, imagine it. Does that mean peace? Then imagine the place where you feel safest. Does it mean perfect joy? Then imagine your greatest happiness. Is there love in your perfect world? Then imagine a place where everyone is completely loved. Whatever heaven means to you, imagine it. Get a good picture in your mind.

And then smile as God reminds you that "no one has ever imagined what God has prepared for those who love him" (1 Corinthians 2:9).

When it comes to heaven, you can't begin to imagine how wonderful it will be.

Growing in Grace

What do you think heaven will look like? On a piece of paper, draw your idea of heaven. As you create, try to think of ways you can bring a little heaven down to earth by what you say and do.

Changed to Look Like Jesus

Who has known the mind of the Lord?

—1 CORINTHIANS 2:16

The differences between our hearts and Jesus' heart seem so huge. He is so good, and we mess up so much. How could we ever hope to have a heart like Jesus?

Are you ready for a surprise? God wants to give you a heart like Jesus. When you become a child of God, He will give you the heart of Jesus. One of the greatest promises of God is simply this: if you give your life to Jesus, He gives Himself to you. He will make your heart His home! Paul said it simply: "Christ [is] living in me" (Galatians 2:20).

Jesus will move into your heart and unpack His bag. And He is ready to change you "to be like him" to bring "more and more glory" (2 Corinthians 3:18).

Growing in Grace

What does change look like? Flatten out a coffee filter. Using washable markers, draw seven or eight rings of different colors on it. Spritz it with water two or three times and watch the colors flow, changing the plain, white filter into something beautiful—just as God's Word changes your ordinary heart into something beautiful!

Choose to Believe

Faith means being sure of the things we hope for. And faith means knowing that something is real even if we do not see it.

—HEBREWS 11:1

Faith is believing that God is real and that God is good. But faith is a choice. You must choose to believe that the God who created everything hasn't left it all—that He is still here and still working. You must choose to believe that He still sends the light of His love to chase away the dark shadows of this world. And you must choose to believe that He still hears and answers your prayers.

Faith is believing that God will do what is right.

God says that the more hopeless things seem to be, the more He will help you. The greater your worries are, the harder you will pray. And the darker your troubles are, the greater your need for His light.

God's help is always near and always ready for you. But His help is only given to those who look for it.

Growing in Grace

Joshua said, "As for me and my family, we will serve the Lord" (Joshua 24:15). Declare your choice with a family banner. On a large piece of paper, write "We will serve the Lord!" Have everyone in your family sign it. Then hang it up for all to see.

A Cut Above

Be quiet and know that I am God.

—PSALM 46:10

The word *holy* means "to separate." The word's meaning can be traced back to ancient times, when it meant "to cut." To be holy, then, is to be a cut above . . . better than the rest . . . extraordinary. That's God. He is a cut above us. What scares us does not scare Him. What troubles us does not trouble Him.

I'm not a great sailor, but I've been in a fishing boat enough times to know how to find land in a storm. You don't aim at another boat—it might float the wrong way. Don't stare at the waves—they're always moving. Set your sights on something that isn't moved by the wind—like a light on the shore—and go straight toward it.

When life is stormy, don't follow your friends—they might go the wrong way. Don't stare at your troubles—they're always moving. Set your sights on the One who never moves—God. He is "a cut above" any storm.

Growing in Grace

Does it matter what you set your sights on? Try this: Grab a football or soccer ball and pick a distant object (like a tree) as your goal. Throw the ball at the goal, but don't look at it. Look to the right or left. Miss your goal? Try again, this time keeping your eyes on the goal. Better? Always keep your eyes on the goal—and on God!

Come and See

Nathanael said to Philip, "Nazareth! Can
anything good come from Nazareth?"
Philip answered, "Come and see."

—JOHN 1:46

Nathanael's question is still being asked today, over two thousand years later. Can anything good come out of Nazareth? Can Jesus be real? Just come and see. Come and see the changed lives: the sad who now have joy; the angry who are now at peace; the shamed who have been forgiven; the hurts that have been healed; the orphans who are hugged; and the prisoners who have been given hope.

Come and see the pierced hand of Jesus. Watch as He touches the most ordinary heart, wipes the tear from the dirtiest face, and forgives the ugliest sin.

Come and see. He welcomes everyone who looks for Him. He ignores no one. He fears no question. Come and see Jesus.

Growing in Grace

What do you see when you look at the homeless person on the street? Or the child with the dirty face and torn clothes? Or the mean kid from your class? Now, what do you think Jesus sees? Someone who needs His touch. Can you share Jesus' touch with someone today?

God's Goodness

The rich and the poor are alike
in that the Lord made them all.

—PROVERBS 22:2

Have you noticed that God doesn't ask you to prove that you will put your time to good use? Have you noticed that God doesn't turn off your air supply when you mess up? Aren't you glad that God doesn't give you only the gifts that you remember to thank Him for?

God is good to you because God *is* good. That is who He is. He blesses you because of His goodness, not because you are worthy of it.

Someone once asked a friend of mine, "Why should we help the poor who don't even want to be Christians?"

My friend simply answered, "God did."

Would God help those who don't love Him? Those who don't even want to know Him? Yes! He did it in the Bible, and He still does it every day for millions of people.

Growing in Grace

God blesses even those who don't like Him. That can be a tough thing for us to do. Can you bless someone who doesn't like you? Can you smile at the grouch? Offer to help the grumpy neighbor? You might just make a new friend.

You or God?

You have been saved by God's grace.

—EPHESIANS 2:5

God is working in your life. When you choose to believe in Him, He saves you with His grace. What does that mean?

It means that when you break one of God's rules—whether it is not obeying your parents, telling a lie, or gossiping with a friend—you have sinned. That sin separates you from God, and that sin must be punished. But because God loves you so much and because He doesn't want to be separated from you, He chose to send Jesus to be punished instead of you. He chose to forgive you and forget your sins. That is grace.

As you think about grace and about all that God does for you, answer these questions: Who is doing the work, you or God? Who is active, you or God? Who is doing the saving, you or God? *God!*

Growing in Grace

God asked Job some tough questions about who was in charge. Take a walk in nature and think about these questions: Have you ever given orders for the morning to begin (Job 38:12)? Can you send lightning bolts on their way (38:35)? Are you the one who commands the eagle to fly (39:27)? It's good to remember that God is God and we are not.

Life Without God

Their thinking became useless. Their foolish
minds were filled with darkness. They said
they were wise, but they became fools.

—ROMANS 1:21-22

There are people who live only to make themselves happy. And because they have never seen God in person, they believe there is no life except the here and now. To them, nothing is real except what they can see. Nothing is important except their own happiness, and there is no Creator and no heaven.

These people say, "Who cares? I may be bad, but so what? What I do is my own business." They are more concerned with having fun than knowing the Father. They are so busy chasing after good times that they have no time for God.

Are they right? Is it okay to spend our days ignoring God and thinking only of ourselves? Absolutely not!

Paul told us in Romans 1 that when we ignore God, we lose more than church on Sundays. We lose the very reason we were created.

Growing in Grace

Many people don't believe that God is real or that He cares. It can be tough to share God's Word with them. But one thing they can't ignore is the way you live. Live like Jesus did—loving others more than yourself. Then God's message will come through loud and clear.

March

Depend on the Lord.
Trust him, and he will take care of you.

—PSALM 37:5

Because of You

No one has ever imagined what God has
prepared for those who love him.

—1 CORINTHIANS 2:9

Think about the day Jesus comes back. There you are in heaven surrounded by all the other Christians who were saved. Though you are one of a crowd, it's as if you and Jesus are all alone.

I wonder if Jesus might say these words to you: "I'm so proud that you let Me use you. Because of you, others are here today. Would you like to meet them?"

And, one by one, they begin to step forward.

The first is that grouchy old lady who lived next door. You didn't think you would see her in heaven! "You never knew I was watching when you did kind things for everyone in the neighborhood," she says, "but I was. And because of you, I am here."

It's not long before you and Jesus are surrounded by all the souls you've touched. Some you know, and some you don't. But you are so happy for each of them. And how wonderful to hear Jesus say, "I am so proud of your faith" (1 Thessalonians 2:19).

Growing in Grace

Someone's always watching what you do—even if you don't know it. So . . . are you the one who cheats on the test? The one who lies about the broken glass? Or are you the one who cleans up the mess you didn't make? The one who picks up the trash from the neighbor's yard? Who are you when no one is watching?

Live a Holy Life

"You should be a light for other people. Live so that they will see the good things you do. Live so that they will praise your Father in heaven."
—MATTHEW 5:16

Do you want to make a difference in your world? Live a holy life. What does that mean? It means you choose to:

Obey your parents.
Be the one at school who refuses to cheat.
Be the neighbor who is helpful and kind.
Be the one who does the chores but never complains.
Be careful with your money and always give some to God.
Enjoy life and keep a smile on your face.
Live like Jesus, not just talk about Him.

People are watching the way you act more than they are listening to what you say. So although it's important to talk about Jesus and to share His Word, it's even more important to live like Jesus.

Growing in Grace

People are more likely to do what you do than what you say. For a real-life example, grab some friends for a game of Simon Says. How easily can you trick your friends into doing what you do instead of what you say? How easily can they trick you?

A Bold Prayer

Let us, then, feel free to come before
God's throne. Here there is grace.

—HEBREWS 4:16

Jesus said, "When you pray, you should pray like this: 'Our Father in heaven, we pray that your name will always be kept holy. We pray that your kingdom will come'" (Matthew 6:9–10).

When you say, "We pray that your kingdom will come," you are inviting God Himself to walk into your world. You are asking Him to be the Lord of your life—your entire life. You are saying that you want His will to rule in your heart. That you want everything you say and do to be pleasing to Him. That you want Him to guide your relationships with your family and friends. And you want Him to take charge of your doubts and fears.

This is no small prayer. You are boldly and bravely asking God to come into every corner of your life.

And who are you to ask such a thing? Who are you to ask God to take control of your world? *You are His child!*

Growing in Grace

The next time you're not sure what to pray, find the Lord's Prayer in Matthew 6:9–13. Jesus prayed for God's kingdom to come and His will to be done, for daily needs, for forgiveness, and for protection from the evil one. Practice praying like Jesus did.

Washing Away Doubt

"Who is more important: the one sitting at the table or the one serving him? You think the one at the table is more important. But I am like a servant among you!"

—LUKE 22:27

In Jesus' day, washing feet was a servant's job. But not just any servant, the lowest of all the servants. No one wanted the job of washing feet. So it was the servant at the bottom of the totem pole who would be on his knees with the towel and the bowl of water.

But at the Passover meal, the One with the towel and the bowl of water was Jesus. The King of the universe was the One kneeling at their feet. The hands that had shaped the stars now washed away filth. Fingers that had formed mountains now rubbed toes. One day all nations will bow down before Him, but on that day He bowed before His disciples.

Hours before His own death on the cross, Jesus thought of only one thing. He wanted His disciples to know how much He loved them. He wasn't just washing away dirt. He was washing away their doubts.

Growing in Grace

What do you think you're too good to do? Take out the trash? Clean up the spill? Wipe a toddler's nose in the nursery? The next time you think you're too good to do something, ask yourself, Would Jesus have been too good to do this?

Only Jesus

"Come to me, all of you who are tired and
have heavy loads. I will give you rest."

—MATTHEW 11:28

As long as Jesus is just one of many choices, you probably won't choose Him.

As long as you think you can handle all of your problems by yourself, you don't need a problem-fixer. As long as you are feeling happy, you don't need comfort. As long as you would rather follow your friends Monday through Saturday and follow Jesus only on Sunday, you're not really following Him at all. Because He wants all of you every day, not just a little bit on Sunday.

But when you realize that you have sinned and your heart breaks because of your sins, Jesus will be waiting for you. When you are ready to give Him all your worries and cares, He will be there. When your problems flash around you like lightning in a storm, Jesus will be right there in the middle of the storm— waiting to save you.

Growing in Grace

Some substitutes are okay—like margarine for butter. But others aren't. Try this: stir up a package of powdered drink mix, but use flour instead of sugar. Did it work? No! Faith is the same way. Some people put their faith in money, friends, or fame, but there's no substitute for Jesus!

A Second Chance

Christ . . . was not guilty, but he died for those who
are guilty. He did this to bring you all to God.

—1 PETER 3:18

What is a second chance? It's the teacher throwing away the failed test and saying, "I know you can do better." It's the friend you've hurt who says, "I forgive you. Now let's go play." It's the parent who hugs you and says, "Let's try that again."

And it's the Savior who loves you so much that He died to save you.

You see, Jesus came to earth for one reason: to give His life to save you, to save me, to save all of us. To give us a second chance. He loves each of us so much that He would have suffered through anything to save us. And He did. He went to the cross.

Jesus—who was perfect and without any sin—gave His perfection to us. And all our sins, all our mistakes and imperfections, were given to Him. Because Jesus was willing to take them, we are forgiven and given a second chance.

Growing in Grace

What does the cross mean to you? It means that when you snap at your sister, God doesn't hold it against you. It means that when you tell a lie, God can forgive you. It means that God loves you when you aren't lovable. Jesus' sacrifice on the cross is your second chance to get it right.

Just in Time

May the God you serve all the time save you!

—DANIEL 6:16

Look at Jonah in the belly of the fish. He's floating around with tummy juices and sucked-in seaweed. He prays. Before he can say amen, the belly rumbles, the fish belches, and Jonah lands face-first on the beach.

Look at Daniel in the lions' den. Things aren't looking good. Jonah was swallowed, and Daniel is about to be.

Or look at Joseph in the pit, a dusty hole in a hot desert. His brothers have pulled the lid over the top and the wool over his eyes. Like Jonah and Daniel, Joseph is trapped. He is out of ideas. No exit. No hope. But even though Joseph's road to the palace takes a turn through a pit and a prison, he ends up at the throne.

The stories of the Bible often go this way. One close call after another. Just when the lion is about to pounce, just when the prison door clangs shut, Calvary comes—and God saves the day! Just in time.

Growing in Grace

Pretend you are Jonah, Daniel, or Joseph. How would it feel to be trapped in the belly of a fish? In a den of hungry lions? Or in a deep, dark, desert pit? Now imagine how wonderful it would feel to be saved by God—just in time!

The Holy Spirit

The true children of God are those who
let God's Spirit lead them.
—ROMANS 8:14

You hear a lot of people talk about God and about Jesus. But when it comes to the Holy Spirit, nobody says much. And sometimes the thought of a "spirit" can be confusing, maybe even frightening. But the truth is, we're confused because no one has taught us about Him. And we're frightened because we don't understand Him.

Let's make things a bit simpler. The Holy Spirit is nothing to be afraid of—He is a gift from God. He is the presence of God living inside us, and He carries on the work of Jesus in our lives.

The Holy Spirit works in three ways: He helps our hearts by giving us the fruit of the Spirit (Galatians 5:22–24). He prays to God for us when we don't know what to say (Romans 8:26). And He pours God's love into our hearts (5:5).

The Holy Spirit is God living in you—and that is nothing to be frightened of!

Growing in Grace

Blow up a balloon and tie a knot in the end. Can you see the air inside it? No. But you can see how it fills the balloon. The Holy Spirit is much like that. You can't see Him. But He fills you up with the presence of God.

God's Will

"We pray that your kingdom will come.
We pray that what you want will be done,
here on earth as it is in heaven."

—MATTHEW 6:10

To pray "Your will be done" is to search for what God wants for you in your life. The word *will* means "strong desire." So what *is* God's strong desire for your life? What is His will? What is His heart's greatest hope? It's no secret. God's greatest desire is to save you. God doesn't hide what He is going to do. In fact, He has gone to a lot of trouble to show us His will. He sent His Son to lead us. He gave us His Word to teach us. And He sent His Holy Spirit to guide us. He even placed the stars in the heavens to prove to us that He is real.

God is not the God of confusion or doubt. Wherever He sees someone who is truly seeking Him, whenever He knows someone's heart is filled with questions, God is there. And you can bet He is doing whatever it takes to help that person see His will. Because when you look for God, He lets you find Him.

Growing in Grace

God's will can be wrapped up in two commands: "Love the Lord your God. Love him with all your heart, all your soul, all your strength, and all your mind" and also "You must love your neighbor as you love yourself" (Luke 10:27). Do these two things, and you'll always be doing the will of God.

Crazy About You

"God even knows how many hairs are on your head."

—MATTHEW 10:30

There are many reasons God saves you. It brings glory to Him. It allows you to come to Him without any sin. It shows that He is Lord of all. But one of the sweetest reasons God saves you is because He is *fond* of you. He likes having you around. He thinks you are the best thing to come along since peanut butter.

If God had a refrigerator, your picture would be on it. If He had a wallet, your photo would be in it. He sends you flowers every spring and a sunrise every morning. Whenever you want to talk, He listens. God can live anywhere in the universe—the highest mountain or the most beautiful beach. But He chooses to live in your heart.

Face it, friend. God is crazy about you!

Growing in Grace

God's crazy about you. Show the world you are crazy about Him too. John 3:16 is the perfect picture of God. Post it on your fridge. Hang it on your wall. Write it on your notebooks. Tell the world what God looks like!

His Mercy

Be kind and loving to each other. Forgive each
other just as God forgave you in Christ.
—EPHESIANS 4:32

When Jesus washed the disciples' feet, He knew the future of those feet. Not one of them would spend the next day following Him or defending Him. Those feet would run for cover at the first flash of a Roman sword. Only one pair of feet wouldn't run away from Him in the garden. Judas wouldn't even make it that far!

So why did He do it? Why did Jesus stoop to wash the disciples' feet? The answer is in one word: *mercy*. Jesus knew what those men were about to do, and He wanted to give them something to remember. He wanted them to remember that He had washed their feet. He wanted them to know that those feet were still clean and that He had forgiven their sin before they even did it. He gave them mercy before they even asked for it.

That mercy is there for you too. When you choose to believe in Jesus and to obey Him, His mercy will make you clean.

Growing in Grace

Mercy is when you deserve to be punished . . . but you are forgiven instead. Jesus gives you mercy for your mistakes. He asks you to do the same for others. Is there someone who has hurt or disappointed you? Ask God to help you show mercy.

Slaves to Goodness

Now you are free from sin and have become
slaves of God. This brings you a life that is only
for God. And this gives you life forever.

—ROMANS 6:22

Before Jesus comes into our lives, we may snap at our brothers and sisters or be selfish with our allowances. Maybe we are slow to obey our parents and teachers. Maybe we don't even know what a mess we are until He comes into our lives.

But then Jesus moves in, and things begin to change. The careless, mean words we throw around are thrown away. The selfishness that clutters up our hearts is cleaned out. Oh, we'll still mess up once in a while. We still might say a wrong word or do a wrong thing. But for the most part Jesus puts our lives in order.

Suddenly we find ourselves wanting to just do good. Do we want to go back to our old selfish ways? Are you kidding? Paul says it this way: "In the past you were slaves to sin—sin controlled you. But thank God, you fully obeyed the things that were taught to you. You were made free from sin, and now you are slaves to goodness" (Romans 6:17–18).

Growing in Grace

Next time you clean your room, clean up your heart too. As you throw out the trash, toss out any anger or jealousy. Clean up the closet and clean out your thoughts. Sweep up the floors as you ask God to sweep away your sins.

Who Would Ask?

"The thing you should seek is God's kingdom. Then all the other things you need will be given to you."

—LUKE 12:31

God loves us so much that He doesn't just give us the things we ask Him for—like good health and help with family and school. God also gives us what we need—a Savior.

And that's a good thing. For who would ever dare to say, "God, would You please take away all my sins and mistakes by hanging Yourself from a wooden cross?" Who would dare to add, "And after You forgive me, could You prepare a place in Your house for me to live forever?"

And if that weren't enough, would you have ever thought to ask, "God, would You please live in my heart and protect me and guide me and bless me with more than I could ever imagine or deserve?"

Honestly, would we have the nerve to ask for that?

Jesus already knows the price of forgiving us. He already knows the cost of grace. But He gives us His grace anyway.

Growing in Grace

To help you know how much God loves you, write John 3:16 on an index card. Fill in your name in the spaces shown: "For God loved [your name] so much that he gave his only Son. God gave his Son so that [your name] may not be lost, but have eternal life."

Jesus Sticks Up for You

Who can say that God's people are guilty? No one! Christ Jesus . . . is on God's right side and is begging God for us.

—ROMANS 8:34

Jesus is praying for you. Right now.

Jesus has spoken, and Satan has listened. In the fight for you, the devil may land a punch or two. He may even win a few rounds. But he never wins the whole fight. Why? Because Jesus sticks up for you. Jesus is "always able to save those who come to God through him. He can do this, because he always lives, ready to help those who come before God" (Hebrews 7:25).

Jesus, at this very second, is protecting you. When the devil comes to tempt you to do wrong, Jesus takes up for you. He helps you to stand strong against the devil. And He will "not let you be tempted more than you can stand. But when you are tempted, God will also give you a way to escape that temptation. Then you will be able to stand it" (1 Corinthians 10:13).

Jesus is on your side. He never stops fighting for you.

Growing in Grace

The next time there's a thunderstorm, think about how powerful it is. The whipping wind and sheets of rain. The booming thunder and crackling lightning. Imagine: Jesus stopped the storm with just a few words. Isn't it great to have the all-powerful Jesus sticking up for you?

The Fire Inside You

Jesus began to explain everything that had been written about himself in the Scriptures.

—LUKE 24:27

After Jesus rose from the grave, He appeared to two of His disciples. At first, they didn't know Him, but when they "saw who he was, he disappeared. They said to each other, 'When Jesus talked to us on the road, it felt like a fire burning in us'" (Luke 24:31–32).

Don't you love that verse? The disciples knew they had been with Jesus because of the fire inside them. This isn't a fireplace kind of fire. It's a spiritual fire. It's an eagerness to learn more about God and to follow Him. God shows us His will for our lives by touching our hearts with spiritual fire.

He gave Jeremiah a spiritual fire for preaching to people who didn't believe. He gave Nehemiah a fire for rebuilding Jerusalem. He gave Abraham a fire to go to a land he'd never seen.

And Jesus comes to set your heart on fire! He touches heart after heart with His flame, warming cold hearts and bitter souls. He burns away sin and lights up the path for you to follow.

Growing in Grace

Share the light of Jesus' fire with some younger children. Offer to help in your church's toddler class and teach them the song "This Little Light of Mine." See those shining, smiling faces? That's being "on fire" for Jesus!

Listen for His Voice

"I will never leave you; I will never forget you."

—HEBREWS 13:5

Let me tell you something very important. There is never a time that Jesus is not speaking. *Never.* There is never a place where Jesus isn't there. *Never.* There is never a room so dark that your greatest Friend is not around. He is always present, always seeking, always tender. It's as if He is gently tapping on the door of your heart—just waiting to be invited in.

Not many people hear His voice. Even fewer people open the door of their hearts to Him.

But that doesn't mean He isn't there. Because He is. He promised He always would be: "You can be sure that I will be with you always. I will continue with you until the end of the world" (Matthew 28:20).

Some people in this world may tell you to stop listening to Jesus. They may tell you that the things He says are wrong aren't really wrong. Don't listen to them. Open up your Bible and listen for Jesus' voice. His Word will speak to you . . . if you will listen.

Growing in Grace

March mornings can still be pretty chilly. Use those chilly mornings to help you remember that God is everywhere. Breathe out and notice the white, puffy clouds. We usually don't see the air, but the cold lets us see it. And just like the air, God is everywhere—even though we don't see Him.

His Gift

All I want is to know Christ and the power of
his rising from death. I want to share in Christ's
sufferings and become like him in his death.

—PHILIPPIANS 3:10

L ook at what Jesus did for us. He swapped the royalty of
heaven for the poorness and hardship of earth. Sometimes
He slept on borrowed blankets; sometimes it was the cold, hard
earth. He depended on the handouts of others. He was sometimes so hungry that He would eat raw grain from the fields or
pick fruit off a tree. He knew what it meant to be homeless. He
was laughed at. His neighbors tried to kill Him. Some called Him
crazy. Sometimes even His friends turned against Him.

He was arrested for a crime that He didn't do. People were
hired to lie about it. The jury had their minds made up before He
was even arrested. And the judge—who was more interested in
politics than in truth—ordered Him to His death.

They killed Jesus. And why? Because He came to give us a
gift that only He could give—salvation.

Growing in Grace

Jesus said that the things you do for the poor, you actually do for Him.
On your next birthday, have a "reverse birthday." Instead of asking for
toys for yourself, ask for toys to give away. After your celebration, take
the toys to a shelter and donate them to the children there.

Doing What's Right

Everyone who is a child of God has the power to win against the world. It is our faith that wins the victory against the world.

—1 JOHN 5:4

D o you ever wonder where the power of God is? Maybe you've been trying to work out a problem—to get rid of a bad habit or a sin—and it just isn't working. Be patient. God is using today's troubles to make you stronger for tomorrow. He is *training* you. The same God who is making you grow taller will help your spirit grow stronger.

Remember that God lives inside you. Think about His power that gives you life. As you think about God living in you, you may change the places you want to go and the things you want to do today.

Do what is right this week. No matter what problems come your way, just do what's right. Maybe no one else is, but *you* do what's right. *You* tell the truth. *You* take a stand against evil. *You* be helpful. After all, even when you mess up, God still does what is right—He keeps His promise to save you with His grace.

Growing in Grace

Write Philippians 4:8 on several index cards: "Think about the things that are good and . . . true and honorable and right and pure and beautiful and respected." Place the cards next to your television, computer, and iPod. Let God's Word help you choose what shows to watch, games to play, and songs to listen to.

A Bowlful of Grace

The blood of the death of Jesus, God's Son,
is making us clean from every sin.
—1 JOHN 1:7

John told us that the blood of Jesus *"is making* us clean from every sin." That means, He *is always making* us clean. This cleansing is not just a promise for someday in the future. It is a fact for right now.

Just let a speck of sin fall on your soul, and it is washed away. Let a spot of filth land on the heart of God's child, and the filth is wiped away.

Jesus kneels down and looks at the most terrible things we have ever said and done. But He doesn't step back in horror. Instead, He reaches out in kindness and says, "I can clean that if you want." And from the bowl of His grace, He scoops out a handful of mercy and washes away our sin.

But that's not all He does. Because Jesus lives in us, you and I can do the same. Because He has forgiven us, we can forgive others.

Growing in Grace

Jesus continually washes away our sins. What's that like? Think of it this way: the next time it rains, wipe off the windshield of your family car while it's still raining. Did you get tired of wiping away those raindrops? Aren't you glad that Jesus never tires of washing away our sins?

A Gift from God

God made you alive with Christ. And God forgave all
our sins. We owed a debt because we broke God's laws.
That debt listed all the rules we failed to follow. . . .
He took away that debt and nailed it to the cross.

—COLOSSIANS 2:13-14

There are many different religions in the world. But they all believe one of two things—they either need God or they don't. They either earn their salvation by doing good things, or it is a gift from God.

People who believe they can save themselves are called *legalists*. They believe you can work your way to heaven if you look right, say the right thing, and belong to the right group. The power to save doesn't come from God; it comes from you.

These people look great on the outside. They say and do all the right things. But look closely. Something is missing. *Joy*. What is there instead? *Fear*. They're afraid they won't work hard enough, be good enough, or do enough good. They're afraid they will fail.

But you don't have to be afraid. Because getting to heaven isn't up to you. It is a gift from God.

Growing in Grace

How long can you go without sinning? Watch the clock and see how long it is before you think a bad thought or say something unkind. Not very long, is it? Aren't you glad salvation depends on who God is—and not what you do?

Jesus Hears Your Prayers

The Lord hears good people when they cry out to
him. He saves them from all their troubles.

—PSALM 34:17

When a friend came to Jesus and told Him that Lazarus was sick, he said, "Lord, the one you love is sick" (John 11:3).

The man didn't come to Jesus and talk about Lazarus's imperfect love for Jesus. He didn't say, "The one *who loves You* is sick." No. He reminded Jesus of His perfect love for Lazarus. He said, "The one *You love* is sick."

When you talk to Jesus in prayer, the power of the prayer is not in you, the one who says the prayer. The power is in the One who hears the prayer.

So when you pray, you can use the same words as Lazarus's friend: "The one You love is sick . . . tired . . . sad . . . hungry . . . lonely . . . afraid." You can pray this way, because *you* are the one Jesus loves.

The words of your prayers may change, but what Jesus does never changes. Your Savior never misses a word. He hears your prayer.

Growing in Grace

Listening to your prayers is just one way Jesus shows His love. Keep a journal this week. Write down all the different ways that Jesus says, "I love you." From the sunrise painted just for you . . . to the air you breathe . . . to the stars that sparkle in the sky.

Dark Nights, God's Light

Pray for all people. Ask God for the things
people need, and be thankful to him.

—1 TIMOTHY 2:1

Do you ever look at the world around you and wonder about some of the things that happen here? As you pray, do you ever wonder about things like . . . starving children, Christians with cancer, and why bad things happen to God's people?

Those are tough questions. They are probably a lot like the questions the disciples must have asked when they were in the middle of the sea during a storm: "Jesus, don't You care?"

All they could see were black skies and black waves as they bounced in the battered boat. Then a figure came to them, walking on the water. It wasn't what they expected, so they almost missed seeing the answer to their prayers.

And unless you look and listen closely, you might make the same mistake. God's answers are like the stars in the night sky—there are billions and billions of them. But some of them you just can't see yet.

Growing in Grace

God often uses His children—that's you!—as answers to tough questions. His children can feed the hungry. His children can visit the hospitals. And His children can comfort the hurting. Ask God what you can do to help others. You just might be the answer to someone's tough question.

The Cloak of Humanity

Jesus told Peter, James, and John to come with him.
Then Jesus began to be very sad and troubled.

—MARK 14:33

While Jesus lived on earth, he prayed to God and asked God for help. He prayed with loud cries and tears to the One who could save him from death" (Hebrews 5:7).

Just imagine . . . Jesus is praying in the garden only hours before His death. Jesus is in pain. Jesus is filled with fear. At this moment, perhaps more than any other, Jesus knows how weak and frail His human body is.

The next time you are really sad, remember Jesus in the garden. The next time you think no one understands how much you are hurting, read this verse again. The next time you are feeling sorry for yourself, kneel down just as Jesus did in the garden. And the next time you wonder if God really understands how hard it is to live on this earth, think of Jesus' pleading prayer in the garden.

Growing in Grace

Think of someone you know very well. Has that person ever surprised you? Probably. But God is never surprised. He knows everything about you—everything! Every thought. Every place you go. Every word you say—before you ever say it! He knows. And because He was once human, He understands.

Perfect

We are made holy through the sacrifice of his body.
Christ made this sacrifice only once, and for all time.

—HEBREWS 10:10

Only those who are holy will see God. To get into heaven, you have to be holy. You have to be perfect to live with God for all eternity. We wish it weren't so. We act like it isn't so. We act like those who are "good people" will see God. Those who try hard will get into heaven. We pretend that we're good if we don't do anything too terrible. And we hope that our goodness is enough to get us into heaven.

That may sound right to us, but it doesn't sound right to God. God says, "You must be perfect, just as your Father in heaven is perfect" (Matthew 5:48).

You see, in God's plan, we have to be perfect. We can't compare ourselves to others. They are just as messed up as we are. The goal is to be like God—perfect. Anything else is just not good enough. Thankfully, God knows that we can't be perfect. So He sent His Son to be perfect for us.

Growing in Grace

Make a bookmark for your Bible by tying beads on one end of a twelve-inch piece of string. Use four beads: black, red, white, and yellow. The black is for our sins. The red is for Jesus' blood that washes us white as snow. The yellow is for the streets of gold in heaven.

The Author of Our Story

"In this world you will have trouble. But be
brave! I have defeated the world!"

—JOHN 16:33

God doesn't keep secrets from us. He told us there would be troubles. Just as Dorothy faced dark forests, twisted roads, and wicked witches on her way to Oz, so we will have troubles on our way to heaven. We will be sick. Our hearts might get broken. People we love will die, and wars will be fought. We should not be surprised by these things, because the devil lives in this world. But just because the devil swoops in like the wicked witch and laughs his evil laugh, we shouldn't panic.

Jesus said, "It is finished" (John 19:30). The battle is over. Keep on the lookout for the devil's tricks, but don't be alarmed. Jesus has already written this book, and He wins in the end. Satan may still play his evil tricks, but only for a little while. Just a few more twists and turns in the yellow brick road, and his story will end.

Growing in Grace

Pretend you're following the yellow brick road—all the way up to heaven. Whom will you meet along the way? How many people can you take with you? How will the devil try to trip you up? Unlike Dorothy, you've got a Helper who goes right along with you—God!

God's Touch

Jesus touched the man and said, "I
want to heal you. Be healed!"

—MATTHEW 8:3

God's touch is a powerful thing! Have you felt it? It's a bit different from your touch or mine. It's the teacher who dried your tears or the friendly hug just when you needed it most. It's the nurse who holds your hand when you get a shot or the friendly face that greets you on your first day in a new class.

Can you offer God's touch to someone?

Maybe you already do. Maybe you have figured out how to touch people with God's love. Your hands pray for the sick, help bake cookies for the shut-ins, and hug the lonely. You have learned the power of a touch.

Or maybe you've never tried to touch others. Your heart is good, but you've forgotten how important one touch can be. Just look at how Jesus reached out to touch others. Aren't you glad He reached out to touch you?

Growing in Grace

Jesus has gone back to heaven, but He still has hands on earth today . . . yours! What can you do to be Jesus' hands today? Help a brother or sister with a chore. Be a friend to someone who needs one. Take cookies to a shut-in. Or simply offer a friendly wave to all you meet.

God Will Take Care of You

Depend on the Lord.
Trust him, and he will take care of you.

—PSALM 37:5

God promises to take care of your needs. Look at all the birds and the flowers. God cares for each of them (Matthew 6:26–30). Don't you think a holy God will take care of His children too?

The writer of Hebrews prayed that "the God of peace will give you every good thing you need so that you can do what he wants" (13:20). If you think about it, you'll see that prayer has already been answered in your life. You may not always have a feast of all your favorite desserts, but don't you always at least have bread to eat? You may not have everything you *want*, but don't you have everything you truly need? And many times, there *is* a feast.

After all, how can you complete the mission He has for you if your needs aren't met? How can you share His Word or teach others if you don't have food, clothes, or shelter? Would God ask you to join His army and then not give you the supplies you need? Of course not!

Growing in Grace

It's easy to forget our blessings sometimes—home, family, friends, clothes, food, books, and toys. Most of us have far more than we really need. Could you share some of your blessings? Gather up some of your clothes, books, and toys to share with needy children at a shelter.

God's Child

The Father has loved us so much! He loved us so much that
we are called children of God. And we really are his children.

—1 JOHN 3:1

Do you know who you are? Let me tell you:

You are the brother or sister of Christ (Romans 8:17).

You are eternal—you will never die—just like the angels
(Luke 20:36).

You have a crown that will last forever (1 Corinthians 9:25).

You are His treasured possession (Exodus 19:5).

But more than any of those things—more important than
any title—is the simple fact that you are God's own child.

"We really are his children," and *you* really are His child.

And because you are His child, if something is important to
you, it's important to God.

Growing in Grace

*There is no problem too small to take to God. No worry, no
mistake, no joy. Nothing is too small to pray about. God wants to
hear it all—no matter what it is. If it's important to you, then it's
important to God.*

Footprints of Discipleship

All people will know that you are my
followers if you love each other.

—JOHN 13:35

Have you ever tried to follow your dad as he walks through the snow or across the sand? Have you tried to step only in the footprints that he has made? Not an easy task! You have to stretch your legs as far as they will go to reach his footprints!

But by following in his footprints, you know which way to go. That's what following God is like. It's called *discipleship*.

As a Christian, you need to follow in someone else's footprints. A parent, grandparent, or teacher. That person's footprints show you the right way to go, what to say and do as a child of God. No one has to walk this path alone.

Did you know that you also leave footprints for others to follow? Even though you are young, you can lead others to Jesus—a younger child, a friend, or someone who is just learning about Jesus. Part of discipleship is not letting someone walk this trail alone.

Growing in Grace

Trace around your feet on a piece of construction paper, and then cut out the footprints. Ask your mom or dad to do the same. Which ones are bigger? The feet of the grown-ups are—they've been growing longer. Your faith should be the same way. The longer it grows, the bigger your "faith footprint" will be.

Hands

He humbled himself and was fully obedient to God. He
obeyed even when that caused his death—death on a cross.
—PHILIPPIANS 2:8

Stop for a minute and think about the cross. Picture the soldiers' hands that nailed Jesus' hands to the cross. But it wasn't really the soldiers' hands who held Jesus' hands there. It was God and His love for each of us that held those hands on the cross.

Those same hands scooped out the oceans and built up the mountains. Those same hands set the sunrise in place and created each cloud. Those same hands designed an incredible plan to save you and me. Those hands could have reached out and called ten thousand angels to save Jesus from the cross.

But He didn't.

Why? Because those hands that made you and placed you on this planet also wrote this promise: "God would give up His only Son to save you." And so He did.

Growing in Grace

God said, "See, I have written your name on my hand" (Isaiah 49:16). Then God sent His Son to the cross. Each time you see a cross, picture Jesus' hands there. Then picture your name written on those hands. He went to that cross to save you. What can you do to thank Him today?

The Shepherd's Voice

"A time is coming when all who are dead and in their graves will hear his voice. Then they will come out of their graves. Those who did good will rise and have life forever."

—JOHN 5:28-29

A day is coming when everyone will hear Jesus' voice. It is the day that Jesus returns from heaven. On that day all other voices will be silent. His voice—and only His voice—will be heard.

Some people will hear His voice for the very first time. It's not that He never spoke to them. It's just that they never listened. Jesus will be a stranger to them. They will hear Him that one time—and then they will never hear Him again. They will spend eternity without Jesus.

But other people will hear Jesus' voice and will know who it is. They have been listening to Him and following Him because they are like the sheep who know the voice of their shepherd. Jesus will call His sheep by their names (John 10:3), and they will follow Him. And this time, they will follow Him into heaven.

Growing in Grace

Sheep follow their shepherd because they know his voice. Play a game of sheep-and-shepherd with a friend. Set up an obstacle course, and blindfold the sheep. Can you make it through the obstacle course just by following the shepherd's voice?

April

Be strong in the Lord and in his great power.

—EPHESIANS 6:10

An Incredible Plan

With the help of evil men you nailed him to a
cross. But God knew all this would happen. This
was God's plan which he made long ago.

—ACTS 2:23

The cross didn't just happen.

Jesus' death was not an accident. The cross wasn't a sad surprise. Calvary was not some cosmic mix-up or galactic goof. It wasn't some failed attempt to save the world. Jesus' death was anything but unexpected.

No, Jesus' death was part of God's incredible plan to save you, to save me, and to save all of His children. And that plan started thousands of years before Jesus came to earth.

The moment that forbidden fruit touched the lips of Eve, God had a plan to save us all. Although the cross wouldn't appear for centuries, the plan for it began in the garden of Eden. And between that moment in the garden and the moment the first nail went into the cross, God's great plan to save us was fulfilled.

Growing in Grace

April 1 is called April Fool's Day. And one day, more than two thousand years ago, Satan became the biggest fool of all. When Jesus died on the cross, Satan thought he had won. But—April Fool!—Jesus rose from the grave, and the devil lost forever.

Jesus Called It Love

John said, "Look, the Lamb of God. He
takes away the sins of the world!"

—JOHN 1:29

Some things are easy to do. But some things just aren't. Things like getting a shot, trying out for the team, even getting a tooth pulled. There are times when we just have to *do* what we know we need to do.

When Jesus went back to Jerusalem for the last time, He knew what He had to do. It wasn't going to be easy. It was by far the hardest thing any person has ever had to do. But He was determined to follow His Father's plan. He was determined to save us from our sins. And He knew He would have to die to do it (Luke 9:51).

Jesus said, "I am the good shepherd. . . . I give my life for the sheep" (John 10:14–15). And that is what He did. He gave His life on the cross to save His sheep—to save you.

Some people call it grace. Some people call it salvation or sacrifice. Jesus called it love. "For God loved the world so much that he gave his only Son. God gave his Son so that whoever believes in him may not be lost, but have eternal life" (John 3:16).

Growing in Grace

Our plans often go wrong. Bikes crash into bushes. Toes get stubbed, and fingers get smashed. But God's plans never go wrong. He is perfect. His timing is perfect. His love is perfect. God even has a perfect plan for your life (Jeremiah 29:11). Ask Him to help you see and follow His plan.

Jesus Prayed for You

Then Jesus went about a stone's throw away
from them. He kneeled down and prayed.

—LUKE 22:41

In the Garden of Gethsemane, Jesus prayed about many things. But did you know that He also prayed about you? Jesus loved you so much that—in His last hours on earth—He just had to talk to God about you. He prayed that you would be with Him and that you would see His glory (John 17:24). And He prayed that God would keep you safe from the evils of this world (John 17:11).

And today, more than two thousand years later, God is still answering Jesus' prayer. He knows the troubles you face, the tough decisions, and even the temptations to do wrong. He knows your every struggle to do the right thing, your every sadness, and your every joy. And He promises that He will always be right there with you to help you through (Matthew 28:20).

Growing in Grace

On the night before He died, Jesus took time to pray for you. Read John 17:6–26. Make a list of all the things Jesus asked God to bless you with. Do you know someone who does not know Jesus? Be like Jesus and pray for that person.

The Facts

Your sins are red like deep red cloth.
But they can be as white as snow.
Your sins are bright red.
But you can be white like wool.

—ISAIAH 1:18

Jesus told us to pray for the forgiveness of our sins and to forgive those who do wrong to us. When He said that, He knew that He would be the One to pay for those sins. He knew that He would hang on the cross. And He knew that He would say, "It is finished"... the debt for your sins is paid (John 19:30).

There are some facts that will never change. One fact is that you are forgiven. If you believe in Christ and follow Him, your sins are covered. When He sees you, He doesn't even see your sins. He sees you as better than you see yourself. And that is a wonderful fact of your life.

Growing in Grace

Read the story of the unforgiving servant in Matthew 18:21–35. Stop and think about all the things that God has forgiven you for. Do you offer that same forgiveness to others? Write a promise to God: "Because You have forgiven me, I will forgive..."

Worship from the Heart

Come, let's bow down and worship him.
Let's kneel before the Lord who made us.

—PSALM 95:6

Worship. In two thousand years we still haven't figured it out. We still struggle with the right words to pray. We don't know when to kneel. We don't know when to stand. We don't know how to pray.

Worship can be confusing.

That's why God gave us Psalms: to help us worship Him. It is a praise book for God's people. And although the psalms talk about many different things, they each have the same purpose: to draw us closer to the heart of God.

Some psalms are bold. Others are humble. Some are to be sung. Others are to be prayed. Some seem written just for you alone. Others seem to be for the whole world to sing.

The fact that there are so many different kinds of psalms reminds us that there are many different kinds of worship. There is no one secret formula, no one right way. Each person worships differently. But each person should worship.

Growing in Grace

Take a stroll through the book of Psalms. Look at all the different titles, such as A Prayer for Protection (Psalm 140 NCV), A Song of Trust in God (Psalm 27 NCV), and God in the Thunderstorm (Psalm 29 NCV). When you don't know what to pray, turn to the psalms.

Say a Prayer

"I pray these things while I am still in the world.
I say these things so that these men can have
my joy. I want them to have all of my joy."

—JOHN 17:13

What Jesus dreamed of doing (saving us all) and what He had to do (face the cross) seemed impossible to Him. So when the time came for Him to go to the cross, Jesus prayed. He prayed for the impossible to happen. That the cross would not be necessary.

The lesson here for us, though, is that Jesus prayed. When it seemed that the world had turned against Him, He prayed. When He felt all alone, He prayed. When it seemed impossible for Him to do what He needed to do, Jesus prayed.

There may come a time when it feels like everyone is against you. Maybe your friends are talking about you behind your back. Say a prayer. There may come a time when you feel all alone and that no one understands. Say a prayer. There may even come a time when it seems impossible for you to do what you know you need to do. Say a prayer . . . just as Jesus did.

Growing in Grace

Jesus prayed in the garden. Where do you go to pray? Not for mealtime or bedtime prayers, but when you really talk to God. Make a special place for prayers—a corner of your room or under a tree. Take time each day to go there and pray.

Jesus Is Able

"I gave you more power than the Enemy has."

—LUKE 10:19

The night that Jesus was arrested, there were many people gathered at Gethsemane. Judas with his kiss of betrayal. Peter with his sword. The soldiers with their weapons. And though these are important, they aren't the most important. The true battle is not between Jesus and the soldiers; it is between God and Satan. Satan has dared to enter yet another garden— the Garden of Gethsemane this time—just as he did in Eden. But God stands up to him, and Satan doesn't have a chance.

There in Gethsemane, Jesus speaks just three simple words—"I am Jesus"—and sends both the devil and members of the world's finest army falling to the ground (John 18:5–6). Neither Satan nor those who do his will can stand before Christ.

When Jesus says He will keep you safe, He means it. The devil will have to get through Him to get to you. Jesus is able to protect you. When He says He will get you home to heaven, He will get you home.

Growing in Grace

The devil can be scary, and he has some scary tricks up his sleeve. But check out Isaiah 41:10: "Don't be afraid, because I am your God. I will make you strong and will help you. I will support you with my right hand that saves you." God's got the devil beat—hands down.

What God Sees

Be strong in the Lord and in his great power.

—EPHESIANS 6:10

When you look in the mirror, what do you see? Do you see your mistakes? Do you see the guy who lied to his mom about the broken picture? Do you see the girl who didn't stand up for a friend when she was being made fun of?

When your eyes look in the mirror, do you see a promise-breaker? A bad friend? Someone who has messed up... again... and again... and again? If you do, then please look once more. But this time look through the eyes of faith. See what God sees. He sees His much-loved child, the one He sent His Son to save.

Your eyes see your mistakes. But God's eyes see the child He loves.

Your eyes see your sin and guilt. But God's eyes see someone washed clean by the sacrifice of Jesus.

Growing in Grace

Is there a bad habit that you can't seem to break? One sin that you just seem to keep doing over and over again? A bad temper? Telling lies? Complaining all the time? God promises to help you stop these bad habits (1 Corinthians 10:13). Pray for His help.

It Was Love

Christ's love is greater than any person can ever know.
But I pray that you will be able to know that love.

—EPHESIANS 3:19

It wasn't right for Judas to betray his friend Jesus. It wasn't right that the ones Jesus came to save were the ones who hit Him, lied about Him, and spat upon Him.

And it wasn't right for the One who had never sinned to be punished for all of our sins.

It wasn't right, but it happened.

Why? It happened so that "he who believes in God's Son [would not be] judged guilty" (John 3:18).

Was it right? No. Was it fair? No. Was it love? Yes. Did it save you? Yes.

Growing in Grace

Sometimes people are put down because of their skin color, where they come from, or a physical handicap. That's not right or fair. God loves all people. And Jesus went to the cross to save all people. Make sure you are a friend to everyone.

Jesus' Broken Heart

[Jesus] saw the crowds of people and felt sorry
for them because they were worried and helpless.
They were like sheep without a shepherd.

—MATTHEW 9:36

Think of all the different people who came to Jesus for help. All kinds of people. Young children and old beggars. The sick and the lame. The kind and the selfish. It seems that everywhere Jesus went, great crowds of people came to Him, wanting His help.

Surely there must have been times when He was tired, when He just wanted to rest. Why didn't He simply turn them away and tell them to come back tomorrow? Why didn't He take a day off now and then? Why?

Could it be that Jesus' heart hurt for those people? Could it be that His heart was—and is—broken for all people who have ever stared up at the heavens and cried out in prayer, "Why is this happening to me?"

Imagine Jesus today: He is leaning over, bending down close to someone who is hurt. He's listening. His eyes fill with tears as He hears that person's troubles. Then His hand gently brushes away a tear. He was hurt once too. He understands.

Growing in Grace

Jesus is never too busy to listen to your prayers. Do you find yourself too busy for others sometimes? The next time your friends need you to listen or to help, take time for them. It's what Jesus would do.

Love on the Cross

"For God loved the world so much that he gave his only Son. God gave his Son so that whoever believes in him may not be lost, but have eternal life."

—JOHN 3:16

It was the day of Jesus' crucifixion. God looked around the hill and saw the scene. Three men hung on three crosses. Arms spread. Heads fallen forward. They moaned with the wind.

Some Roman soldiers sat on the ground near the three crosses. Heartbroken women huddled at the foot of the hill . . . their faces streaked with tears.

The Bible tells us that all heaven stood ready to fight—"12 armies of angels" could have been sent to save Jesus (Matthew 26:53). All nature rose up, ready to rescue Him as darkness covered the "whole country" and "the earth shook and rocks broke apart" (Matthew 27:45, 51). Still the angels waited to protect. But the Creator never gave the order to save His Son.

Imagine the scene in heaven: "It must be done," God said, as He turned away. The angel whispered, "It would be less painful if . . ." But the Creator interrupted softly, "But it wouldn't be love."

Growing in Grace

What does love mean to you? Is it just hugs and kisses and presents on holidays? God's love is so much more. It's giving up what you want so you can give to another. It's choosing to be last so another can be first. It's helping even when it's hard. That's what love is.

God's Message

Jesus tasted the vinegar. Then he said, "It is
finished." He bowed his head and died.

—JOHN 19:30

Pretend you are at the foot of the cross. Listen for a moment. Let these words from Scripture soak into your heart. Imagine the sound of Jesus' cry from the cross. The sky is dark. The other two men are moaning on their crosses. The loud jeers of the crowd are finally silent. Perhaps there is thunder. Perhaps there is crying. Perhaps there is silence. Then Jesus draws a deep breath, pushes His feet downward on that Roman nail, and cries, "It is finished!"

What was finished?

God's plan for saving all of mankind was finished. The plan that had started all the way back in the garden of Eden was done at last. God had given His greatest gift to each of us. He had washed away our every sin and will one day take us home to heaven. And with that gift came God's message of how very much He loves each and every one of us.

Growing in Grace

The cross is God's message of love to you. Draw a cross on a large piece of paper. All around write your messages of love to God. Tell Him all the things you are thankful for and how very much you love Him.

The Keystone

We believe that Jesus died and that he rose
again. So, because of Jesus, God will bring
together with Jesus those who have died.

—1 THESSALONIANS 4:14

The *keystone* is the stone at the top of an arch. It holds the
whole thing up. In the same way, Jesus' being raised from the
dead is the *keystone* of Christianity. It holds the whole thing up.

You see, God's promise to those who choose to follow Jesus is a
simple one: because Jesus was raised from the dead—*resurrected*—
we, too, will rise from death and go to live in heaven with Him.

But can we trust that promise? How do we know the resurrection was real? That isn't just a good question. It is *the* best question.
Paul wrote, "If Christ has not been raised, then your faith is for
nothing; you are still guilty of your sins" (1 Corinthians 15:17).

In other words, if Christ has been raised from the dead, then
His followers will join Him in heaven. But if He has not been
raised, then His followers are lost forever.

Aren't you glad the tomb really was *empty*?

Growing in Grace

*Some people question whether or not the tomb was really empty.
Read Matthew 28 and Luke 24. Several people saw the empty tomb
with their own eyes, including the Roman soldiers (Matthew 28:4).
Can you count how many people saw the empty tomb? That many
people couldn't be wrong!*

No Greater Reason

At dawn on the first day, Mary Magdalene and another
woman named Mary went to look at the tomb.

—MATTHEW 28:1

Mary and Mary Magdalene made their way up the mountain toward Jesus' tomb. They were taking spices to put on His body. It was something that needed to be done. They didn't expect anything in return. After all, what could Jesus give them? What could a dead man offer them? These two women weren't going to Jesus' tomb to *get* anything; they were going to *give*. They were going because they wanted to serve Him . . . because they loved Him.

There is no greater reason.

At the tomb that day, Mary and Mary Magdalene were acting out of love—the greatest service of all. It is what we are called to do as Jesus' disciples. It is truly following Him.

Growing in Grace

It's easy to think some jobs in the church are more important. But tidying up a classroom or drawing a card for someone who is sick is just as important as preaching and teaching. Everyone—young and old—is part of the church. And every person has an important job to do (1 Corinthians 12:12–26).

God Still Knows

Everything you say and everything you do
should all be done for Jesus your Lord.

—COLOSSIANS 3:17

Mary and Mary Magdalene knew what needed to be done. Jesus' body needed to be anointed—or covered—with special spices before He could be buried. That's what the Jews did for people who had died. And it was the last thing that the women could do for their Lord. Peter didn't offer to do it. Andrew didn't volunteer to do it. So the two Marys decided to do it (Mark 16:1–2).

What would have happened if, on the way to the tomb, they had changed their minds? What if they had given up? What if one had thrown up her hands and moaned, "I'm tired of being the only one who cares. Let Andrew do something for a change. Let Nathanael take a turn"?

It would have been so sad if they had given up and decided to quit. You see, we know something they didn't. We know the Father was watching. Mary and Mary thought they were alone. They weren't. They thought no one knew about their journey. They were wrong. God knew—just as He knows all the good that you do.

Growing in Grace

Sometimes it can seem like no one even notices how hard you're trying. You do the right thing, but you get no reward. Don't give up! Keep doing the right thing, because "your Father can see what is done in secret, and he will reward you" (Matthew 6:4).

The Only Way

*"I am the way. And I am the truth and the life.
The only way to the Father is through me."*

—JOHN 14:6

Tolerance. It's a big word that you hear a lot these days. The world thinks that tolerance means accepting other people no matter what they believe about religion. It is a sign that you are intelligent—or at least that's what the world says.

Jesus believed in tolerance too. But for Jesus, tolerance meant being kind to those who didn't understand His truth. And it meant helping them to understand. For example, He was tolerant of the disciples when they doubted, He was tolerant of the crowds when they misunderstood, and He is tolerant of us when we sin.

But there is one thing about which Jesus was not—and is not—tolerant. He is not tolerant about other ideas of how to get to heaven.

Some people believe if they do enough good things, or if they are strong enough or brave enough, they'll get to heaven. Others believe there are many different ways to heaven. But the truth is that there is only one way to heaven—by believing in and obeying Jesus.

Growing in Grace

Pick out a place you would love to visit. Now take out a map and figure out how to get there. How many different roads could you take? Maybe you could even fly or go by train. But there is only one way to heaven—through Jesus!

Never Enough

*A person cannot do any work that will
make him right with God.*

—ROMANS 4:5

Pretend you have a bank account in heaven—a "holiness account."

In order to get into heaven, your holiness account must be full. So you try to fill your account by doing as many good things as you can. Maybe you say something nice to a friend, or help your neighbor rake up leaves, or help out in the church nursery. Maybe you lead prayers or memorize Bible verses. Surely doing more good things will earn you some extra holiness, right? That should fill up your holiness account, right?

Wrong. When it comes to goodness, you can never do enough. You can never earn enough holiness. To get to heaven, God demands that your holiness account be full—and you just can't do that on your own. So how *do* you get to heaven? Jesus.

When you choose to believe in Jesus and to obey Him, He fills up your holiness account for you. It's called *grace*—and it's His gift to you.

Growing in Grace

You simply can't earn your way to heaven. It is a gift from God. Your gift to God is worship. Make up your own song of worship and praise to God, thanking Him for His gift.

Not Perfect, but Forgiven

Christ had no sin. But God made him become sin. God did
this for us so that in Christ we could become right with God.

—2 CORINTHIANS 5:21

Many people believe that it was the iron nails that held Jesus on the cross. But it wasn't. Not really.

Love held Jesus on the cross.

Jesus knew that our sins had to be punished, and He loved us so much that He took our punishment for us. Jesus—who had never sinned—took on all of our sins and let them die on the cross with Him.

God could have sent His army of angels to save Jesus, but He didn't. He didn't, because God would rather give up His Son than give up on getting us to heaven.

No matter what you've done or said, no matter how big the mistake was, it's not too late to talk to God about it, to ask for forgiveness, and to be free from all sin and guilt.

What makes you a Christian is not that you're perfect but that you're *forgiven*.

Growing in Grace

Give your sins to God. On a chalkboard or dry erase board, write down all the things that you know you've done wrong. Pray about each one and ask God to forgive you. Then erase them all from the board—just as God erases them all from your heart.

I Wonder . . .

"She will have a son, and they will name him Immanuel." This name means "God is with us."

—MATTHEW 1:23

The white space between the lines of the Bible verses leaves room for lots of questions. You can hardly read Scripture without whispering, "I wonder..."

"I wonder if Eve ever ate any more fruit."
"I wonder if Noah had trouble sleeping during thunderstorms."
"I wonder if Jonah ever wanted to eat fish for dinner."

But in your wonderings, there are some questions you never need to ask: Does God care? Do you matter to God? Does He still love His children?

God sent a tiny baby to be born in a stable. That was the proof that, yes, God cares.

Yes, your sins are forgiven. Yes, your name is written in heaven. And, yes, God is in your world.

Immanuel means "God is with us"... and He is.

Growing in Grace

What things do you wonder about? How the sun rises? Why birds sing? What makes stars twinkle? Go to the library and see what answers you can find. Thank God for the wonders of His creation and that you never have to wonder about His love for you.

The Fire in Your Heart

My God, I want to do what you want.
Your teachings are in my heart.

—PSALM 40:8

Want to know God's will for your life? Then answer this question: What sets your heart on fire? That is, what do you feel that you just *have to do* to show God's love or to help others? Is it helping orphans? Or the homeless? Or people who don't know Jesus?

Pay attention to the fire in your heart! Do you love to sing more than anything? Then sing! Does your heart hurt for the sick and the lonely? Then comfort them!

As a young man, I felt that God wanted me to preach. But I wasn't sure if I understood God's will correctly. So I talked to a minister whom I looked up to. His advice to me was, "Don't preach unless you *have* to."

As I thought about his words, I found my answer. "I have to preach. If I don't, this fire in my heart will burn me up. If I don't preach, I'll spend the rest of my life wishing that I had."

What is the fire in your heart? What is it that you just *have to do* for God?

Growing in Grace

Make a list of all the things that you love to do. Do you love to play ball? To sing? Do crafts? Paint or read? Ask God to show you how you can worship Him and share His Word by using the things you love to do.

Time Just for God

*Jesus often slipped away to other places
to be alone so that he could pray.*

—LUKE 5:16

How long has it been since you let God have your full attention?

I mean *really* have all of your attention. How long since you gave Him a part of your day—without any computers or television or telephones? How long since you just listened for His voice and did nothing else? That's what Jesus did. He set aside time to spend time with God—just God.

If you read about the life of Jesus in the Bible, you'll see that He made time with God a habit. He spent time with God regularly, praying and listening. Mark said, "Early the next morning, Jesus woke and left the house while it was still dark. He went to a place to be alone and pray" (Mark 1:35).

Let me ask you a question. If Jesus—the Son of God, the Savior who never sinned—thought He needed to take time to pray, wouldn't we be smart to do the same?

Growing in Grace

How much time do you give to God? Make a list of all you do in a day—sleep, eat, study, play with friends. How much time do you spend on each of those things? Now, how much time do you give to God? Do you need to make some changes?

God's Greatest Work

We know that when Christ comes again, we will
be like him. We will see him as he really is.

—1 JOHN 3:2

When you get to heaven, something wonderful will happen. One final change will happen. You will be just like Jesus. Of all the blessings in heaven, one of the greatest will be you! You will be God's *magnum opus*. That means that you will be His masterpiece, His *greatest* work of art. The angels will gasp in amazement. God's work in you will be complete. As last you will have a heart just like His.

You will love with a perfect love.

You will worship with a joyful face.

You'll hear each word God speaks.

Your heart and your thoughts will be pure; your words will
be like jewels—beautiful gifts to those who hear them.

You will be just like Jesus. Finally, you will have a heart like
His.

Growing in Grace

You don't have to wait for heaven to make your words as beautiful as jewels. Put a handful of pebbles in your pocket. Throughout the day, try to say kind things to those around you. Each time you do, secretly drop a pebble on the ground. How quickly can you empty your pocket?

Peace with God

"I don't call you servants now. . . . Now I call you friends."

—JOHN 15:15

Because of Jesus' sacrifice on the cross, our past sins are forgiven and our future in heaven is certain. "We have been made right with God because of our faith. So we have peace with God through our Lord Jesus Christ" (Romans 5:1).

Peace with God. What will that be like? Have you even been in a gym filled with people screaming for their favorite team? Or at a concert filled with loud music and loud fans? Or stuck between two people arguing at the top of their voices? And then . . . you stepped outside. Your heart stopped pounding, your breathing slowed. How quiet, how . . . peaceful.

Peace with God will be a zillion times better than that. When you get to heaven, there will be no more screaming, loudness, or arguing. There will be only love and joy and peace. It will be better than peace between countries, better than peace between friends, and better than peace at home. We will have peace with God.

Growing in Grace

Peace with God is the most important kind of peace. But some special people also try to keep peace for our country—our soldiers. Write a letter or put together a care package for a soldier who's been sent to a foreign country. Send a little bit of home and hope today.

Confess Your Sins

Happy is the person
whose sins are forgiven,
whose wrongs are pardoned.

—PSALM 32:1

If we are already forgiven for our sins, then why does Jesus want us to confess them—to tell them to Him? Why does He teach us to pray, "Forgive the sins we have done" (Matthew 6:12)?

For the very same reason your parents and teacher make you say you are sorry when you do something wrong. If my own children break a rule, I don't kick them out of the house or tell them to change their last name. But I do want them to be honest about what they did and to apologize. And until they do, our relationship will suffer. I will still be their dad, and they will still be my children, but we will not be as close. There will be a wall between us.

The same thing happens in your walk with God. Confessing sins does not create a relationship with God. You will always be His child. But it does make it better. Confessing your sins gets you closer to God.

Growing in Grace

Is there something you need to confess? Perhaps something you've hidden from your parents? Don't wait a minute longer! Go and tell them. Apologize and make it right. Then ask God to forgive you too. You'll feel a whole lot better when you do.

The Nature of God

There are things about God that people cannot see. . . . But since the beginning of the world those things have been easy to understand. They are made clear by what God has made.

—ROMANS 1:20

God doesn't keep the way to heaven a secret. His Word tells us how to get to heaven. But even those people who have never heard of Jesus are given a message about God: "The heavens tell the glory of God" (Psalm 19:1).

Nature is God's first missionary. Where there is no Bible, there are sparkling stars. If a person has nothing but nature, then nature is enough to tell him something about God. For "day after day [the heavens] tell the story. . . . They have no speech or words. They don't make any sound to be heard. But their message goes out through all the world. It goes everywhere on earth" (Psalm 19:2–4).

The wonders of nature can cause those who don't know God to wonder about their Creator. And God promises that those who search for Him with all their hearts will find Him (Jeremiah 29:13).

Growing in Grace

God's messages in nature are for you too. Take a nature walk and look for God's messages. When you see a bird, thank God for His care. Look at the springtime flowers and thank God for His creativity. Feel the wind and thank God for His power. God's messages are all around you—just open your eyes and see.

Courage

All you who put your hope in the Lord
be strong and brave.

—PSALM 31:24

A legend from India tells about a mouse who was terrified of cats until a magician agreed to change him into a cat. That fixed his fear . . . until he met a dog. So the magician changed him into a dog. The mouse-turned-cat-turned-dog was happy . . . until he met a tiger. So, once again, the magician changed him into what he feared. But when the tiger came complaining that he had met a hunter, the magician would not help. "I will make you into a mouse again, for even though you have the body of a tiger, you still have the heart of a mouse."

Like that tiger, lots of people look big and tough on the outside, but inside they are trembling with fear. We fight our fears, and we try to make ourselves safe by wearing the right clothes, hanging out with the right friends, and having the right stuff. But does that really work? Are we any less frightened?

Courage comes from who we are inside—God's children—not what we have on the outside.

Growing in Grace

God is your "rock and [your] protection" (Psalm 31:3). Head out to a park. Find the biggest rock you can and hide behind it. Can anything get to you through that rock? God is even stronger than that rock. Hide yourself in Him, and the devil can't touch you!

One of a Kind

You made my whole being.
You formed me in my mother's body.

—PSALM 139:13

In my closet hangs a sweater that I never wear. It is too small. I should throw that sweater away. But *love* won't let me.

My mom made it for me. Each stitch shows her love for me. Each strand was chosen with care. Each thread was picked with affection. It is special not because of what it is, but because of who made it.

That must have been what the writer of Psalm 139 was thinking when he wrote, "You knit me together in my mother's womb" (v. 13 NIV).

Think about those words. You were knit together by God. You aren't an accident. You weren't made on some galactic assembly line. You aren't just another kid.

You were deliberately planned, specially gifted, and lovingly placed on this earth by God. In a world that decides your worth by the clothes you wear or the sports you play, let me tell you something—you are valuable because God created you.

Growing in Grace

What makes you you? Make a list of all the things that make you unique. Your hair and eye color. Your talents. Your personality. Then thank God for each part of you, for you are "amazing and wonderful" (Psalm 139:14)!

Just Like the Thief

"Listen! What I say is true: Today you
will be with me in paradise!"

—LUKE 23:43

Tell me, what did the thief on the cross do to deserve help? He had wasted his life. Who was he to beg for forgiveness? He had publicly made fun of Jesus. What right did he have to pray, "Jesus, remember me when you come into your kingdom!" (Luke 23:42)?

Do you really want to know? He had the same right to ask Jesus to save him as we do.

Have we used every second of our time as we should? Probably not. Have we ever laughed at someone or made fun of them? Probably so. Do we deserve Jesus' help? Definitely not.

We can't take out our list of all the good things we've done, because we could never do enough good to get us to heaven. In the single most important way of all, we are just like that thief— our only hope of getting into heaven is Jesus.

So, just like the thief, we pray, "Jesus, remember me."

And just like the thief, we hear the voice of Jesus say, "You will be with me in paradise!"

Growing in Grace

When you find yourself in need of forgiveness, try this prayer: "God, be merciful to me because you are loving. Because you are always ready to be merciful, wipe out all my wrongs. Wash away all my guilt and make me clean again" (Psalm 51:1–2).

Only You

Come near to God, and God will come near to you.

—JAMES 4:8

Some of us have tried to have a quiet time with God every day, but we have not stuck with it. Others of us have a hard time being still and quiet. And all of us are busy. So rather than spend time with God, listening for His voice, we let others do it and then tell us what God said. After all, isn't that what preachers and parents are for?

If that's what you're thinking—if your ideas about God come only from others and not from spending time with Him yourself—think about this: Do you do that with other parts of your life?

Do you let other people go on vacation for you? Do you let other people play with your friends for you? You don't let someone else eat for you, do you? There are some things that no one else can do for you. Only you can.

And one of those things is spending time with God.

Growing in Grace

Make God's message your own. Next Sunday, listen carefully to what the preacher or Bible class teacher says. Write down all the Bible verses that you hear. When you get home, look them up for yourself. See what God's Word has to say to you.

We All Need Grace

"Give us the food we need for each day.
Forgive the sins we have done,
just as we have forgiven those who did wrong to us."
—MATTHEW 6:11-12

We are all sinners. We all mess up and need grace and forgiveness from God. Jesus teaches us to pray, "Forgive the sins we have done . . . [and] do not cause us to be tested" (Matthew 6:12–13).

We've all made mistakes, and we'll all make some more. Paul asked, "So why do you judge your brother in Christ? And why do you think that you are better than he is? We will all stand before God, and he will judge us all" (Romans 14:10).

Do you have a brother or sister who could use some grace from you? Maybe your sister needs your forgiveness just as you need forgiveness from God. It's better to forgive rather than to try to get even. Sometimes tattling and getting revenge only make things worse. And as for your brother, there comes a time when the best thing you can do is love him. Offer him the same grace and forgiveness that you've been given.

Growing in Grace

Getting along with brothers and sisters can be tough. Next time you have a fuss, instead of tattling or getting even, take a time-out. Go to another room and pray. Ask God to help you make things right. Then go to your brother or sister and do just that.

May

Your word is like a lamp for my feet
and a light for my way.

—PSALM 119:105

Your Prayers

The Lord sees the good people.
He listens to their prayers.

—1 PETER 3:12

You and I live in a loud world. It's not easy to get someone's attention. That person must be willing to turn down the radio, turn away from the computer, turn the corner of the page and put down the book. When someone in our world is willing to turn off everything else to listen to us, it is a gift. A very rare gift.

But in heaven God is always listening. Your prayers are like precious jewels to Him. Your words rise up to God like a soft breeze—and they don't stop until they reach His throne.

Your prayers on earth stir up God's power in heaven, and "what [God wants] will be done, here on earth as it is in heaven" (Matthew 6:10).

Your prayers move God to change the world. You may not understand the power and the mystery of prayer. You don't need to. But this much is clear: God is always listening, and He is always answering.

Growing in Grace

God always stops to listen to you. Do the same for Him today. Stop. Turn off the television and the computer. Pull out the earphones. Put down the phone. Be still and quiet. God speaks in a whisper. So listen carefully.

We Look to God

Peter said, "Lord, if that is really you, then
tell me to come to you on the water."

—MATTHEW 14:28

When Peter asked to walk out on the water, he was not testing Jesus—he was begging Jesus. Stepping into a stormy sea did not make sense. It was a desperate move. Peter grabbed the edge of the boat. He threw out one leg and then followed with the other leg. Several steps were taken. It was if an invisible pathway of rocks ran under his feet. At the end of the path was the glowing face of an "I'll-never-give-up-on-you" Friend—Jesus.

We do the same thing, don't we? We try to do it all on our own—to fix our own problems and even to earn our own way to heaven. We only pray to Jesus when we realize that we need Him. When we realize we can never save ourselves, we call out to Him and beg Him to save us.

But the wonderful news is that when we do call out to Jesus, He answers us just as He answered Peter. He says, "Come" (Matthew 14:29).

Growing in Grace

Next time you visit a lake, dip your hand in the water. Think about Peter stepping out of the boat onto a stormy sea. Think of how deep and dark the water must have been. Even when Peter began to sink, he knew where to look for help—Jesus!

Sometimes God Says No

Continue praying and keep alert. And
when you pray, always thank God.

—COLOSSIANS 4:2

Can you imagine what would happen if your parents gave you everything you asked for on your next trip? You'd end up crawling with a bloated belly from one ice-cream store to the next.

Can you imagine the mess there would be if God gave us everything we asked for?

"God did not *choose* us to suffer his anger, but to have salvation through our Lord Jesus Christ" (1 Thessalonians 5:9).

In this verse, what does it say God chooses for your life? Salvation. God's greatest want is that you reach heaven. His plan includes stops that will help you on your journey to heaven. He frowns on stops that slow you down. When His perfect plan and your earthly plan crash together, a choice must be made. Who's in charge of this journey? You or God?

It's God. And I'm glad He chose heaven for us all.

Growing in Grace

Parents have to say no sometimes. The next time your parents tell you no—before you get upset—stop and think about why they said no. Could it be that saying no was best for you? Want to really shock them? Thank them for caring enough to say no!

God's Plan

Your word is like a lamp for my feet
and a light for my way.

—PSALM 119:105

God gave us the Bible so that He could tell us His plan for us. The Bible tells us that we are all lost and need to be saved. And it tells us that Jesus is God in human form and that He was sent to save God's children.

The Bible was written by at least forty different authors spread out over sixteen hundred years. But it has just one message: salvation comes through faith in Jesus. The first words of the Bible were written by Moses in the lonely desert of Arabia, and the last words were written by John on the lonely island of Patmos. Yet one thread holds the whole Bible together: God's love for His children and God's plan to save them.

The Bible is like your compass for your journey through life. Check your compass, and you'll journey safely. Forget to use your compass—forget to study your Bible—and who knows where you'll end up.

Growing in Grace

God's Word is the light for your path. To see how His light can overcome the darkness, grab a flashlight. When it's dark outside, go for a flashlight walk. The light shows you where you can safely go— just as God's Word does.

Not Guilty!

Who can accuse the people that God has chosen?
No one! God is the One who makes them right.

—ROMANS 8:33

E very moment of your life, your accuser—Satan, the biggest tattletale of all time—is taking notes. He has noticed every mistake and written down each slip-up. Try to forget your past; he'll remind you. Try to fix your mistakes; he will trip you up.

Satan has no greater goal than to take you to God's courtroom and press charges. He yells, "This one You call Your child, God, he doesn't deserve Your forgiveness. He's made too many mistakes."

As he speaks, you hang your head. You know he is right. "I plead guilty, Your Honor," you mumble.

"What is the sentence?" Satan asks.

"The punishment for sin is death," explains the Judge, "but Jesus Christ died as payment for this person's sins."

Satan suddenly has nothing to say. And you are suddenly filled with joy. You have stood before the Judge and heard Him say, "Not guilty!"

Growing in Grace

God has a plan to save you—and His plan is Jesus. Believe in Him and obey Him, and you won't have to worry about the devil's tattling. But God also has a plan for your life. Pray and ask Him to show you the next step in His plan for you.

God's in Charge

God's Spirit, who is in you, is greater than
the devil, who is in the world.

—1 JOHN 4:4

Sometimes it may seem like Satan is winning the battle for this world and that he is in charge. But God is in *complete* control, and He has an amazing way of using Satan's evil plans to do good. Satan thought he had won when Jesus died on the cross. But God raised Jesus from the dead and gave the gift of salvation to His people.

Many Christians in the early church were thrown in prison or killed. Many others left their homes and ran away to other lands. But God used those hard times to spread His word to other countries. Sad things and even bad things happen to all people—to those who believe in God and those who don't. But God has a special promise for His children: "In everything God works for the good of those who love him" (Romans 8:28).

When you see sad things or even bad things in your life, when it seems like Satan is winning, remember that God will somehow use those things for good. Because God is in charge.

Growing in Grace

Believing in Jesus can be risky. Some people may laugh at you. You may lose a friend when you refuse to do something wrong that everyone else is doing. Yes, following Jesus has its risks, but the rewards are amazing!

Why Go Back?

He gave himself for us; he died to free us from all evil. He
died to make us pure people who belong only to him.

—TITUS 2:14

Do you ever give in and decide to sin today, thinking, *Oh, I'll
just confess tomorrow?*

It's easy to be like the girl who steals a dollar from her mom's
purse, knowing she won't get caught. Or the kid who sneaks into
the scary movie on Saturday afternoon, knowing he's going
to church on Sunday morning. It's easy to say, "I'm going to do
whatever I want, because God will forgive me anyway."

But is that the purpose of grace? Of God's forgiveness? Did
God give up His Son just so that we could get away with disobeying Him? Nope. The Bible tells us that "God's grace . . . teaches
us not to live against God and not to do the evil things the world
wants to do. That grace teaches us to live on earth now in a wise
and right way" (Titus 2:11–12).

God's grace washes away all our selfish and sinful mistakes.
Once we are clean, why would we want to go back to being dirty?

Growing in Grace

*Pretend you're a pig. You've been stuck in the mud, and now mud
is all over you—even in your ears and in your nose. It's getting itchy.
But then the rain comes and washes you clean. Do you want to go
back to the mud? No! But God says that's just what we do when we
go back to sinful ways (2 Peter 2:20–22).*

Who Are You to Judge?

"You will be judged in the same way that you judge others."

—MATTHEW 7:2

We laugh at the boy who stumbles this morning, but we didn't see how hard he was hit yesterday. We make fun of the girl with the limp, but we cannot see the rock in her shoe.

Is someone too loud? Maybe he is afraid of being ignored again. Is someone else scared? Maybe she is afraid of failing again. Are others moving too slowly? Maybe they fell the last time they ran. We don't know. Only the One who is always watching them can know.

Not only do we not know about their yesterdays, but we don't know about their tomorrows either. We must leave the judging to God. Our job is to "love each other" and to "be kind and humble" to each other (1 Peter 3:8). Remember, "God began doing a good work in you. And he will continue it until it is finished when Jesus Christ comes again" (Philippians 1:6). God's not finished with you—or them—yet!

Growing in Grace

Pick up a book that doesn't have any pictures. Can you tell what kind of story is inside? No! People are much the same way. You only see the outside, but the inside is where the story is. Don't judge a book—or a person—by the cover.

Listening for God

A rule here, a rule there.
A lesson here, a lesson there.

—ISAIAH 28:10

If you have the right tools, you can learn to listen to God. What are those tools? Here are the ones I have found helpful:

The first is *a regular time and place*. Pick a time in your day and a corner of your world, and make that your time and place for God. You may want to listen to God first thing in the morning. Or you may like nighttime better.

A second tool you need is *an open Bible*. God speaks to you through His Word. The first step in reading the Bible is to ask God to help you understand it. Search God's Word for what He is really telling you, not what you want Him to say.

The third tool is *a listening heart*. If you want to be just like Jesus, work on hearing God's voice. Spend time listening for Him until He tells you His lesson for the day—and then go out and live that lesson.

Growing in Grace

To help you remember the tools you'll need to listen to God, make a "ruler tool." Find a wooden ruler and a permanent marker. Write on your ruler the three tools you'll need: Time and Place, Open Bible, and Listening Heart. Use your ruler as a Bible bookmark.

Because You Believe

So let us come near to God with a sincere
heart and a sure faith. We have been cleansed
and made free from feelings of guilt.

—HEBREWS 10:22

Faith is not something that you can trade for. You can't come to God on Sunday morning and say, "Okay, I've been nice to fifteen people this week, obeyed my parents twenty-one times, and done twelve good deeds. I'll trade You all that for one ticket to heaven."

Sounds silly, doesn't it? That's because it is silly. You can't trade your good works for His salvation. Yes, God wants you to do good things, but the truth is you can never do *enough* good things to trade your way into heaven.

What *does* get you into heaven? The apostle Paul answered that question: "You have been saved by grace because you believe. You did not save yourselves. It was a gift from God. You cannot brag that you are saved by the work you have done" (Ephesians 2:8–9). Heaven is God's gift to those who *believe* that His grace will get them there.

Growing in Grace

Grace is God's greatest gift to us. It means we can live with Him in heaven forever. But grace is not God's only gift to us. Make a list of as many of His gifts as you can think of. Here are a couple to get you started: a family that loves you and the air that you breathe.

Personal Grace

The Lord knows those who belong to him.

—2 TIMOTHY 2:19

Just imagine. You are standing before the judgment seat of Christ. The book of your life is opened, and the reading begins—each sin, each lie, each moment of anger and selfishness. But as soon as the sin is read, grace and forgiveness are given.

The result? God's mercy will be heard throughout the universe. For the first time in history, we will understand how great His goodness is. Not just a one-size-fits-all grace. But personal grace. Just for you. Specific kindness. Individual forgiveness. We will stand in awe as one sin after another is read and then forgiven.

The devil will hide. The angels will sing. And we will stand tall in God's grace. As we see how much He has forgiven us, we will see how much He loves us. And we will worship Him.

Growing in Grace

God knows you. You. As an individual. A unique person. He even knows you better than you know yourself. Don't believe it? Try this: count the number of hairs on your head. Can you do it? God can. He already knows the answer—He told us so in Matthew 10:30.

A Better Way

I keep trying to reach the goal and get the prize. That prize is mine because God called me through Christ to the life above.

—PHILIPPIANS 3:14

Life at camp is a lot different from life at home. The first day or two, it's great. Nobody cares if you leave your socks on the floor or take a shower or brush your teeth. You can be a total slob, and no one cares.

About the middle of the week, things start to change. You get tired of stepping over your dirty clothes and everyone else's. You really wish you had a clean bed. And that smell you've been smelling—it's you! By the end of the week, you can't take it anymore. Out come the soap and toothpaste, and up go the socks and towels.

What happened? Simple. You knew there was a better way.

Isn't that what Jesus does for us? Before we knew Jesus, our lives were sloppy and selfish. But suddenly now we want to do good—even when no one is looking! Go back to the old mess? Are you kidding? Not a chance. There's a better way.

Growing in Grace

Do some cleaning up and help others at the same time. Hold a car wash in your neighborhood or at your church. Send the money you raise to missionaries to help them teach others about Jesus and His better way.

Who Am I?

Jesus asked, "Who do you say I am?"

—MARK 8:29

Jesus turned to His disciples and asked them a question. *The* question. "Who do you say I am?"

He didn't ask, "What do you think about all the miracles I've done?" He asked, "Who do you say I am?"

He didn't ask, "Who do your friends think I am? Or your parents? Or who does the preacher think I am?" Instead He asked a very personal question, "Who do *you* think I am?"

You will be asked some important questions in your life:

What do you want to be when you grow up?
Who will you marry?
Where will you live?

But the greatest, most important question of all these kinds of questions is an anthill compared to the mountain of a question that Jesus asked in Mark 8:29.

Who do you say I am?

Growing in Grace

Who do you say Jesus is? Take a poster board and fill it with words and drawings that describe Jesus. Here are a few ideas to get you started: Savior, Prince of Peace, and Almighty King!

God's Mountains

*"My grace is enough for you. When you are weak,
then my power is made perfect in you."*

—2 CORINTHIANS 12:9

Life is a lot like mountain climbing. There are some mountains that you just can't climb on your own. Mountains like wiping away your sins and getting to heaven. Those are God's mountains, the ones that only He can climb. It's not that you aren't welcome to try; it's just that you aren't able.

You aren't supposed to fix all your own problems, or run the whole world, or get yourself to heaven.

Oh, some of you try. You think you can just work a little harder and climb a little faster. That may be enough when it comes to making all As or winning a race. But you can't work hard enough or climb fast enough to get over the mountain of your own sins and mistakes. You don't have that kind of power. You need God to map out the way, to guide your hands and feet, and to hold the ropes so that you don't fall.

Growing in Grace

Have you ever noticed all the gear that mountain climbers have? They have all kinds of safety harnesses and ropes that protect them from falling. God is kind of like that safety gear. He gives you the strength and confidence to climb, and He keeps you safe from falling.

The Right Answer

The person who is made right with
God by faith will live forever.

—ROMANS 1:17

At the moment I don't feel too smart. I just got off the wrong plane at the wrong airport in the wrong city. I went east instead of west and ended up in Texas instead of Colorado. Oops.

It didn't look like the wrong plane, but it was. I walked through the wrong gate, fell asleep on the wrong flight, and ended up in the wrong place.

Paul said we've all done the same thing. Not with airplanes and airports, but with our lives and with God. He said: "There is no one without sin. None!" (Romans 3:10). "All people have sinned and are not good enough for God's glory" (v. 23).

It's like we are all on the wrong plane. All of us. Boy and girl. Grown-up and child. Every person has taken the wrong turn at some point. And we need help. The wrong answers are selfishness and chasing after fun (Romans 1 and 2). The right answer is Christ Jesus (3:21–26).

Growing in Grace

Visit an airport. Notice how all the planes look pretty much the same. Only certain people know the right one—the people in charge. That's true with a lot of choices. Sometimes bad choices look like good ones. Only the One in charge knows the difference. Check with Him before you choose.

This Isn't Home

"I have chosen you out of the world. So you don't belong to it."

—JOHN 15:19

We all know what it's like to be in a house that's not yours. Maybe you've spent time at a friend's house or grandparent's house. Maybe you've slept in a bunk bed at camp or a hotel room on vacation. They have beds and tables. They may have food, and they may be warm, but they are not "your father's house."

Your father's house is where your father is. And your true home is where your heavenly Father is.

You may not always feel welcome here on earth. You may wonder if there is a place here for you. People can make you feel unwanted. Like a stranger in a house that's not yours. You won't always feel welcome here.

You shouldn't. This isn't your home. This language you speak, it's not yours. This body you wear, it isn't the real you. And the world you live in, this isn't home. Where is your real home? Heaven—and it's waiting for you.

Growing in Grace

When you are a child of God, you can take a little bit of your heavenly home with you wherever you go—God's Word. Ask your parents for a small pocket Bible of your own. Keep it in your purse or backpack. Whenever you're feeling homesick, read a little bit about "home."

Working with God

We are God's workers, working together.

—1 CORINTHIANS 3:9 NCV

I t's a wonderful day when we stop working *for* God and start working *with* God.

For years I thought of God as the boss of a big company— a nice guy, but definitely *The Boss*. And I was just one of His loyal helpers. He had His office, and I had mine. I went out to do His work and then reported back. I could call Him as much as I wanted. He was always just a phone call or e-mail away. He encouraged me, cheered me on, and supported me, but He didn't go with me. At least I didn't think He did. Then I read 2 Corinthians 6:1: "We are workers together with God."

Workers *with* God? Working *together*? God and I working together? Wow! We don't just report back to God; we work with God. We don't check in with Him and leave; we check in with Him and then follow. We are always in the presence of God. Every moment is sacred!

Growing in Grace

As you work today—doing your chores or your homework, or serving God—think about who is working next to you. God is. Does that make you want to do things a little differently? A little better? Do all things as if you were doing them for God (Colossians 3:23).

Found, Called, and Adopted

"Healthy people don't need a doctor. Only the
sick need a doctor. . . . I did not come to invite
good people. I came to invite sinners."

—MATTHEW 9:12–13

God didn't look at our messed-up, mixed-up lives and say, "I'll die for you when you deserve it."

No, in spite of all our sins, in spite of our not obeying His Word, He chose to adopt us. And for God, there's no going back.

God's grace is a come-as-you-are promise from a one-of-a-kind God. You've been *found*. You've been *called*—His Spirit has touched your heart and made you want to follow Him. And you've been *adopted* by Him.

So trust your Father and claim this verse as your own: "Christ died for us while we were still sinners. In this way God shows his great love for us" (Romans 5:8). You've been adopted by God! "You are God's child, and God will give you what he promised, because you are his child" (Galatians 4:7).

Growing in Grace

Let's dig a little deeper into these words. Found—it means God came looking for you (Luke 19:10). Called—it means He spoke to your heart (Romans 1:6). Adopted—He chose you to be His child (8:16–17). Not an accident, not a mistake. You are His choice.

God Is for You

If God is for us, who can be against us?

—ROMANS 8:31 NIV

The question is not simply, "Who can be against us?" You could answer that one. Who is against you? The bully in gym class, the mean girl, sickness, sadness, tiredness, loneliness—and all those other "ness-es" that make such messes in our lives.

If Paul's question were only "Who can be against us?" we could list our enemies. It would be much easier for us to simply list them than to fight them. But that is not the question. The question is, "If God is for us, who can be against us?"

God *is* for you. A bully may have picked on you, your teachers may have overlooked you, your brothers and sisters may not speak to you, but within earshot of your prayers is the One who made the oceans—God! He is for you, and He fights for you!

Growing in Grace

What are the problems that pester you? Write them down on a piece of paper, and then tear it into tiny pieces. Now take a look at all those pieces. No matter how huge your problems may seem, they're just tiny scraps compared to the power of God.

God's Anger

So put all evil things out of your life....
These things make God angry.

—COLOSSIANS 3:5-6

Many people don't understand God's anger. They confuse the anger of God with the anger of people. But the two are very different. People's anger is usually selfish. It shows itself in explosions of temper and violence. We get upset because we've been ignored, skipped over, or cheated. When we don't get what we want, we get mad. This is the anger of people. It is not, however, the anger of God.

God doesn't get angry because He doesn't get His way. He gets angry because we disobey Him. And He knows that by disobeying Him, we will always end up getting hurt. After all, what kind of father sits by and watches his child hurt himself? Not God!

Growing in Grace

Spend an hour helping in your church's toddler class. Pick out one youngster who is just learning to walk. How hard is it to keep him from falling and hurting himself? Just as you follow close behind that toddler to protect him, God follows close behind you—to protect you.

God Knows Your Name

I have written your name on my hand.

—ISAIAH 49:16

What a thought! Your name is written on God's hand. Your name is on God's lips. Maybe you've seen your name in some special places. On an award or a trophy. But to think that your name is on God's hand and on God's lips . . . Wow! Could it be?

Or maybe you have never had your name honored. Maybe you've never made the honor roll. Or won the trophy. Or been chosen for the team. If so, it may be even harder for you to believe that God knows your name.

But He does. It's written on His hand. Spoken by His mouth. Whispered by His lips. *Your name.*

Growing in Grace

Close your eyes and picture God gently calling your name. Do you hear Him? Do you see your name written in beautiful letters on the palm of His hand? Read Psalm 139 to discover just how well the Lord knows you—and how much He loves you.

Hold On

Our time on earth is like a shadow.

—1 CHRONICLES 29:15

God lives forever. He has no beginning and no end. But He knows the beginning and end of everyone who has ever lived. He knows every moment of their lives. And He knows the answer to their every question.

"How long am I going to be without a friend?"

"How long am I going to be sick?"

"How long am I going to struggle to get along with my family?"

Do you really want God to answer? He could, you know. He could answer exactly how many weeks, or days, or hours. "A few more months without a friend." "Two more years of illness." "The rest of your life with your family."

But God doesn't usually do that. He asks us to trust Him. He uses our times of loneliness, sickness, and struggle to teach us to turn to Him for help. Although our troubles sometimes seem to last forever, they really don't—but heaven does. So hold on.

Growing in Grace

God's time is very different from our time. To us, one bad day seems like a thousand years. But because God is eternal, a thousand years are just like one day (2 Peter 3:8). Think of it this way: your day is like a grain of sand, but God's day is like the whole beach!

Stick Together

We pray that the Lord will lead your hearts
into God's love and Christ's patience.
—2 THESSALONIANS 3:5

All people will know that you are my followers if you love each other" (John 13:35). Stop and think about this verse for a minute. Could it be that *unity*—loving one another and sticking together—is the way we can tell the world about Jesus?

If unity is the key to reaching others, shouldn't it have an important place in our prayers? Shouldn't we, as Paul said, "do all [we] can to continue together" (Ephesians 4:3)? If sticking together matters to God, then shouldn't sticking together matter to us? If unity is important in heaven, then shouldn't it be important on earth?

Nobody wants to be around people who fuss and fight. So if God's people want to help others learn about Jesus, we must first show them that we love each other. That means we don't talk badly about each other. We treat each other with kindness and respect. We help each other, and we stick together. God's people must love each other *before* they can love others.

Growing in Grace

Unity—sticking together—is important for churches, but it's also important for families and friendships. Ephesians 4:2 is the perfect recipe for keeping unity: "Always be humble and gentle. Be patient and accept each other with love."

Sorry for Sin

If we confess our sins, he will forgive our sins.
We can trust God. He does what is right.

—1 JOHN 1:9

I f we confess our sins . . ." The biggest word in the Bible just might be that tiny two-letter one *if.* Confessing sins—admitting we have messed up—is exactly what we often don't want to do. We don't want to admit we've failed. We are prisoners of our own pride.

"Me? A sinner? Oh sure, I get in a little trouble once in a while, but I'm a pretty good kid."

"Hey, listen! I'm just as good as Amy, and I'm definitely better than Jake."

Pretty good. Just as good. Better than. Sound familiar? We all say these things. We compare ourselves to others, and we look good. But in heaven, pretty good just isn't good enough.

When you get to the point of being sorry for your sins, when you admit that Jesus is your only choice, then confess. Tell Him about your sins, and give all your cares to Him. He is waiting for you.

Growing in Grace

Who do you compare yourself to? Your parents? Your friends? Or maybe it's the star of your favorite sports team? Or the latest, greatest singer? Try comparing yourself to Jesus instead. Make being like Him your goal.

Courage

I was given mercy so that in me Christ Jesus could show
that he has patience without limit. And he showed
his patience with me, the worst of all sinners.

—1 TIMOTHY 1:16

During the early days of the Civil War, a Union soldier was arrested for sneaking away and leaving the army. Unable to prove that he was innocent, he was sentenced to die. His plea for mercy found its way to the desk of President Abraham Lincoln. The president felt sorry for the soldier and signed a pardon. The soldier returned to service, fought the rest of the war, and was killed in the last battle. After his death, the signed letter from the president was found inside his shirt pocket.

Close to the heart of the soldier were his leader's words of pardon. The soldier found courage in the grace of the president.

But we have an even greater pardon from an even greater Leader—the pardon of all our sins from our heavenly King. Let God's grace give you the courage to do the right thing.

Growing in Grace

Write your own letter of pardon from your Leader. Write down these words from 1 John 1:9, and then tuck them in your backpack or purse: "If we confess our sins, [God] will forgive our sins. We can trust God. He does what is right. He will make us clean from all the wrongs we have done."

God Still Comes

The Lord is close to the brokenhearted.
He saves those whose spirits have been crushed.

—PSALM 34:18

The Bible is not just a collection of Sunday school stories. These are not made-up fairy tales.

These are actual moments in history when a real God helped real people in real pain so we could answer the question, "Where is God when I hurt?"

How does God react to broken dreams? Read the story of Jairus and his dying daughter (Luke 8:40–56). How does God feel about those who are sick? Picture yourself at the pool of Bethesda as He heals the crippled man (John 5:1–9). Do you wish God would speak to your lonely heart? Then listen as He speaks to the disciples on the road to Emmaus (Luke 24:13–35).

He's not doing it just for them. He's doing it for me. He's doing it for you.

The God who spoke to them still speaks. The God who came to them still comes. He comes into your world. He comes to do what you can't.

Growing in Grace

The Bible is God's Word to His people. And "every word of God can be trusted" (Proverbs 30:5). But how did we get the Bible? Ask your parents or one of your church's ministers to help you find out how we got the Bible we have today.

Close to God

A deer thirsts for a stream of water.
In the same way, I thirst for you, God.

—PSALM 42:1

Jesus didn't act unless He saw His Father act. He didn't judge until He heard His Father judge. He never did or said anything without His Father's guidance.

Because Jesus could hear what others couldn't—His Father's voice—He acted differently than they did. Do you remember in the Bible when everyone was troubled about the man born blind? Jesus wasn't. He knew that the blindness would reveal God's power (John 9:3). Remember the time when everyone was upset about Lazarus's illness and death? Jesus wasn't. It was as if Jesus could hear the thoughts of His Father telling Him that Lazarus would live.

Do you think the Father wants the same kind of hearing for us? Yes! God wants the same closeness with you that He had with His Son. All it takes is spending time with Him.

Growing in Grace

Turn everything off. Go outside. Be still and listen. What do you hear? A dog barking, the wind sighing, a bee buzzing. You hear so much more when you are still and quiet and listening. You can hear your Father when you are "quiet and know that [He is] God" (Psalm 46:10).

A Work in Progress

Jesus will keep you strong until the end. He will keep
you strong, so that there will be no wrong in you on
the day our Lord Jesus Christ comes again.

—1 CORINTHIANS 1:8

God is not finished with you yet. Oh, you may think He is. You
may think you're right where you need to be. You may think
you've got life all figured out.

If so, think again. You've still got a lot of growing to do.

"God began doing a good work in you. And he will continue it until it is finished when Jesus Christ comes again"
(Philippians 1:6).

Did you see what God is doing? *A good work in you.* Did you
see when He will be finished? *When Jesus comes again.* Let me
make God's message clear for you: *God ain't finished with you yet.*

Growing in Grace

*God ain't finished with you yet. But what will you look like—and
be like—when He is? Paint your best self-portrait. Just the way you
look right now. Then paint another portrait. This time show how
you think you'll look when God is finished with you—in heaven.*

A Loving God

Many people who have already died will live again. Some of them will wake up to have life forever. But some will wake up to find shame and disgrace forever.

—DANIEL 12:2

There are those who say hell is not real. That a loving God just wouldn't send anyone there. But let's think about that. If you take punishment out of the Bible, then you also take away God's justice. It's as if you're saying that God doesn't care if people lie or steal or murder. And that He doesn't care about those who have been hurt by the liars, thieves, and murderers. But God says, "I am the One who punishes" (Romans 12:19).

And think about this: if everyone gets into heaven, then why did God send Jesus to wash away our sins? Jesus Himself said, "The only way to the Father is through me" (John 14:6).

If we say there is no punishment for those who refuse to follow Jesus, then we are saying that the Bible is a lie. Because over and over the Bible tells us that some will be lost and some will saved (for example, Matthew 25:33). Punishment for our sins is real. We *must* choose to follow Jesus to be saved.

Growing in Grace

Hell is described as a "lake of fire" (Revelation 20:15). What a terrible place to spend forever! To see how heaven is described, read Revelation 21:10–27. What lights the city of heaven? What are the streets made of? The gates? Sing a song praising God for inviting you to heaven.

He Still Does

[Jesus] felt sorry for them and healed those who were sick.

—MATTHEW 14:14

Matthew wrote that Jesus "healed those who were sick." Not some of the sick. Not just the good people among the sick. Not the deserving among the sick. But "those who were sick."

Surely, among the many thousands, there were a few people who didn't deserve good health. The same God who gave Jesus the power to heal also gave Him the power to see into people's hearts. I wonder if Jesus was ever tempted to say to the liar, "Get out of here, buddy, and take your tales with you."

And Jesus could not only see their past, but He could also see their future. There were surely those in the crowds who would use their new health to hurt others. Jesus healed tongues that might someday curse. He gave sight to eyes that could covet their neighbor's things. He healed hands that could kill.

Each time Jesus healed, He had to overlook the future and the past. Something, by the way, that He still does today—for us.

Growing in Grace

It's easy to help the lovable, the kind, the thankful. It's not so fun to help the grumpy, the mean, the ungrateful. But that's just what Jesus would do. Find a way to reach out to those whom others don't want to help—the prisoners, the homeless, or the poor.

The Best That You Can

I praise you because you made me in an
amazing and wonderful way.

—PSALM 139:14

Antonio Stradivari was a violin maker in the 1700s. His name in its Latin form, *Stradivarius*, has come to mean "excellence." He once said that to make a violin less than his best would be to rob God, who could not make Antonio Stradivari's violins without Antonio.

He was right. God could not make Stradivarius violins without Antonio Stradivari. Certain gifts were given to that craftsman that no other violin maker possessed.

In the same way, there are certain things you can do that no one else can. Perhaps it is encouraging your friends, playing basketball, or drawing the beauty of God's creation. There are things that only *you* can do, and you were put here by God to do them. Pretend that life is a great orchestra and you have been given an instrument and a song. You owe it to God to play them both the very best that you can.

Growing in Grace

What great talent has God blessed you with? Not sure? Ask a parent, grandparent, or friend to help you find your talent. Then figure out a way to use your talent for God.

June

What we see will last only a short time. But what we cannot see will last forever.

—2 CORINTHIANS 4:18

God's Favorite Word

Jesus said, "Come follow me."

—MATTHEW 4:19

Everyone likes to be invited—to a friend's house, to a party, to be part of the team. But the best invitations of all don't come from friends. They come from God.

You see, our God is an inviting God. He invited Mary to birth His Son, the disciples to fish for men, the woman caught in sin to start over, and Thomas to touch His wounds. God is the King who prepares the palace, sets the table, and invites His people to come in.

In fact, it seems His favorite word is *come*.

"*Come*, we will talk these things over. Your sins are red like deep red cloth. But they can be as white as snow" (Isaiah 1:18).

"All you who are thirsty, *come* and drink" (Isaiah 55:1).

"*Come* to me, all of you who are tired and have heavy loads. I will give you rest" (Matthew 11:28).

God is a God who invites. God is a God who reaches out. God is reaching out to you.

Growing in Grace

Have you ever felt left out? Was there a party you weren't invited to? Were plans made that didn't include you? Just think, God never leaves you out of His plans. Give someone else that same gift. Invite someone who is often left out.

The Branch and the Vine

"Remain in me, and I will remain in you. No branch can produce fruit alone. It must remain in the vine."

—JOHN 15:4

Abranch is connected to a vine. One is a part of the other. It's impossible to tell where the branch starts and the vine ends.

The branch isn't connected to the vine only when it bears fruit. The gardener doesn't keep the branches in a box and then—on the day he wants grapes—run out and glue the branches to the vine. No, the branch lives on the vine and gets its strength from the vine.

That's the kind of relationship God wants with you. God doesn't want you to turn to Him only when you need something or when something is wrong. God wants your thoughts and your heart to be with Him always.

If a branch is cut off the vine, it begins to dry up. It has lost the source of its life. In the same way, when you are cut off from God, your heart begins to dry up. You have lost the source of your life.

Stay connected to the vine—to God—and He will keep you strong.

Growing in Grace

With your parents' permission, cut a small branch from a tree. Place it where you will see it every day. What happens after a few hours? A few days? Now imagine you are the branch and God is the tree. If you cut yourself off from Him, how will you change?

A Hidden Hero

I have learned the secret of being happy at
any time in everything that happens.

—PHILIPPIANS 4:12

Peek into the prison and see Paul for yourself: bent over and frail, chained to the arm of a Roman guard. Look and see this apostle of God. He's alone. No family. No property. He can't see well and he's worn out. Doesn't look like a hero, does he?

Doesn't sound like one either. He called himself the worst sinner in history. He was a Christian-killer before he was a Christian leader. At times his heart was so heavy, Paul's pen dragged itself across the page. "What a miserable man I am! Who will save me from this body that brings me death?" (Romans 7:24).

Only heaven knows how long Paul stared at that question before he found the courage to write, "I thank [God] for saving me through Jesus Christ our Lord!" (Romans 7:25).

Yes, look and see this apostle of God. Look and see this true hero of faith.

Growing in Grace

Look at the heroes around you. Not the sports stars. Not the movie stars. The real heroes. The ones with calluses on their hands and love in their hearts. The parents and grandparents, the preachers and teachers. The ones who do what is right simply because it is right. Now, go be like them.

Power

The wisdom of this world is foolishness to God.

—1 CORINTHIANS 3:19

Power comes in many forms.

It's the boy who refuses to be kind to his sister.

It's the teacher who plays favorites with grades and praise.

It's the popular kid who gives the silent treatment to anyone who doesn't follow the crowd.

It might be the taking of someone's turn, or it might be the taking of someone's life.

But they are all spelled the same: P-O-W-E-R. They all have the same goal: "I will get what I want even if it hurts you."

And they all have the same end: uselessness. It's useless. Absolute power is not possible. When you make it to the top—if there even is a top—the only way left to go is down. And the fall is often painful.

A thousand years from now, will it matter what the world thought of you? Will it matter if you went first or not? No, but it will make a difference what God thought of you. And that's what really matters.

Growing in Grace

Does it really matter? Ask yourself that question the next time someone cuts in line or flings hateful words at you. Will it matter next week or next year? Focus your time and energy on the things that last—like being a child of God.

God's Mighty Hand

Through his power all things were made—things in
heaven and on earth, things seen and unseen.

—COLOSSIANS 1:16

L et there be..."
With those three words, history began. Time began. "Let
there be..." light. And "let there be..." day and night, sky and earth.
And then on this earth the mighty hand of God went to work.

He carved out the canyons and dug the deepest oceans. He
made mountains burst out of the flatlands. He flung the stars
into the sky and made the universe sparkle with His light.

Do you want to see God's might? Look at the mountains.
Want to see His gentleness? Touch His wildflowers. Want to
hear His power? Listen to the thunder.

Today you will come face-to-face with God's creation.
When you see the beauty of nature all around you, let it remind
you to give thanks to God for the world He made.

Growing in Grace

*June can be a beautiful time of year, a time when we can really
enjoy nature. Go outside. Take a walk. Pick a flower. Feel the breeze.
Praise God for the creative work of His mighty hand.*

Growing Up

I made you and will take care of you.
I will carry you, and I will save you.

—ISAIAH 46:4

Growing up can be dangerous. It's like hiking on a rocky trail with lots of chances to trip and fall. The devil would love to knock you down or get you lost on the wrong path. So it's smart to be prepared.

As you grow up, you'll start making more and more decisions for yourself. You'll face some tough choices. And you'll have to decide which way your life will go and which way it won't. But God doesn't leave you on your own. "I made you and will take care of you," He promises.

Look in His Word; He gives you plenty of advice. And look around you; He gives you plenty of good examples to follow.

The choices that you make now will prepare you for the choices you must make as a grown-up. And they all start with choosing God.

Growing in Grace

Look at the teenagers and grown-ups around you. Who are the ones you admire? Who are the ones serving God? When you don't know what to do, don't be afraid to ask questions and ask for help from those who've already traveled this same path.

God Will Get You Home

*What we see will last only a short time. But
what we cannot see will last forever.*

—2 CORINTHIANS 4:18

We will all face tough times in our lives. Even as kids, some of you already have. Maybe you've been made fun of and made to feel that you didn't fit in. Maybe you've had to move or had friends who moved away. Maybe those around you don't understand your faith. Maybe you've even lost someone you love. Some days the hurts seem to outnumber the hugs.

Those days can leave you feeling tired and all alone. They can make you just want to give up. But don't.

When you're having a tough day, God can seem far away, and getting to Him can seem like an impossible journey. But it isn't. Let me cheer you on and give you hope. God never said the journey would always be easy. But He did say that if you trust in Him, He will get you home to heaven.

Growing in Grace

God's promises are wonderful, especially when you're feeling alone. Start a journal and write down the promises of God as you discover them in His Word. Here are a couple to get you started: Psalm 34:4 for when you are afraid and Joshua 1:5 for when you are feeling all alone.

John the Baptist

*If a person wants to be a friend of the world,
he makes himself God's enemy.*

—JAMES 4:4

John the Baptist would never get hired as a preacher today. What would the people think? Can't you just hear them whispering? "His clothes are 'made from camel's hair' (Mark 1:6)! Did you see him? He 'ate locusts and wild honey' (Mark 1:6)! I'm not sitting next to him in Sunday school!"

John's message was as no-nonsense as his dress: confess your sins and turn away from them because the Lord is on His way (Matthew 3:2). John the Baptist set himself apart from the rest for one reason—to tell others about Jesus. Everything about John focused on that one task. His dress. His food. His words. His actions.

You don't have to be like the world to make a difference in the world. You don't have to be like the crowd to change the crowd. You don't have to lower yourself down to their level to lift them up to God's level.

Holiness doesn't try to fit in. Holiness tries to be like God.

Growing in Grace

Take a good look at yourself. What kinds of things are you doing just to fit in with the crowd? What are you wearing or watching? Is it worth it? Are these things pleasing to God? Or are there some things you need to change?

God Lets Us Choose

We all have wandered away like sheep.
Each of us has gone his own way.

—ISAIAH 53:6

How could a loving God punish people for all eternity? People often ask that question. But we need to get a couple of things straight.

First, *God* does not choose to punish people. God tells us what will happen if we do not obey His Word, and then He lets *us* choose. If we choose not to follow His Word, then we choose to be punished. But if we choose to obey His Word, then He rewards us with heaven. The choice is ours. God simply respects our choice.

Second, God does not punish *people*. God punishes sinners. He punishes those who have chosen to do wrong and disobey Him.

And, last, no one *has* to be punished. God offers a way for everyone to get to heaven. All we have to do is believe in His Son and obey His Word. But God won't force us to believe—it has to be our choice.

Growing in Grace

Waiting until you have to choose makes it harder to make the right decision. So decide now. What will you do if a friend offers you drugs or alcohol? What if you're tempted to lie? Will you cheat to get what you want? Deciding today makes choosing a lot easier tomorrow.

Shortcuts

"They continue saying things that mean nothing. They think that God will hear them because of the many things they say."

—MATTHEW 6:7

I love short sentences. Below are some of my favorite short sentences. Keep the ones you like. Forget the ones you don't. Share them when you can.

- Pray all the time. You don't even have to use words!
- God forgets the past. Be like Him.
- I've often been sorry for being greedy. But for giving? Never.
- Don't ask God to do what you want. Ask God to help you do what is right.
- No one is useless to God. No one.
- Nails didn't hold Jesus on the cross. Love did.
- You will never forgive anyone more than God has already forgiven you.

Growing in Grace

Take one of these sentences and really think about it this week. What does it mean? How does it make you live your life differently? How does it make you think about your parents, friends, even strangers on the street?

Who's in Charge?

Give all your worries to him, because he cares for you.

—1 PETER 5:7

Worry makes you forget who's in charge. And when you focus on yourself, you worry. You become anxious about many things. You worry that:

Your parents won't understand.
Your classmates will make fun of you.
You won't ever be as gifted as your friends are.
You won't ever make a difference.

Worry makes you think about the things *you* want rather than the things *God* wants for you. You become more interested in what others think of you than what God thinks of you. You may even find yourself jealous of a friend's gifts and doubting God's plan.

God has given you talents. He has done the same for your friend. If you focus on your friend's talents, you won't see your own. But if you focus on *your* talents—on the gifts that God has given to you—you could inspire both yourself and your friend.

Growing in Grace

What are your talents? Not just the singing and dancing kind of talents. But the spiritual talents. Are you good at listening? Or encouraging? Or teaching? Everyone has different talents. But they are all wonderful gifts from God. Ask God to show you ways to use your talents today.

Walking with God

You were taught to be made new in your hearts. You
were taught to become a new person . . . made to
be like God—made to be truly good and holy.

—EPHESIANS 4:23–24

Healthy families love each other. They are kind and tender
with each other, and they are honest with each other. As
we spend time with our families, we become like them. God
designed our homes to be the place where we can always go to
find love.

The same is true in our relationship with God. Sometimes
we go to Him with our joys, and sometimes we go with our hurts.
But we always go, and we always find His love. And the more we
go, the more we become like Him. Paul said, "This change in us
brings more and more glory" (2 Corinthians 3:18).

People who live long lives together begin to sound alike,
to talk alike, even to think alike. As we grow closer to God, we
begin to sound like Him and think more like Him. And hope-
fully our hearts begin to look more like His every day.

Growing in Grace

*Look at your grandparents or another older couple who've been
married a long time. Ask if you can see some photos of them
through the years. Have they started to look alike? Are there habits
that they both have? Do they even finish each other's sentences?*

A Promised Home

*And I saw the holy city coming down out of heaven
from God. This holy city is the new Jerusalem. It was
prepared like a bride dressed for her husband.*

—REVELATION 21:2

In the book of Revelation, John said that the city of heaven is like "a bride dressed for her husband."

How can a city be like a bride? Well, even though you're a long way from being a bride or a groom, you've seen brides, haven't you? Is there anything more beautiful than a bride?

Maybe it is her beautiful dress or the way her eyes sparkle like diamonds. Or maybe it's the blush of love that colors her cheeks or the flowers that she carries in her arms.

A bride. She is like a beautiful promise, saying to her groom, "I'll be with you forever."

Heaven, too, is a beautiful promise. It is God's promised reward for His children. Heaven is your promised home.

Growing in Grace

Imagine your wedding day. What are the promises made at a wedding? To love, honor, and cherish? Those are the very same promises that God makes to you. When you become His child, He promises to love, honor, and cherish you . . . always.

The Story of God

"I am the Lord. I am the God of every person on the earth. You know that nothing is impossible for me."

—JEREMIAH 32:27

Corrie ten Boom was a Dutch Christian who, along with her family, helped Jews escape the Nazis. She used to say, "When the train goes through a tunnel and the world gets dark, do you jump out? Of course not. You sit still and trust the engineer to get you through."

We need to hear that God is still in control. We need to hear that it's not over until He says so. We need to hear that life's troubles and trials are not a reason to jump off the train. They are a reason to sit still and trust the Great Engineer to get us through.

What do you do when you're feeling sad and alone? What do you do when you're facing a tough time? Go back and read the story of God. Read His Word again and again. Let God remind you that you aren't the first person to be sad or to need help. Let God remind you of how He helps His children.

Read the story of God and remember that its message is for you!

Growing in Grace

Life can feel like a roller coaster—racing up and down, this way and that at breakneck speeds. All you can do is sit tight, hang on, and trust God to get you through. Next time you're zooming along on a real roller coaster, think about hanging on—to the safety bar and to God.

The Big Choice

Maybe you don't want to serve the Lord. You must choose for yourselves today. You must decide whom you will serve.

—JOSHUA 24:15

God's invitation to us is clear. It's simple. God is clear about what He asks of us—to obey Him—and clear about what He offers—to live with Him in heaven forever. But whether or not we say yes to His invitation is our choice.

Isn't it incredible that God leaves the choice to us? Think about it. There are many things in life we can't choose. We can't, for example, choose our family. We can't choose the weather. We can't choose whether or not we are born with a big nose or blue eyes or curly hair. We can't even choose how people act toward us.

But we can choose where we spend eternity. The big choice God leaves to us. The most important choice is ours.

And it's the only choice that really matters.

Growing in Grace

As you grow up, you'll make lots of decisions, but the most important is deciding to become a Christian. As you decide, read through Scriptures such as John 3, Mark 16, and Romans 8. Talk to parents, preachers, or a good Christian friend. And pray.

Needed: One Great Savior

All people have sinned and are not good enough
for God's glory. People are made right with
God by his grace, which is a free gift.

—ROMANS 3:23-24

It is only God's grace that can save us. Not what we do. Not our talents. Not our feelings. Not our strength.

Like Paul on the road to Damascus, we need to know two things: we are great sinners, and we need a great savior.

And like Peter when he stepped out of the boat and onto the stormy water, we need to know two facts: we are going down, and Jesus is still standing up. There is nothing we can do to save ourselves. We need to reach out for Jesus' hand and hold on to His grace that saves us.

Grace is when God steps in and fills our stormy lives with His peaceful presence. We hear His voice, saying, "Don't be afraid. It is I" (John 6:20). He wants us to let go of all our past mistakes, all our worries and fears, and hold on to Him.

And amazingly, when we do, all our failures are forgiven. And God is not only within sight, He is within reach.

Growing in Grace

When you're at the pool or the lake this summer, think about that life jacket you're wearing. That float you're holding. No matter what the waves do, cling to it and you'll stay afloat. Kind of like Jesus. No matter what crashes down on you, cling to Him, and you'll stay afloat.

Dealing with Anger

Don't get angry.
Don't be upset; it only leads to trouble.

—PSALM 37:8

Anger. It's loud. It's loud in your heart. It's loud in your mind. And it can be just plain loud.

The louder it gets, the more desperate we become.

Some of you are thinking, *You don't have any idea how hard my life is. Homework. Tryouts. Bullies. Fighting parents.* You're right. I don't know how tough your life is right now. But I have a very clear idea of how miserable your future will be if you don't deal with your anger.

Anger is like a dark thundercloud: black, threatening, and terrible. It's like a storm in your heart that is threatening to turn into a tornado. You can't change what other people do, but you can change how you act toward them. You can't always help being angry, but you can control what you do with your anger. Ask God to help you—because He will.

Growing in Grace

There will always be things—and people—that make you angry. Like the bully who always picks on you, piles of homework, or being laughed at. Being angry is okay, but sinning is not. Avoid sin by deciding now what you will do the next time something makes you angry.

Give a Little Grace

"Lord, when my brother sins against me, how many times must I forgive him?" . . . Jesus answered, . . . "You must forgive him even if he does wrong to you 70 times 7."

—MATTHEW 18:21-22

Seems to me that God gives us a lot more grace than we could ever imagine.

Seems to me that we could do the same for others.

You know that you're not perfect. And, thankfully, God doesn't ask you to be. That's what His grace is for—it washes away all those times that you're not perfect.

When God gives you His grace, He then asks you to do something for Him: *remember that no one else is perfect either.* Give a little grace to those around you.

Because it's going to happen. Your brother or sister will say something mean. Your best friend will hurt your feelings. Once in a while even your mom or dad might snap at you. When those things happen, don't hold a grudge. Forgive them, and give a little grace—because God has given you a whole lot.

Growing in Grace

God asks you to give others the same grace that He gives you, but He also wants you to give grace to yourself. You're not perfect, and you will mess up. Someday you will do that thing you said you wouldn't do. And when you do, ask God to forgive you. Just don't forget to forgive yourself too.

Making God Part of Your Day

Pray in the Spirit at all times. Pray with all kinds
of prayers, and ask for everything you need.

—EPHESIANS 6:18

How do you make God a part of your day, all day long? How do you know when His unseen hand is on your shoulder and His whispering voice is in your ear? How can you and I learn to hear and know the voice of God? Here are a few ideas:

Give God your waking-up thoughts. Before you face the day, face the Father. Before you step out of bed, pray that God will guide your steps this day.

Give God your waiting thoughts. Spend time with Him being still and quiet. Wait to hear His voice.

Give God your whispering thoughts. Just imagine: every moment is a chance to talk to God.

Give God your end-of-day thoughts. As you settle into bed, let your mind settle on Him. End the day as you started it—talking to God.

Growing in Grace

Learn to pray "at all times" by creating times to pray. For example, before you get out of bed, pray, "God, lead me today." At shower time, pray that He will wash away your sins. In the car, pray, "God, show me the right way." At bedtime, thank Him for your day.

Listening for the Right Answer

"Continue to ask, and God will give to you.
Continue to search, and you will find. Continue
to knock, and the door will open for you."

—MATTHEW 7:7

John the Baptist was in prison, and he was beginning to doubt. Why wasn't Jesus coming to save him? So he sent Jesus a question: "Are you the one who was to come, or should we expect someone else?" (Matthew 11:3 NIV).

Jesus understood. He didn't scold John for his doubt. Instead, Jesus said, "Go back to John and tell him about the things you hear and see: The blind can see. The crippled can walk. . . . And the Good News is told to the poor'" (Matthew 11:4–5).

Now John understood. It wasn't that Jesus was silent. John had just been listening for the wrong answer. John had been listening for an answer to his earthly problems—a way out of prison. But Jesus was busy taking care of John's heavenly problem—a way into heaven. Remember that the next time you think God hasn't answered your prayers.

Growing in Grace

We may not always see God working in our lives, but He is. Even when bad things happen, God can use them for good. Romans 8:28 promises, "God works for the good of those who love him." Next time something bad happens, ask God to show you the good He can do with it.

God Calls Your Name

This is what the Lord God says: I, myself, will
search for my sheep. I will take care of them.

—EZEKIEL 34:11

Let's imagine God standing on the porch of heaven. He's waiting for you, hoping, searching the horizon for a glimpse of His child. You're the one God is looking for.

God is the waiting Father, the caring Shepherd in search of His lost lamb. His legs are scratched, His feet are sore, and His eyes are burning. He climbs the cliffs and crosses the fields. He explores the caves. He cups His hand to His mouth and calls down into the canyon.

And the name He calls is yours.

God doesn't just sit up in heaven and hope that you'll come looking for Him. He comes looking for you. There is nowhere you can go that He cannot find you. He wants to save you. He is calling out your name. Not just any name—*your name*. All you have to do is answer Him.

Growing in Grace

Think of your favorite hiding places when you play hide-and-seek. You have some good ones, don't you? But did you know there is nowhere you can hide from God? Not behind the couch. Not under the bed. Not even in the belly of a whale—just ask Jonah!

A Little Light, Please

Jesus came to them. He was walking on the water. . . .
[T]hey were afraid . . . and cried out in fear.

—MATTHEW 14:25–26

Every so often a storm will come along, and I'll look up into the dark sky and say, "God, a little light, please?"

That's probably what the disciples were asking as the storm tossed their boat around the sea. And the light did come for the disciples. A figure came to them walking on the water. It wasn't what they expected. Maybe they were looking for angels to come down or heaven to open up. We don't know what they were looking for. But one thing is for sure, they weren't looking for Jesus to come walking on the water!

And because Jesus came in a way they didn't expect, they almost missed seeing the answer to their prayers.

And unless we look and listen closely, we risk making the same mistake. Just like real thunderstorms, sometimes our lives become stormy, and bad things happen. But God's lights in our dark storms are as bright as the stars—if only we'll look for them.

Growing in Grace

A little light can go a long way. Take a flashlight into a dark room and close the door. See how that one little light brightens up the whole room? You can do the same thing. Be the light of Jesus in this world of darkness.

Decide to Love

Be sure that no one pays back wrong for wrong. But always try to do what is good for each other and for all people.

—1 THESSALONIANS 5:15

It's important to know that no friendship is perfect, no family is perfect, no person is perfect. And you're not perfect. So when you decide to make a relationship work—to get along—you have to remember that people will still make mistakes, will still get on your nerves sometimes, will still hurt your feelings.

So how do you get along with others? Look at what God says in Romans 12:10–18: "Give your brothers and sisters more honor than you want for yourselves. . . . Wish good for those who do bad things to you. . . . Be happy with those who are happy. Be sad with those who are sad. . . . If someone does wrong to you, do not pay him back by doing wrong to him. . . . Do your best to live in peace with everyone."

In other words . . . *choose to love.*

Growing in Grace

Agape love is "anyway love." It is a choice, not just a warm, fuzzy feeling. It's the kind of love that says, I'll do what's best for you even when you hurt my feelings, or trick me, or laugh at me. I'll treat you the way I wish you would treat me.

The Most Important Mission

So go and make followers of all people in
the world. Baptize them in the name of the
Father and the Son and the Holy Spirit.

—MATTHEW 28:19

Look at the words used to describe heaven in Revelation 21:
"It was shining with the glory of God" (v. 11). "The city was
made of pure gold" (v. 18). "Each gate was made from a single
pearl. The street of the city was made of pure gold" (v. 21). "There
is no night there" (v. 25). Now look at the words used to describe
hell: it is a "lake of fire that burns with sulfur" (Revelation 19:20).

The fact is we all have to spend eternity somewhere—either
heaven or hell. Seems like an easy choice to me! And when we
choose to obey God, His *mercy* saves us from hell, and His *grace*
blesses us with heaven.

But what about all the people who don't know God? They'll
spend an eternity somewhere too. Knowing that should make
us want to pray more. Serve more. Reach out to those who don't
know God more. Helping others choose heaven is the most
important mission we'll ever have.

Growing in Grace

*Is there someone you care about who does not know Jesus? Start
praying for that person every day. Ask God to open his or her heart.
And ask Him to show you how to be a good example. Then invite
that person to come with you to church.*

The Cost of Greed

"A man's life is not measured by the many things he owns."

—LUKE 12:15

Jesus had a definition for greed. He called it "measuring who you are by what you have." In other words, a person's worth is equal to the person's purse. 1. You have a lot. = You are a lot. 2. You have a little. = You are a little.

The result of this kind of thinking is easy to guess: If you are what you own, then by all means own it all! No price is too high. No payment is too much. Go ahead, gossip to be popular. Lie to get the new shoes. Steal to get the new game. If you *have* more, then you'll *be* more—more important, more popular, more happy. Right?

No. *Not* right. Greed costs a lot—and not just a lot of money. Gossip will cost you friendships. Lies and stealing will cost you the trust of your family. And all of those things will pull you away from God.

When you believe that you are what you own, you actually lose the things that are truly important—friends, family, and faith. And nothing is worth that.

Growing in Grace

This world encourages us to be greedy. To have the newest clothes, the newest game, the newest bike or skateboard. But what does greed cost you? Not just money, but peace and happiness. Instead of always wishing for something new, enjoy the things you have.

Falling

God is strong and can help you not to fall.

—JUDE 24

In some ways, living a Christian life is like climbing a great wall. The wall is high, and the risk is higher. You take your first step up the day you confess Jesus as the Son of God. He gives you His safety harness—the Holy Spirit. He hands you a rope—His Word.

Your first steps up are sure and strong. But as the climb goes on, you become tired. And as you climb higher, you become afraid. You lose your focus. You lose your grip, and you fall. You do that thing you know you shouldn't do. And for a moment—which seems like forever—you fall. Tumbling wildly. Dizzy. Out of control.

But then the rope tightens, and the fall stops. You hang there in the safety harness and find that it is strong. You hold on to the rope and trust it to hold you up. And although you can't see your Guide, you know Him—Jesus. He is strong. And He is able to keep you from falling.

Growing in Grace

Falling can be frightening—a tummy-tightening, teeth-gritting terror. Unless you're on one of those giant, bouncy inflatables! Next time you're bouncing around, think about that tummy-tightening fall—and then about how wonderful it is to bounce back up again. Just as God lifts you up again when you fall into sin.

Looking Like God

Our faces, then, are not covered. We all show the Lord's
glory, and we are being changed to be like him.

—2 CORINTHIANS 3:18

Did you know that worship changes your face?

That is exactly what happened to Jesus on the mountain. His face was changed, and it "became bright like the sun" (Matthew 17:2).

When we worship, our face becomes filled with the light and love of God.

The link between the face and worship is no accident. Our face is the most seen part of our bodies. It is covered less than any other part. It is also the way people know who we are. We don't fill a school yearbook with pictures of people's feet. We fill it with pictures of faces. God wants to take our faces—the most seen and the most easily remembered part of us—and use them like a mirror to reflect His goodness.

Take some time to worship God today, and let Him change your face.

Growing in Grace

Look in the mirror. Who do you see? Do you look like your mom? Do you look like your dad? Maybe you even look like your great-grandparents. But what God most wants to see is how much you look like Him.

Put Out the Fire

If you suffer for doing good, and you are
patient, then that pleases God.

—1 PETER 2:20

What do you do when people mistreat you or those you love?
Do you feel anger bubble inside you? Do flames of hate
burn your heart? Does your face burn red and hot?

Or do you reach up to Jesus? Do you ask Him to help you
control the angry fire? Do you pull out a bucket of mercy—and
throw it on the angry flames? Do you put out the fire?

Don't get on the roller coaster of anger. Be the one who says,
"Yes, he treated me wrong, but I am going to be like Christ. I'll be
the one who says, 'Father, forgive them. They don't know what
they are doing'" (Luke 23:34).

If Jesus could look down from the cross and say those words,
then so can you. Ask Him to help you put out the fire.

Growing in Grace

*The next time you feel like you can't forgive someone, picture Jesus
on the cross. He didn't die there so that you could hold a grudge.
Pray for His help to forgive those who have done you wrong.*

Some People

Be holy in all that you do, just as God is holy.
God is the One who called you.

—1 PETER 1:15

In this world, some people will try to get you to go a different way. A way that doesn't include God. Sometimes those people are on TV. Sometimes their messages are in the songs you listen to. Sometimes they are sitting right next to you at the lunch table.

They will tell you to swap your honesty for a good grade on a test. They will tell you it's okay to wear clothes that show too much. They will tell you it's okay to make fun of others if it makes you look good. They will even tell you it's okay to turn away from God in order to be more popular.

They will whisper, tease, and torment. "Go ahead. It's okay," they say. "Don't worry. No one will know."

When some people tempt and tease you to do wrong, remember what God says: "Be careful. Continue strong in the faith . . . and be strong" (1 Corinthians 16:13). God will give you the strength to stand strong against "some people."

Growing in Grace

Peer pressure is the pressure to do wrong just because everyone else is. Because you want to fit in. Fight peer pressure with God's Word. Read a verse from Proverbs every day, and remember these words: "I have hidden your word in my heart that I might not sin against you" (Psalm 119:11 NIV).

A Simple Plan

"He who believes in the Son has eternal life. But he who does not obey the Son will never have that life."

—JOHN 3:36

When do we have salvation? When we look to Jesus. When we believe that He is our Savior and we choose to obey Him. It's really very simple, isn't it? Read the great promise of John 3:16: "For God loved the world so much that he gave his only Son. God gave his Son so that whoever believes in him may not be lost, but have eternal life." That is *your* promise from God.

Wow! What a promise! Salvation. New life. All just for following Jesus. But even though God's plan is so simple, there are still those who don't believe. They don't trust His promise.

That's where you come in. Show the world what a follower of Jesus looks like. Show those who don't believe in Him the joy and hope that come from following Him. Show them that His power to help and to save people in this world is real. And show them that He wants to save them too.

Growing in Grace

People who don't know God may not feel comfortable coming to church. An invitation to Sunday school might even be scary. Try inviting them to hang out with some of your friends from church or to go to a devotional at someone's home. It might be just the thing to make them more comfortable with Jesus.

July

Jesus quickly spoke to them. He said, "Have courage! It is I! Don't be afraid."

—MATTHEW 14:27

God's Job

Wait for the Lord. He will make things right.

—PROVERBS 20:22

Some of you are still arguing. Still whining and complaining. You're complaining to your parents, to the teacher, to friends, to anyone who will listen. Every chance you get, you're going over those same hurt feelings again and again.

I have one question for you: Who made you God? I don't mean to sound like a smart aleck, but why are you doing His work for Him?

"I will punish those who do wrong," God declared. "I will repay them" (Hebrews 10:30).

Judging people is God's job—not yours. To think something else is to think that God can't do it.

Revenge is unholy. To forgive someone is to show them God's holiness. Forgiveness is not saying that the one who hurt you was right. Forgiveness is saying that you know God is faithful and *He* will do what is right.

Growing in Grace

To help yourself let go of past hurts, write them on a rock. Then throw that rock as far as you can into a lake or river. Notice how the rock sinks out of sight? How the water covers over it? Let your hurt feelings sink with it as you forgive the one who spoke unkindly or treated you badly.

Your Whispering Thoughts

God, examine me and know my heart.
Test me and know my thoughts.

—PSALM 139:23

Imagine—what if you thought of every second of every day as a chance to talk to God?

By the time your life is over, you will have spent six months waiting at stoplights, a year and a half looking for lost stuff, and a whopping five years standing in lines.

Why don't you give these "lost" moments to God? By giving God your thoughts during these moments, the ordinary becomes extraordinary. Your prayers don't need to be out loud. Your eyes don't have to be closed. Prayers can simply be silent whispers—just between you and God.

Simple prayers—such as "Thank You, Father," "Be with me this day, God," and "I trust You, Jesus"—can turn a car ride into worship. You don't need a special place. Just pray where you are. Let the kitchen become a church and the classroom become a chapel. Give God your whispering thoughts.

Growing in Grace

Do you only pray at church and at home? Only before meals and at bedtime? Try a "pray where you are" challenge today. How many different places can you remember to pray to God? Can you make it five, or ten, or even twenty?

God Changes Our Faces

He put a new song in my mouth.
It was a song of praise to our God.

—PSALM 40:3

God wants to spend time with us so that He can change our face. And He wants to change our face so that it shows His glory. But the change isn't easy. The sculptor who carved the presidents' faces into Mount Rushmore had an easier job than God does. But our God is able to do it.

God loves to change the faces of His children. His fingers rub away the wrinkles of worry and fear. Shadows of shame become smiles of grace. He softens clenched jaws and gritted teeth. He smoothes away lines of anger. His touch gives rest to weary eyes, and tears of sadness become tears of peace and relief.

How does God do that? Through worship and praise.

You'd think it would be harder, wouldn't you? Maybe spending forty days without food like Moses did and Jesus did. Or memorizing the entire book of Leviticus. But no. God's plan is simpler. When we praise Him and worship Him, He changes our faces and fills them with joy.

Growing in Grace

Find a quiet place outside and lift your face to heaven. Let the sun's warmth remind you of the warmth of God's love. Let the breeze whisper that He is always with you. Let the sounds of creation fill you with awe at His power. And let Him change your face as you worship Him.

Finding God's Grace

You gave me life and showed me kindness.
And in your care you watched over my life.

—JOB 10:12

Punishment is easy for me to understand. *You break the rules, and you pay the price.* But God's grace? That's not as easy to understand. *You break the rules, but Jesus pays the price.* Want examples?

- David the psalmist became David the murderer, but by God's grace, he became David the psalmist again.
- Peter denied Jesus three times before he preached Jesus.
- Zacchaeus was a crook. He stole money, and his heart was dirty with greed. But Jesus still had time for him.
- The thief on the cross was headed for hell and hung out to die one minute, but he was heaven-bound and smiling the next.

Story after story. Prayer after prayer. It seems that God is looking more for ways to get us home to heaven than for ways to keep us out.

Growing in Grace

Can you think of other examples of God's grace from the Bible? How have you been given grace in your own life—by God, by family, or by friends? How does this make you feel about giving grace to those who wrong you?

The Prison of Bitterness

"If you forgive others for the things they do wrong, then your Father in heaven will also forgive you for the things you do wrong."

—MATTHEW 6:14

Bitterness is hurt and anger that you hold on to. It is that wish for revenge against those who have wronged you. And it is its own prison.

The walls of this prison are slippery with hatred. Puddles of muddy anger darken the floor. The stench of betrayal fills the air and stings the eyes. And a cloud of self-pity blocks out the light.

Bitterness can trap you when you've been lied to, betrayed by friends, or bullied by enemies. It will trap you when you choose to hold on to the hurt. When you choose not to forgive. When you choose to hate. Bitterness will trap your heart in a prison just as real as one with iron bars.

But you can escape from that prison. How? Choose to let go of the hurt. Choose to forgive. Choose to accept God's love and grace, and then give it to others.

Growing in Grace

What does bitterness do to your heart? Try this: take a half of a lemon and squeeze the bitter juice into your mouth. What happens to your tongue? Does it feel like it's shriveling up inside your mouth? That's just what bitterness does—it shrivels up your heart.

The Perfect Priest

On the day when the Lord Jesus comes . . . all the
people who have believed will be amazed at Jesus.

—2 THESSALONIANS 1:10

When we see Jesus, what will we see? We will see the perfect Priest.

In Bible times, a priest was the one who presented people to God and God to people. Revelation says that, in heaven, Jesus "was dressed in a long robe. He had a gold band around his chest" (1:13). That is the type of robe and gold band that only priests used to wear. Jesus was wearing the clothing of a priest.

You have known other priests. They may or may not have been church leaders, but they were all people who wanted to bring you to God. But even these people needed a priest. These people, like you, were sinful. But not Jesus. "Jesus is the kind of high priest that we need. He is holy; he has no sin in him. He is pure and not influenced by sinners. And he is raised above the heavens" (Hebrews 7:26).

Jesus is the perfect Priest.

Growing in Grace

Who are the people who try to bring you closer to God? Family, Bible teachers, friends? Do three things for them: Thank God for each of them. Go and thank them in person. And then try to be like them and help bring others closer to God.

Closer Than You Think

Jesus quickly spoke to them. He said, "Have courage! It is I! Don't be afraid."

—MATTHEW 14:27

The storm at sea was terrible. The wind howled. The waves beat against the boat. And the disciples battled for their lives. They were already frightened. So when they saw Jesus walking toward them on the water, they called him a ghost. A phantom. To them, the glow was anything but God.

When we see gentle lights in the middle of the stormy parts of life, we often think the same thing. We see the kindness, the helping hand, the answer. But we think they are just an accident, a chance happening, or good luck. We think they are anything but God.

But God doesn't burst into the room with ten thousand angels to help you. When you're in the middle of a bad day or a bad problem, He uses the people around you to help. That friendly hug, that offer to help, that unexpected answer just when you needed it—they aren't accidents. They are God. He is closer than you think.

Growing in Grace

The prophet Elijah looked for God in the mighty wind, the earthquake, and the fire. But God was not in any of these. At last came a "quiet, gentle voice," and this was God (1 Kings 19:11–13). You can hear God's quiet, gentle voice too—in a sunrise, a kind word, a helping hand.

He Kept the Faith

Continue to have faith and do what you know is right. Some people have not done this. Their faith has been destroyed.

—1 TIMOTHY 1:19

Imagine you are in Bible times. You have traveled back in time to talk to a man on death row. He is Jewish by birth. A tent-maker. An apostle of Christ. His name is Paul, and his days are numbered. You wonder what it is that keeps this man going as he nears his death. So you ask him some questions.

Do you have family, Paul? *I have none.*

How is your health? *My body has been beaten, and I am tired.*

Have you gotten any awards? *Not on earth.*

Then what do you have, Paul? No awards. No family. What do you have that matters? *I have my faith in Jesus. It's all I have. But it's all I need. I have kept the faith.*

Then Paul leans back against the wall of his cell and smiles. Paul smiles because he knows God's promise: "If you are faithful, I will give you the crown of life" (Revelation 2:10).

Growing in Grace

Faith is like a seed. It starts out small, but with care, it grows and blooms. As it blooms, it provides food and shelter for those around it. Make a "faith picture" of a blooming flower by gluing dried beans, popcorn, or sunflower seeds to a piece of cardboard.

A Newborn

God is being patient with you. He does not want anyone to
be lost. He wants everyone to change his heart and life.

—2 PETER 3:9

To those who believe that Jesus is our Savior, He has promised a new birth into a new life with God. It's a life free of the shame of past mistakes and a life full of the hope of heaven.

Does that mean that your old, sinful side will never show its ugly head again? Or that you'll never be tempted to do wrong again?

To answer that question, compare your new birth in Jesus to a newborn baby. Can a baby walk? Or feed himself? Or sing or read or speak? No, but someday he will.

It takes time for a baby to grow and learn. But in the hospital delivery room, is the parent ashamed of the baby? Is the mom embarrassed that the baby can't spell . . . or walk . . . or stand up and give a speech? Of course not. The parents aren't ashamed; they are proud. They know the baby will grow and learn with time. God knows you will grow and learn too.

Growing in Grace

*Look back through your baby pictures. See how much you've
changed, grown, and learned? Your parents didn't toss you out of
the house when you stumbled as a toddler. God won't either. He'll
lift you up, dust you off, and help you take the next step.*

Why Am I Here?

"Love the Lord your God with all your heart, soul and mind."
—MATTHEW 22:37

Dig deep enough in every heart and you'll find it: the wish to understand why God created you. As surely as you breathe, you will someday wonder, "Why am I here? Why did God make me?"

Some people search for the answer in their work. These people believe that who they are is what they *do*, so they do a lot. "I am here to be an A+ student." That's a great goal, but not exactly a reason for living.

For other people, who they are is what they *have*. They find meaning in the right clothes, right house, right toys. They believe their reason for being here is tied to the things they own. Others try to have all the fun they possibly can, and still others try to be the sports star or the movie star.

But none of these things are the right answer to the question "Why am I here?" We only have one purpose in life. One reason for being here. To praise God.

So shouldn't we do just that?

Growing in Grace

How do you want people to describe you? As cool, or as committed to Christ? Write down words you think describe Jesus, like patient, kind, loving, selfless. Now try to live so that people will say those same things about you. That's the kind of life that will praise God.

A Big View of God

Holy, holy, holy is the Lord God All-Powerful.
He was, he is, and he is coming.

—REVELATION 4:8

Exactly what is *praise*? I like King David's definition: "Tell the greatness of the Lord with me. Let us praise his name together" (Psalm 34:3).

Praise is telling the Lord how great He is. It is *magnifying* Him. That is, praise is making our view of God—His power, His might, and His majesty—even bigger. Growing our understanding of Him. Kind of like stepping into the cockpit of creation to see where God the Pilot sits and to watch how He works.

Of course, God's size doesn't change, but our understanding of Him does. As we draw nearer, He seems larger. And isn't that what we need? A *big* view of God? Don't we have *big* challenges, *big* worries, *big* questions? Of course we do. So we need a big view of God.

Praise gives us that. When we sing words such as "holy, holy, holy," they help us focus on how big and wonderful God really is.

Growing in Grace

Take a look through a magnifying glass. What does it do? It brings the object closer and makes it look bigger so you can see it more clearly. That's what worshiping God does—God is brought closer and you can see Him more clearly.

Spiritual U-Turns

Perhaps you do not understand that God is kind to
you so that you will change your hearts and lives.

—ROMANS 2:4

Have you ever heard the word *repent*? Christians use that word a lot, but what does it really mean? *Repent* means more than just saying we're sorry. *Repent* means we stop doing what is wrong and we try to do what is right. It is turning away from selfishness and sin and turning to God. It's like a spiritual U-turn.

When we repent, the sadness we feel on the *inside* shows itself in the way we act on the *outside*.

You look at the love of God and compare it to your sins. You can't believe He loves you like He does—with all your mess-ups and mix-ups. And knowing this makes you want to change the way you live. That is what it means to repent.

Growing in Grace

Have you ever been in the car with your parents when they realized they were going the wrong way? Do they just keep going? No, they stop. But they don't just stop. They turn around and start going the right way. That's repentance—not just stopping, but turning around and going the right way.

Knowing God

"Everyone who sees the Son and believes in him has
eternal life. . . . This is what my Father wants."

—JOHN 6:40

We learn God's will for our lives by spending time with
Him. The key to knowing God's heart is having a relationship with Him. A *personal* relationship. God will speak to you
differently than He will speak to others.

Just because God spoke to Moses through a burning bush
doesn't mean we should all sit next to a bush waiting for God to
speak. God used a fish to get Jonah's attention. Does that mean
we should have worship services at Sea World? No. God reveals
His heart personally—in a different way—to each person.

That is why the time you spend with God is so important.
You can't know His heart just by having a quick chat once in a
while or a weekly visit. You learn God's will as you spend time
with Him every single day.

Hang out with God long enough, and you will come to know
His heart.

Growing in Grace

*Who is your best friend? What is his or her favorite song? Favorite
color? Favorite movie? How did you find out these things? Did you
just know them? Of course not. You spent time together. In the same
way, you'll learn more about God as you spend time with Him.*

God's Signature

Before I made you in your mother's womb, I chose you.

—JEREMIAH 1:5

You aren't an accident or something that just happened. You are a gift to the world, a divine work of art signed by God.

One of the greatest gifts I ever received is a football signed by thirty former professional quarterbacks. There is nothing unique or special about the ball itself. For all I know it was bought at a discount sporting goods store. What makes it special are the signatures.

The same is true with us. If you look at all of nature, *Homo sapiens* (people) are not unique. We aren't the only creatures with flesh and hair and blood and hearts. What makes us special is not our body but the signature of God on our lives. We are His works of art. We are created in His image to do good deeds. We are important and valuable, not because of what we do but because of whose we are.

Growing in Grace

Take a look at your refrigerator. Chances are some of your drawings are there. Yes, they are wonderful. But is that why your mom gives them star treatment? No, they hang in a place of honor not because of what they are but because of who made them.

Believing in What You Don't See

Faith means being sure of the things we hope for. And faith means knowing that something is real even if we do not see it.

—HEBREWS 11:1

Faith is trusting what our eyes can't see.

- Human eyes see the prowling lions. Daniel's faith sees the angel close the lions' mouths.
- Human eyes see storms. Noah's faith sees the rainbow.
- Human eyes see a giant. David's faith sees the giant Goliath fall.
- Your eyes see your faults. Your faith sees Jesus your Savior.

When you look in the mirror, do you see your mistakes, your sins? It's easy for our human eyes to only see what is wrong. We need to use our "eyes of faith"—the way God sees things—to see what is right. Look in the mirror again, using your eyes of faith. I can tell you what God sees there—His beloved child, the one He has promised all of heaven to.

Growing in Grace

We trust our eyes to show us what is real and what is not. But our eyes can't see everything. What are some real but invisible things? Wind. Love. Kindness. Electricity. Can you think of others? You may not be able to see them, but you can see what they do—just like you can see what God does.

All God's Children

*If they could be made God's people by what they did,
then God's gift of grace would not really be a gift.*

—ROMANS 11:6

To whom does God offer His gift of grace and forgiveness? To the smartest? The most beautiful or the funniest? No. His gift is for us all—rich and poor, popular and unpopular, sports stars and science geeks. All God's children.

And God wants each of us so badly that He'll take us no matter what shape we're in. He wants us "as is"—just as we are—with all our mistakes, all our worries and fears, and all our imperfections.

God isn't about to wait for us to be perfect before He saves us. (He knows we'll *never* be perfect!) Do you think He's waiting until we are no longer tempted to sin? Not hardly. Remember, Jesus died for us *while* we were still sinners. His sacrifice—and our salvation—does not depend on what we do. It depends on who God is.

Growing in Grace

Leftovers are . . . well . . . what's left over after everyone else has taken the best parts. The leftover part in the school play, the leftover pizza with all the pepperoni gone. But God's gifts—love, mercy, and understanding—are the same for all His children. No one gets leftovers.

God Is on Your Side

The Lord himself will go before you. He will be
with you. He will not leave you or forget you.

—DEUTERONOMY 31:8

When I was seven years old, I ran away from home. I'd had enough of my father's rules. With my clothes in a paper bag, I stormed out the back gate and marched down the alley. But I didn't go far. I got to the end of the alley and realized I was hungry, so I went back home.

Although my disobedience was brief, it was still disobedience. And if you had stopped me in that alley, I just might have told you how I felt: "I don't need a father. I'm too big for his rules."

I didn't hear the rooster crow like Peter did. Or the fish belch like Jonah did. I didn't get a robe like the prodigal son did. But I learned from my earthly father what they learned from their heavenly Father: I can count on God to be on my side no matter what I do. You can too.

Growing in Grace

Every family has its own rules. Be kind. Wipe your feet. Respect everyone. Wash your hands. Say please and thank you. God's family has its rules too. Just two of them. Find out what they are in Luke 10:27.

Jesus Walks Among Us

He took our suffering on him.
And he felt our pain for us.

—MATTHEW 8:17

Imagine the pool of Bethesda. In Bible times, it was the place where the hopelessly sick came (John 5:1–9). It was, they believed, their one last chance to be healed. For at a certain time, an angel would stir the waters of the pool. Whoever stepped in first, after the waters were stirred, would be healed.

But imagine all those who weren't healed. Imagine walking by the pool. The ground around it must have looked like a battlefield covered with wounded bodies.

As people passed by, what did they hear? An endless wave of groans. What did they see? A field of faceless needs. What did they do? Most just walked past. But not Jesus. The people needed Him, so He was there.

Little did they know that this was God—walking slowly, stepping carefully between the beggars and the blind. Because wherever His hurting children are, that is where God is.

Growing in Grace

Our world is still home to the hopelessly sick and crippled, to the beggars and the blind. And although Jesus no longer walks the earth among them, He uses His people to help them now. Talk with your family about sponsoring a child through Compassion International or World Vision.

Just a Band-Aid, Please

If we say that we have no sin, we are fooling
ourselves, and the truth is not in us.

—1 JOHN 1:8

We are lying to ourselves if we pretend that our sins aren't really sins or that perhaps they're not really so bad after all.

Some time ago my daughter Andrea got a splinter in her finger. I took her to get the first aid kit. I set out some tweezers, ointment, and a Band-Aid.

She didn't like what she saw. "I just want the Band-Aid, Daddy."

Sometimes we are just like Andrea. We come to Jesus with our sins, but all we want is for them to be covered up. We want to skip the treatment. We want to hide our sin. And one has to wonder if God—even in His great mercy—will heal what we just try to hide.

How can God heal what we say isn't even there? How can God touch what we cover up? Tell God all about your messes. Your sins. Your mistakes. He can fix them—and He won't even need a Band-Aid.

Growing in Grace

Grab a Band-Aid and put it on your hand. Band-Aids are wonderful, aren't they? When you have a bump or bruise, sometimes just putting one on is enough to help you feel better. But there are no Band-Aids for sins. There is only one fix—God's mercy. Just ask for it.

Seeing Jesus Clearly

Now we see as if we are looking into a dark mirror.
But at that time, in the future, we shall see clearly.

—1 CORINTHIANS 13:12

What will it be like to finally see Jesus face-to-face? How will it feel?

I believe it will be greater than anything we could ever imagine. But I like to imagine anyway. And I imagine it will be better than Christmas morning, better than a birthday, better than an ice-cream sundae—all rolled into one!

When we see Jesus face-to-face, we will be looking into the eyes of One who loves us more than anyone else ever could. And His love will fill us with complete joy and peace.

All our sins and mistakes will be completely washed away forever. There will be no more guilt or shame, no more loneliness or being left out. We will never mess up again or stumble again or doubt again. Why? Because "when Christ comes again, we will be like him" (1 John 3:2).

And I can't wait!

Growing in Grace

First Corinthians 13:12 says, "Now we see as if we are looking into a dark mirror. But [then] . . . we shall see clearly." Take a mirror into a dark room. A little hard to see your reflection, isn't it? Now turn on the light. Much clearer! That's what heaven will be like—we'll be able to see Jesus clearly.

God on the Hunt

Come back to the Lord your God.
He is kind and shows mercy.
He doesn't become angry quickly.
He has great love.
He would rather forgive than punish.

—JOEL 2:13

How far do you want God to go to get your attention? If God has to choose between your eternity in heaven and your happiness on earth, which do you hope He chooses?

What if God moved you to another land? (As He did Abraham.) What if you were kidnapped, made a slave, and then thrown into prison. (Remember Joseph?) How about being struck blind on the side of the road like Paul was?

God does whatever it takes to get our attention. Isn't that the message of the Bible? God's never-ending, all-out pursuit of us. God on the hunt. God in the search. Peeking under the bed for hiding kids, searching in the classrooms and on the practice fields for those who are lost. Looking for you because He wants you with Him forever.

Growing in Grace

Gather up five or six of your stuffed animals. Ask your mom or dad to hide them all over the house while you cover your eyes. How quickly can you find them all? Did you have to look high and low? Now imagine—that's just the way God looks for you!

If Only . . .

So now you are not a slave; you are God's child, and God will give you what he promised, because you are his child.

—GALATIANS 4:7

It's easy to look at the world around you and say, "If only . . . If only I could make the team . . . If only I could be popular . . . If only I had the right clothes or the right friends . . . If only we had more money . . . If only my family were different . . ."

Your list could go on and on and on.

I believe God has an "if only" list too. His list probably goes something like this: "If only he knew how much I love him . . . If only she would ask for My help . . . If only he would trust Me . . . If only she would let Me save her . . ."

There are a lot of "if only" things that you can't do anything about. But you can choose to do something about God's "if only" list. You can choose to believe in Him and to obey His Word—and you can make God's "if onlys" come true.

Growing in Grace

You decide what kind of person you will be. Whether you were blessed with a great family or a not-so-great one, you get to decide if you want to be like them. But God is most interested in how much you want to be like Him. It's your choice.

Time-Tested Rules for Life

Honor God and obey his commands.
This is the most important thing people can do.
—ECCLESIASTES 12:13

On the first day of school, most teachers will give you a list of classroom rules. Rules that help the school day go much more smoothly. It's good to have some rules for the other parts of your life too. Here are some God-given, time-tested rules for life that will make all your days go much more smoothly:

- Love God more than anything else.
- Live like someone is watching even when no one is.
- Do your best, at home and away from home.
- Obey your parents.
- Be kind and respectful to everyone.
- Don't spend money that you don't have yet.
- Pray twice as much as you think you need to.
- Forgive yourself because God has forgiven you.
- Remember that God always loves you . . . *always.*

Growing in Grace

Next time you're in the car, take a look at the stoplights. Use them to help you remember to live for God. On red, remember that Jesus' blood takes away our sins. On yellow, be careful about what you do and say. And on green, praise God every chance you get.

Praise Him

Honor and glory to the King that rules forever! He cannot be destroyed and cannot be seen. Honor and glory forever and ever to the only God.

—1 TIMOTHY 1:17

Praise. Honor. Glorify. What do all these words really mean? Well, these are all just fancy words that mean telling God how wonderful He is. Telling Him that you know He is all-powerful. Telling Him how grateful you are for all that He does. And simply telling Him how very much you love Him.

We were created to praise, honor, and glorify God. But how do we *do* that? There are many different ways. You can praise God with the songs you sing. You can honor Him with your gifts of time and service and money. You can glorify Him by helping others. But that's not all. Pray to Him. Study Him. Notice His work in nature. There are so many different ways to praise God.

But the most important thing is simply to praise Him—each and every day.

Growing in Grace

In your private prayer time, try some of the different ways of praying that are mentioned in the Bible. Lift up holy hands as in 1 Timothy 2:8. Lie down as Moses did in Deuteronomy 9:25. Kneel as Daniel did in Daniel 6:10. There is no one way to pray. Just pray.

How Big Is God?

"God can do all things."
—MATTHEW 19:26

Do you want to know who God is? Just look up at the night sky and see what He has done. Do you want to know His power? Take a look at His creation. Are you curious about His strength? Pay a visit to His home address:

1 Billion Starry Sky Avenue

God is not just big; He is perfect and all-powerful. He is not touched by even a hint of sin, not limited by the time line of history, not weakened by the tiredness of a body.

What controls you doesn't control God. What troubles you doesn't trouble Him. What tires you doesn't tire Him. Is an eagle bothered by a bump in the road? No, he rises above it. Is the whale troubled by the hurricane? Of course not! He dives beneath it. Is the lion irritated by the mouse standing in his way? No, he steps over it.

How much more is God able to rise above, dive beneath, and step over the troubles of the earth!

Growing in Grace

Can you measure the wind? Count the stars? Number the sand on the seashore? God can. God is bigger, stronger, more powerful than we can ever imagine. Sing "My God Is So Big" as you think of the many ways He truly is so big.

What Is Unity?

Do not be angry with each other, but forgive each
other. If someone does wrong to you, then forgive him.
Forgive each other because the Lord forgave you.

—COLOSSIANS 3:13

What is *unity*? Unity is choosing to get along. And though it
may sound simple, it isn't always easy to do.

What does having unity mean?

It means thinking about what others want and need—not
just what you want and need.

It means that when someone makes you angry, you choose
to let that anger go.

It means that when someone hurts your feelings, you don't
hurt them back.

It means forgiving when you don't want to.

It means being kind when you would rather not.

It means being patient when you want to be mad.

Unity means sticking together when the selfish ways of this
world want to pull you apart. Doesn't unity sound like one of
God's great ideas?

Growing in Grace

*Unity isn't just for churches. It's for families too. Instead of focusing on
the things you don't like about one another, think about the ways you
are all alike. Maybe you all share the same house, or you all like peanut
butter and chocolate ice cream. And you are all God's children!*

Just One Goal

"The Son of Man did not come to be served.
He came to serve. The Son of Man came to
give his life to save many people."

—MARK 10:45

One of Jesus' greatest skills was His ability to stay on target, to stay focused. His life never got distracted or off track. He kept His life headed in the right direction.

As Jesus looked out at His future, He could see many choices. He could have chased after any one of them, and He could have been a success at any one of them. He could have been a warrior and fought the Romans to free the Jewish people. He could have been happy as a teacher in the temple and educated the people. But in the end He chose to be a Savior and save souls.

Anyone who was with Him for any length of time heard it from Jesus Himself: "The Son of Man came to find lost people and save them" (Luke 19:10). The heart of Jesus was focused on just one thing. The day He left the carpentry shop of Nazareth He had one goal—the cross.

Growing in Grace

What are your goals for your life? Is there a certain school you want to go to? A job you want to have when you grow up? A place you want to live? Keep a journal of these goals and how they change as you grow older. But remember, your greatest goal should be to be like Jesus.

Trusting God

The person who trusts in the Lord will be blessed.

—JEREMIAH 17:7

Just before His crucifixion on the cross, Jesus told His disciples that He would be leaving them. "Where I am going you cannot follow now. But you will follow later" (John 13:36).

Saying something like that left the disciples with some questions. Peter spoke for the others and asked, "Lord, why can't I follow you now?" (John 13:37).

Jesus' answer was tender, just as a parent is tender when answering a child. "Don't let your hearts be troubled. Trust in God. And trust in me. There are many rooms in my Father's house. I would not tell you this if it were not true. I am going there to prepare a place for you. . . . I will come back. Then I will take you to be with me so that you may be where I am" (John 14:1–3).

That whole paragraph could be put into just one sentence: "You trust in Me, and I'll take care of you."

Growing in Grace

What are some things you trust your parents to do for you? Things like pay for your home, provide food, wash clothes, and make sure you're healthy. If your parents—who are not perfect—know how to take care of you, how much more will God—who is perfect—take care of you?

When You Need Courage

I am the Lord your God.
I am holding your right hand.
And I tell you, "Don't be afraid.
I will help you."

—ISAIAH 41:13

Could you use some courage? Jesus understands when you do. After all, He chased the butterflies out of the stomachs of His nervous disciples.

We need to remember that the disciples were ordinary men given an extraordinary task. Long before they were pictured in the stained-glass windows of our churches, they were trying to make a living and raise a family. They didn't come from a long line of priests, and they weren't superheroes. But they loved Jesus more than they were afraid, and because of that, they did some extraordinary things.

When you choose to follow Jesus, He will take care of your earthly fears. He will help you to be brave. Remember, Jesus gave courage and strength to His disciples, and He'll give it to you too.

Growing in Grace

What are you afraid of? Monsters under the bed? Parents fighting? Not having a friend? Some things we fear are real, some are imaginary—but all fears are frightening. When you're afraid, remember these words: "The Lord protects those who truly believe" (Psalm 31:23).

"As You Love Yourself"

"The work that I ask you to accept is easy. The
load I give you to carry is not heavy."

—MATTHEW 11:30

Jesus tells us to do two things. First, "Love the Lord your God with all your heart, soul and mind." And, second, "Love your neighbor as you love yourself" (Matthew 22:37–39).

Let's take a look at that second command: "Love your neighbor as you love yourself." Who is your neighbor? Well, Jesus answered that in Matthew 22: your neighbor is everyone around you. That's the part of the verse that most people talk about. But they don't usually talk about the second part of that verse: "as you love yourself." Jesus said that you are supposed to love yourself.

Now, Jesus wasn't talking about an "I'm-better-than-you" kind of love. He's talking about loving yourself because you are an amazing creation of God.

The simple fact is that you have to love yourself and know how you want to be treated *before* you can know how to love your neighbor. And when you don't love yourself, it becomes easier for others to be unkind to you. So, love your neighbor . . . *as you love yourself.*

Growing in Grace

There are days when we all feel unloved, unneeded, and unimportant. Look up these verses and write them on slips of paper—Psalm 139:14; 1 John 3:1; Matthew 6:31–33; Zephaniah 3:17. Tuck them into a jar and pull one out the next time you're having a bad day.

He's Coming Back

Christ was first to be raised. When Christ comes again,
those who belong to him will be raised to life.

—1 CORINTHIANS 15:23

Jesus made a promise to us: "I will come back." And when He returns, it will be a frightening time for people who didn't follow Jesus. They will be judged by the One they refused to worship. But children of God do not need to be afraid because Jesus has promised to take us home to heaven with Him.

But can we believe Jesus' promise? How can we know He will do what He said? How can we believe He will save us and set us free from our sins? How can we know He will come back?

Because He's already come back once. Because the stone was rolled away and His tomb was empty. Because Jesus lives.

Growing in Grace

What will it be like when Jesus returns? Check out 1 Corinthians 15:52 for a glimpse of what will happen:

It will only take a second. We will be changed as quickly as an eye blinks. . . . The trumpet will sound and those who have died will be raised to live forever.

August

Grow in the grace and knowledge of our
Lord and Savior Jesus Christ.

—2 PETER 3:18

Nothing on Earth

When we came into the world, we brought nothing.
And when we die, we can take nothing out. So, if we
have food and clothes, we will be satisfied with that.

—1 TIMOTHY 6:7-8

Satisfied? That is one thing we are not. We are not happy with what we have. We take the vacation of our dreams. We enjoy every kind of fun in the sun. But we are not even on the way home before we dread the end of the trip and begin wishing for the next one.

We are not content. We are not happy. We are not satisfied.

As a kid we say, "If only I were a teenager." As a teen we say, "If only I were an adult." As an adult, "If only I were married." As a married person, "If only I had kids."

We are not satisfied. Why is it so hard to be content?

Because there is nothing on earth that can satisfy our deepest want—to see God. Everything in His creation is whispering that we will see Him, and we won't be content until we do.

Growing in Grace

What are you waiting for? What do you think you need to be truly happy? While you are wishing for something more, time is passing by. Look for the joy in the things of today—like hugs from loved ones, playing with your pet, and quiet moments with the God who loves you.

The Master Builder

He restores my soul;
He leads me in the paths of righteousness
For His name's sake.

—PSALM 23:3 NKJV

I t's hard to see things grow old. The town in which I grew up is growing old. Some of the buildings are boarded up. Some of the houses are torn down. The old movie theater where I went with my friends has "For Sale" up on its sign.

I wish I could make it all new again. I wish I could blow the dust off the streets, but I can't.

I can't. Just like I can't dust the sin off my soul or erase my mistakes. But God can. "He restores my soul," wrote the shepherd. God doesn't change our souls. He *restores* them. He makes them new again. He doesn't just cover up the old; He makes the old new. The Master Builder will pull out the original plan and make it just like new. He will restore the liveliness. He will restore the energy. He will restore the hope. He will restore your soul.

Growing in Grace

Sometimes the things we love grow old. And sometimes we grow too old for the things we love. Take a look at your toys. Are there some you no longer play with? Restore them with a little cleaning up and fixing up. Then share them with a child who will love them again.

A Raging Fire

Since God has shown us great mercy, I beg you to
offer your lives as a living sacrifice to him.

—ROMANS 12:1

Anger and hate make our blood pump faster and our hearts
race. As time goes by, we need more and more anger and
hate to keep our blood pumping faster.

There is a dangerous point at which anger stops being an
emotion and becomes the reason we do what we do—and what
we do is usually the wrong thing. A person who only cares
about getting even moves further and further away from being
able to forgive. And that moves him further and further away
from God.

Hatred is like a rabid dog that turns and bites its owner.

Revenge is like a raging fire that burns up the one who set it.

Anger is like a trap that catches the hunter.

And mercy is the choice that can set them all free.

Growing in Grace

*The next time you're red in the face with anger, try these tips: First,
take a deep breath and do nothing. That's right—nothing. Take a
time-out to think about what you should do and say. Second, pray
for God's wisdom. And, third, forgive—even if you don't want to.*

The Joy of God's Heart

As a man is very happy about his new wife,
so your God will be happy with you.

—ISAIAH 62:5

Have you ever seen the way a groom looks at his bride during the wedding? I have. Perhaps it's because of where I'm standing. As the minister at the wedding, I'm standing right next to the groom.

If the light is just right, I can see a tiny reflection in his eyes. Her reflection. And the sight of her reminds him why he is here. His jaw softens, and his smile becomes real again. He forgets he's wearing a tux. He forgets his sweat-soaked shirt. When he sees her, any thought of running away becomes a joke. For it's written all over his face, "I can't live without my bride!"

And those are the exact same feelings Jesus has. Look long enough into His eyes, and you will see the reflection of someone. Dressed in white. Clothed in pure grace.

And who is this person Jesus is waiting for? *It's you!* You are the joy of God's heart.

Growing in Grace

You are the light of God's world. The joy of His heart. The apple of His eye. Want proof? Ask a parent to slice an apple in half across the middle. What do you see in the center? A star. Just another reminder that you are the shining star of God's creation.

God's Plan for Your Life

Enjoy serving the Lord.
And he will give you what you want.

—PSALM 37:4

When we choose to follow God's plans, we can trust our wants and desires. Our life's mission—our purpose—is found at the place where God's plan and our pleasures meet. *What do you love to do? What makes you happy? What gives you a sense of satisfaction?* God will use those things in His plan for your life.

Some people feel a need to help the poor. Others enjoy leading others at church. Each of us has been made to serve God in our own special way.

The things you enjoy doing are no accidents. They are important messages. The things you love to do shouldn't be ignored; they should be respected. Just as the wind turns the direction of the weather vane, so God uses the things you love to do to turn the direction of your life. God is too kind to ask you to do something you hate.

Growing in Grace

As you search for your life's mission, ask yourself these questions: What do you love to do? What is your favorite part of church? What makes you smile the most? Now find people in your church who have those same interests and ask them how they use their interests to serve God.

An Inside Job

Fix your attention on God. You'll be
changed from the inside out.

—ROMANS 12:2 MSG

Real change is an inside job. What does that mean? It means that you can change the way you look on the outside with money and clothes and stuff, but changing *who* you are—changing your heart—that's an *inside* job.

That's because our problem is not on the outside. It's not money, clothes, or stuff. Our problem is on the inside: our sin. Sin is when we do what we know is wrong. It is disobeying our Creator. And because God is perfect and has no sin in Him, He cannot be around us when we have sin inside us. Our sin keeps us from getting close to God.

But—and here's the really great news—God loves us so much that He doesn't want to be cut off from us. So He gave us a way to get rid of the sin inside us. He gave us His Son. When we choose to follow Jesus, He washes away all our sins. Jesus changes us from the *inside* out.

Growing in Grace

What "inside" things would you like to change about yourself?
Think about the ways you want to change so that you can be more
like Jesus. Ask for God's help. He always gives to those who ask:
"If any of you needs wisdom, you should ask God for it. God is
generous. He enjoys giving to all people" (James 1:5).

Truth in Love

Your kingdom is built on what is right and fair.
Love and truth are in all you do.

—PSALM 89:14

The single most difficult goal is to have truth *and* love.

Love by itself is a difficult goal to reach. Especially *agape* love—the kind of love that wants the best for others.

Truth is a tough one too. Not the who-really-broke-the-glass kind of truth. But the kind of truth that wants to lead others to God.

But put them together, try to have truth and love at the same time, and—whew!—you've got your work cut out for you.

Love in truth. Truth in love. Never one without the other.

You see, you can't just accept what someone believes about God if it doesn't match the truth of the Bible. Sometimes you *do* need to help others see what God's Word really says. But it's important to help for the right reason—because you love them—and not just because you want to be right.

Growing in Grace

When you are tempted to tell someone they're wrong about something they believe, ask yourself why you are doing it. Is it because you love that person and want to build up his or her faith? Or because you love yourself and want to feel that you're better than someone else? Ask yourself, What would Jesus say?

Safe to Believe

When Jesus was raised from the dead it was a
signal of the end of death-as-the-end.

—ROMANS 6:9-10 MSG

Don't you just love that verse? "When Jesus was raised from the dead it was a signal"—a signal that He had defeated death!

The resurrection of Jesus is like an exploding signal flare shot into the sky. It tells all of us who are truly searching for Christ that it is safe to believe. Safe to believe in eternal justice. Safe to believe in eternal life. Safe to believe in heaven as our home and the earth as its front porch. Safe to believe in a time when questions and worries won't keep us awake. Safe to believe in a time when pain and sickness won't keep us down. Safe to believe in endless days and real praise.

Because we can believe the resurrection story, it is safe to believe the rest of God's story.

Growing in Grace

Reread one of your favorite Bible stories. Maybe it's the story of Daniel and the lions, Paul on the road to Damascus, or Jesus calming the storm. After you read it, take time to think about how these aren't just stories like Cinderella and Aladdin. These were real people and real events—serving a real God.

He Saves Us

The followers went to Jesus and woke him. They
said, "Lord, save us! We will drown!"
Jesus answered, "Why are you afraid?"

—MATTHEW 8:25-26

The Bible says that after Jesus calmed the storm, "those who were in the boat worshiped Jesus and said, 'Truly you are the Son of God!'" (Matthew 14:33).

After the storm, the disciples worshiped Him. As far as we know, they had never, as a group, done that before. Never. Check it out. Open your Bible. Search for a time when the disciples all joined together and praised Jesus. You won't find it.

You won't find them worshiping when He healed the leper. Reached out to the woman at the well. Preached to the masses. They were willing to follow. Willing to leave family. Willing to cast out demons. Willing to be in the Lord's army.

But only after Jesus stilled the storm on the sea did they worship Him. Why?

Simple. This time they knew *they* were the ones who had been saved.

Growing in Grace

God's saving love isn't just for people in general. It is for you—you personally. Don't believe it? Check out Isaiah 43:1: "I have saved you. I have called you by name, and you are mine." God is calling your name—so answer Him.

Prayers for Parents

All your children will be taught by the Lord.
And they will have much peace.
—ISAIAH 54:13

Pay attention to the prayers of a Christian parent. Pay attention to the power that comes when a parent asks God to be with or help a child. Who knows what prayers will be answered in your life ten or twenty years from now because of your parents' faithful prayers right now? God listens to thoughtful parents.

And God listens to thoughtful children. Just as your parents pray for you, take time to pray for your parents. They are God's children too. They need His help, His guidance, His wisdom just as much as you do. There is nothing more special, more precious than the time that a child spends struggling with prayers to God. Your prayers are heard—and answered—in heaven.

Growing in Grace

It doesn't matter how old you are, there are few things more wonderful than hearing your name lifted up in prayer. Ask your parents if you can pray together. Listen as they pray for you—and let them hear your prayers for them.

God's Big Power

The Lord gives strength to those who are tired.
He gives more power to those who are weak.

—ISAIAH 40:29

Do you ever think God is too small to do the big things we ask of him? Do you ever think your problem is just too enormous, even for God to handle? Do you ever think to yourself: *There's no way out of this mess.* Or, *God can't help me. This problem is just too big.*

If you've had thoughts like that, listen to what His Word says: "With God's power working in us, God can do much, much more than anything we can ask or think of" (Ephesians 3:20).

Did you get that? You can't even *begin* to imagine what God will do for you and through you—when you let His power work in you. When your problems seem bigger than the answers, ask your big God to help. Keep praying and trusting Him with everything in your life. See what He will do!

Growing in Grace

How can you let God's big power help you? Try a prayer like this: "God, You are bigger and stronger and more powerful than anything I can even imagine. I don't know how You can fix this problem, but I know that You can—and I can't wait to see how You do it! Thank You, God, for answering my prayer—because I know that You will. In Jesus' name, amen."

Be Patient with Yourself

Patience produces character, and character produces hope. And this hope will never disappoint us.

—ROMANS 5:4-5

God is often more patient and more forgiving with us than we are with ourselves. We may believe that if we mess up—if we sin—then we aren't truly saved. If we struggle and stumble, then we aren't really His children. We are supposed to be "made new" when we belong to Christ (2 Corinthians 5:17). So if we sometimes still fall back to our old selfish ways, then we might think, *Uh-oh. Maybe I wasn't made new after all.*

If you are worried about these things, please remember that "God began doing a good work in you. And he will continue it until it is finished when Jesus Christ comes again" (Philippians 1:6).

In other words, don't worry. God's still working on you.

Growing in Grace

God is still working on you. You aren't perfect. And you won't be perfect this side of heaven. But there are some things you can do every day to be a little more like Jesus. Pray every day. Read the Bible every day. And follow Jesus' example—you guessed it— every day.

Give It to God

When I kept things to myself,
I felt weak deep inside me.

—PSALM 32:3

Ask yourself two questions:

Is there any sin in my life that I have not confessed and given to God?

Confession is telling God you did the thing He saw you do. He doesn't need to hear it—He already knows. But He also knows you need to say it. Whether you think it's too small to be mentioned or too big to be forgiven doesn't matter. It's not your decision. Your job is to be honest with God.

Are there any worries in my heart that I haven't given to God?

"Give all your worries to him, because he cares for you" (1 Peter 5:7). The German word for *worry* means "to strangle." The Greek word means "to divide the mind." Both are right. Worry is like a noose around your neck that won't let you breathe. Worry confuses your mind. Neither of these things will lead you to the joy God wants you to have.

Growing in Grace

Nothing is too small to give to God—no worry, no fear, no confession of sin. After all, this is the God who created each grain of sand, the tiniest of wildflowers, and, yes, the most microscopic of amoebas. What other tiny things did God take time to create?

What Are Your Strengths?

We all have different gifts. Each gift came
because of the grace that God gave us.

—ROMANS 12:6

There are some things we want to do but simply aren't able to do. I, for example, would love to sing. Singing for others would fill me with joy and satisfaction. The problem is, I'm not the best singer, so it would not give the same joy and satisfaction to those listening to me.

Paul gave good advice in Romans 12:3: "Do not think that you are better than you are. You must see yourself as you really are."

In other words, know your strengths. Know your talents. Know what you are good at. When you help in the nursery, do the toddlers follow your every step? You may be a teacher. When you offer to serve, do other kids follow your example? You may be a leader. Where are you able to do the most good for God? Find out your strengths, and then focus on them. Failing to focus on your strengths may keep you from doing the very thing that God has created you to do.

Growing in Grace

God has a job for you. He put you here on earth for a reason. And your first task is to find out what that job is. So don't be afraid to try new things. One of them just might be the very thing God is calling you to do. What new way can you serve Him this week?

God's Temple

You should know that your body is a temple for the Holy
Spirit. The Holy Spirit is in you. You have received the
Holy Spirit from God. You do not own yourselves.

—1 CORINTHIANS 6:19

You will live forever in your body—or at least in a perfect version of your body. What is now crooked will be straightened. What is now broken will be fixed. Your body will be different, but you won't have a different body. You will have this one. It will be made new and perfect, but it will be the same one. Does that change the view you have of your body? I hope so.

God created your body, and He loves His creation. You should as well. Respect your body. I did not say worship it, but I did say respect it. After all, the Bible tells us that the human body is the temple of God—the place where the Holy Spirit of God lives. Be careful how you feed it, use it, and take care of it. You wouldn't want anyone trashing your home, would you? Well, God doesn't want anyone trashing His either. After all, it is *His* temple, isn't it?

Growing in Grace

All those things your mom tells you to do—like brush your teeth, eat your veggies, go outside and play—are really about keeping you healthy. Try to add one healthy habit this week. Turn off the TV and shoot some hoops. Choose fruit for your after-school snack. Take care of God's temple.

God Sees Our Value

God does not see the same way people see. People look at the outside of a person, but the Lord looks at the heart.

—1 SAMUEL 16:7

God sees us with the eyes of a Father. He sees our faults, our mistakes, and our imperfections. But He also sees our value, how much we are worth.

What did Jesus know that made Him able to do what He did on the cross?

Here's part of the answer. He knew the value of people. He knew that each human being is a treasure. And because He did, people did not make Him worried and stressed. They made Him joyful.

So when Jesus looks at you, He is able to look past all your faults, your mistakes, and your imperfections. He does not see you as one big mess of stress. You are His source of joy.

Growing in Grace

Think of the things that make you smile. Grab some old magazines and find pictures of those things. Cut them out and use them to make a collage for your room. Then think about this: If Jesus made a poster like that, your picture would be on it. Because you make Him smile.

Only a Great God

God will always give mercy
to those who worship him.

—LUKE 1:50

God does not save us because of what we've done.
Only a weak, puny god could be bought with our gifts and offerings. Only an uncaring god would be impressed with our pain. Only a heartless god would sell salvation to the highest bidders.

And only a great God would do for His children what they can't do for themselves—save them. God gives you His joy when you give yourself up to Him, not when He defeats you. The first step to getting His joy is to ask for His help, to admit that you have sinned, to realize that you aren't good enough for heaven.

Those who choose to follow God understand that they can't get to heaven without His help. Those who choose to follow God ask for His forgiveness for all the wrongs they have done.

And because God is so great, He doesn't just forgive them—He calls them His children.

Growing in Grace

There are lots of different religions, but only one way to the true God and heaven—through Jesus. When you hear about another religion, ask your parents to help you compare its beliefs to what God's Word teaches. Pray that those who follow other gods will come to know the true God.

Look-Alikes

He will keep his agreement of love for a thousand lifetimes. He does this for people who love him and obey his commands.

—DEUTERONOMY 7:9

We are God's idea. We are His. His face. His eyes. His hands. His touch. We are Him. Look deeply into the face of every human being on earth, and you will see His likeness. We are all created in the image of God.

We are—amazingly and incredibly—the body of Christ. And although we may not always act like our Father, there is no greater truth than this: we are His. That cannot change. He loves us with a love that never dies. Nothing can separate us from the love of Christ (see Romans 8:38–39).

Nothing can separate *you* from the love of Christ.

Growing in Grace

Make a list of things that separate. There are things you can see, like walls, doors, and mountains. And there are things you can't see, like anger and hatred. But not one of those things can separate you from the love of Jesus.

God's Mountaintop

The Lord will always lead you.

—ISAIAH 58:11

Imagine climbing to the top of a beautiful mountain. Turn your back on this noisy world and climb up the rocks that God Himself created. Listen to His voice whispering to you in the wind. No crowds of people. No school. No practice. Just you and God.

God gently invites you to sit on that high rock, far above the trees, and look out with Him at the ancient mountain peaks that will never be worn down. He asks you to listen as He says:

"The things that are needed for your salvation will always be there for you."

"There is nowhere you can go tomorrow that I have not already been."

"My truth will always win out over evil."

"The victory—heaven—is yours."

Spend some quiet time in prayer on God's sacred summit, His mountaintop. It's an unchanging place in an ever-changing world.

Growing in Grace

Think of all the things you can count on to always be true, to always happen. Things like the sun will rise and the morning will come, the earth will spin around the sun, and your parents will love you. And God's perfect plan will save you.

Four Habits Worth Having

Grow in the grace and knowledge of our
Lord and Savior Jesus Christ.

—2 PETER 3:18

Growing a stronger faith should be the goal of every Christian. Maturing is a must.

If you stopped growing taller, your parents would be worried, right? They would try to get help for you.

When a Christian's faith stops growing, help is needed too. If you are the same Christian you were last year, be careful. You might need to get a checkup. Not on your body, but on your heart. Not a physical, but a spiritual.

May I suggest one?

Why don't you check your habits? Make these four habits part of your daily activities, and see what happens.

First, the habit of prayer. Second, the habit of Bible study. Third, the habit of giving both your time and your money to God's work here on earth. And, last, the habit of fellowship and friendship with other Christians.

Growing in Grace

Make a checklist of the four habits (prayer, Bible study, giving, and fellowship) and post it where you will see it every day. Check off each item at least once a day. Although a checklist won't get you into heaven, it can bring a bit of heaven into your life each day.

Faith Starts at Home

Work as if you were working for the Lord, not for men.

—COLOSSIANS 3:23

When do we get our first clue that Jesus knew He is the Son of God? In the temple of Jerusalem. He was twelve years old. His parents were three days into their return trip to Nazareth before they noticed He was missing. They found Him in the temple studying with the leaders.

As a young boy, Jesus already heard the call of God. But what did He do when He left the temple? Start rounding up apostles and preaching sermons and performing miracles? No, He went home with His folks, learned the family business, and finished growing up.

And that is exactly what you should do. Want to bring focus to your life? Do what Jesus did. Be home, love your family, and take care of the business of growing up. "But, Mr. Lucado, I want to be a missionary when I grow up," you might say. Your first mission field is at home. To be able to show love to people overseas, you first need to be able to show love to the people who live across the hall.

Growing in Grace

How do you want to reach out to those who don't know Christ? With a smile or a glare? With a kind word or a grunt and a groan? With gentleness or a snappy comeback? Reach out to your own family in the same way. Faith starts at home.

A New Leader

When I was helpless, he saved me.

—PSALM 116:6

When I was growing up, all of us kids in the neighborhood would play street football. The minute we got home from school, we'd hit the pavement. One kid had a dad with a great arm and a love for football. As soon as he'd pull in the driveway from work, we'd start yelling for him to come and play ball. He couldn't resist. Out of fairness he'd always ask, "Which team is losing?" Then he would join that team, which often seemed to be mine.

When he joined the huddle, the whole game changed. He was confident, strong, and, most of all, he had a plan. He'd look at us and say, "Okay, boys, here is what we are going to do." The other side was groaning before we left the huddle. You see, we not only had a new plan, but we also had a new leader. He brought new life to our team.

God does the same thing. In this sinful world, we don't need a new play; we need a new plan. We don't need to trade positions; we need a new player. That player is Jesus.

Growing in Grace

Grab some friends for a game of Follow the Leader. Take turns being the leader. Notice how each person's style of leading is just a bit different? Let Jesus be your leader through life. He'll show you a whole new way of doing things.

Perfect

Their sins and the evil things they do—
I will not remember anymore.

—HEBREWS 10:17

With one sacrifice he made perfect forever those who are being made holy" (Hebrews 10:14).

Underline the word *perfect*. Note that the word is not *better*. Not *improving*. Not *looking brighter*. God doesn't just improve; He perfects. He doesn't make better; He completes.

Now I know that in one way we're not perfect. We still make mistakes. We still mess up. We still do exactly what we don't want to do, what we're trying so hard not to do. And that part of us is the part that God says is "being made holy."

But when it comes to our place before God, we're perfect. When He sees each of us, He sees one who has been made perfect through the One who is perfect—Jesus Christ.

Growing in Grace

Look up the word perfect *in the dictionary. Does that describe you? Nope, and it doesn't describe me either. But that is exactly how God chooses to see us when we believe in and obey His Son.*

Who Do You Want to Be?

The Spirit gives love, joy, peace, patience, kindness, goodness, faithfulness, gentleness, self-control.

—GALATIANS 5:22–23

A lot of people will ask you, "What do you want to be when you grow up?" But a more important question is: "*Who* do you want to be when you grow up?"

When it comes to choosing what you want to be, there are hundreds of choices—from architect to zookeeper and everything in between. But when it comes to choosing *who* you want to be, there are only two choices: you can either be a person of the world or a person of God.

A person of the world thinks, *What do I want to do?* But a person of God thinks, *What does God want me to do?* See the difference?

A person of the world is selfish, bragging, and always demanding his or her own way. But a person of God tries to obey these words from Philippians 2:3: "Do not let selfishness or pride be your guide. Be humble and give more honor to others than to yourselves."

Growing in Grace

Take a good look at yourself. Not at the way you look, but at the way you act. Are you loud, annoying, bragging, or always demanding your own way? Or are you kind, gentle, patient, and faithful? Today, try to be a child of God—not the world—in all that you do and say.

Saved from the Storm

"I tell you the truth. Whoever hears what I say and believes in the One who sent me has eternal life."

—JOHN 5:24

When you realize that God has saved you, you'll want to praise Him like never before.

But you're young, so maybe you haven't yet seen some of the tougher, stormier parts of life. If you haven't needed God to rescue you, you might have an easier time keeping Him at a distance. Sure He's important, but so are your grades. Your friends. Your sports and hobbies.

But maybe you *have* seen some of life's storms, some of its troubles. The move to a new school. The divorce. The lost friend. Sadness might have fallen over you like a fog. In your heart, you weren't sure where to turn to feel better.

Turn to your friends for help? Only if you want to hide from the storm instead of escape it. Lean on your grades for strength? A storm isn't impressed with how much you know.

Only God can help you through all of life's storms.

Growing in Grace

People face life's storms every day. And every day God is there to rescue them. There are also those here on earth who try to rescue the hurting. Whenever you see a police car, ambulance, or fire truck, pray for those rescuers and for those they are trying to save.

Saved!

You have begun to live the new life. In your
new life you are being made new. You are
becoming like the One who made you.

—COLOSSIANS 3:10

The Bible calls Jesus the Shepherd and calls us His sheep. I wonder if Jesus doesn't give a slight grin as He sees one of His lost sheep come dragging into the fold—the beaten, broken, dirty sheep who stands at the door looking up at the Shepherd and asking, "Can I come in?" The Shepherd looks down at the sheep and says, "Come in. This is your home."

Jesus has given you salvation. No one can take it away from you. But *sanctification*—being made holy—will happen your whole life. Sanctification is being changed to be just a little bit more holy, just a little bit more like Jesus each day. It is putting away the old sinfulness and taking on the new holiness.

The psalmist David told us that those who have been *redeemed*—who have been saved—will say so! If we're not saying so, maybe it's because we've forgotten what it is like to be saved. Let's tell the world how we are saved!

Growing in Grace

Are you redeemed? Then say so! Say it with a song you write yourself. Say it with a prayer. Say it with a picture of praise that you create. Say it with a smile for everyone you meet. Find a way every day to tell the world you are saved.

Paul's Strength

We continue to preach Christ to all men. We use all
wisdom to warn and to teach everyone. We are trying to
bring each one into God's presence as a mature person
in Christ. To do this, I work and struggle, using Christ's
great strength that works so powerfully in me.

—COLOSSIANS 1:28–29

Look at Paul's goal: *to bring each one into God's presence as a
mature person in Christ.* Paul dreamed of the day that each
person would be safe in Christ. What was his way of doing this?
Warning and *teaching* others. What were Paul's tools? Verbs.
Nouns. Sentences. Lessons. The same tools that you and I have.

Was it easier back then to teach others than it is now? I don't
think so. Paul called it work. "To do this, I work and struggle," he
wrote. *Struggle* means it was hard. *Work* means homes visited,
people taught, classes prepared.

How did Paul do it? What was his source of strength? It was
Jesus—"Christ's great strength that works so powerfully in me."

As Paul worked, so did God. And as you work, so does the
Father.

Growing in Grace

*Yes, you are young, but you have the same tools that Paul did—nouns,
verbs, sentences. Put them to use! Invite someone to church or a Bible
class. Teach a lesson. Write a puppet show for younger kids. Send a
note to cheer up someone who is struggling. Put your words to work.*

God Knows What's Best

Trust the Lord with all your heart.
Don't depend on your own understanding.

—PROVERBS 3:5

This world just doesn't fit right. Oh, it will do for now, but it isn't made to fit us. We were made to live with God in heaven, but on earth we must live by trusting in God. We were made to live forever, but on earth we live for just a moment.

We must trust God, that He will do what is best and that He knows what is ahead. Look at Isaiah 57:1–2: "Good people are taken away, but no one understands. Those who do right are being taken away from evil and are given peace" (NCV).

Wow! What a thought. God takes good people away from the evil. Could death be part of God's grace? It isn't always easy to understand the things that happen on this earth—why good people get sick, or hurt, or even die. But we can always believe that God does what is best for each of His children. He is always taking care of us—especially in times of sickness and death.

Trust in God, Jesus encourages us, *and trust in Me.*

Growing in Grace

Make a list of all the things you won't need anymore when you get to heaven. Things like glasses (you'll have perfect vision in heaven), Band-Aids (no suffering), hospitals (no sickness), and tissues (no tears). What else will you not need in heaven?

Our Wounds Are Healed

He will change our simple bodies and make them
like his own glorious body. Christ can do this by his
power. With that power he is able to rule all things.

—PHILIPPIANS 3:21

What do we know about how our bodies will look in heaven? Will we look so different that others won't know who we are? Maybe. (We may need name tags.)

Will we be walking through walls and on water? Chances are we'll be doing much more than that.

Will we still have the scars from this life? The bumps and bruises. The signs of disease. The jagged scars of bike wrecks and broken arms. Will these still be on our bodies? That's a good question. Jesus kept the wounds on His hands, His feet, and His side for at least forty days. Will we keep ours? For this question, we have only opinions, and my opinion is no. Peter told us "we are healed because of his wounds" (1 Peter 2:24). In heaven, only one wound is worthy of being remembered—the wound of Jesus.

Our wounds and hurts will be healed.

Growing in Grace

Bullying is a terrible sin. It causes wounds that are every bit as serious as wounds to the body. As you go back to school this year, be careful not to hurt those around you. And when you see someone who is hurt by bullying, offer him or her healing words of kindness.

A Witness for Christ

"You will be my witnesses—in Jerusalem, in all of
Judea, in Samaria, and in every part of the world."

—ACTS 1:8

Have you ever seen a courtroom scene on television? One where a witness is telling the court what he has seen or heard? We are witnesses too. And we are called to testify just like witnesses in a courtroom. We are to tell others what we have seen and heard about Jesus. Our job is not to stretch the truth or make things seem different from what they are. Our job is to tell the truth. Period.

There is, however, one difference between the witness in court and the witness for Christ. Sooner or later, the witness in court will step down from the witness chair. He will be finished. But as a witness for Christ, you never step down. You are never finished.

Because the promises of Jesus are always on trial, you must always be a witness. You must always tell the world who He is, what He has done for you, and what He wants to do for the world.

And you must always tell the truth.

Growing in Grace

Did you know that when you live by God's Word, you become a living Bible? A walking example of His Word? Some people don't own a Bible, don't go to church, and don't know God. You may be the only Bible they'll ever "read." Make sure you're a good one.

A Simple Story

I will make you my promised bride forever.
I will be good and fair.
I will show you my love and mercy.

—HOSEA 2:19

For all its strange names and unusual events, the Bible has a simple story: God made people. People turned away from God. God won't give up until He wins His people back. God will whisper. He will shout. He will touch and tug. He will take away our worries and fears. He will even take away our blessings. If there are 1,000 steps between us and Him, He will take 999. But He will leave the last step for us to take. The choice is ours.

Please understand. God's goal is not to make you happy. His goal is to make you His. His goal is not to get you what you want. It is to get you what you need—a faith in His Son that will get you to heaven.

Growing in Grace

Use a roll of craft paper or sheets of paper taped together to make a mural of the story of Jesus. Begin with His birth and go all the way to the Resurrection. But don't stop there. Draw what Jesus means to you. Hang your mural on the wall or roll it into a scroll.

September

Let us hold firmly to the hope that we have confessed.
We can trust God to do what he promised.

—HEBREWS 10:23

Thirsty for God

Create in me a pure heart, God.
Make my spirit right again.

—PSALM 51:10

We are thirsty.

Not for fame, or for stuff, or for popularity. Oh, we think that's what we want. Maybe we've tried those things. Maybe we've tasted those waters. But they are like saltwater in the desert. They won't quench our thirst—they just make us thirstier. Why? Because we aren't thirsty for the things of this world. We are thirsty for God and His goodness.

Matthew 5:6 says, "Those who want to do right more than anything else are happy."

Those who want to do right—that's righteousness. That's it. That's what we are actually thirsty for. We're thirsty for a clean heart. We crave a "do over." When we mess up, we want a fresh start. So we pray that God will reach down and do for us the one thing we can't do for ourselves—make us right again. And when we ask Him to, He promises that He will.

Growing in Grace

What does "thirst for righteousness" mean? Try eating a salty snack—like pretzels or chips. Now, how long can you go without getting a drink? Feel your throat tighten, your tongue stick to the roof of your mouth. That's how your soul feels without God. That's thirsting for righteousness.

Free in God

In Christ we are set free by the blood of his death. And so we have forgiveness of sins because of God's rich grace.

—EPHESIANS 1:7

Jesus talked about freedom, but it's a different kind of freedom. His freedom doesn't come through having more rights and power, but through giving up yours. It's not about controlling everything, but giving up your control to Him. And it's not about collecting the stuff of this world, but giving it away.

Sounds a little strange, doesn't it? God wants to *free* His people by having them surrender to Him. You see, God wants us to be His sons and daughters, not slaves to the stuff of this world. He wants us to be ruled by His love.

By believing that Jesus died for our salvation, we are freed from trying to work our way to heaven. We are free to pray and to love God with all our hearts. And we are free from our sins because we have been forgiven by the only One who can call us guilty. We are truly free!

Growing in Grace

How do you feel when the school bell rings? When class is dismissed and the school day is over? Free from the rules and demands of others? Free to play? Multiply that feeling times a million-gazillion, and you'll get a tiny taste of what it's like to be free in God.

Chasing the World

"Your heart will be where your treasure is."

—MATTHEW 6:21

The most powerful life is the most simple life. It's the life that knows God is its source of strength. It's the life that stays free of clutter and busyness.

Being busy is not a sin. Jesus was busy. Paul was busy. Peter was busy. Nothing important happens without hard work and tiredness. No, being busy is not a sin.

But what are we being busy about? Is it an endless chase to get more stuff—the newest, the greatest, the latest? Or an endless search for popularity—be the best, look the best? That kind of busyness will only leave you empty inside. That isn't pleasing to God.

Chasing after the things of this world just makes you tired. Stuff can't make you happy, because there is always more stuff to chase after. Your stuff, your pride, your popularity—these are just things. When you try to make a life out of things instead of God, you only make yourself tired and unhappy.

Growing in Grace

It's okay to have stuff. To want stuff. But it's not okay when stuff is all you think about. Next time you want to buy something, try making yourself wait a week or even two. You may find you don't need that stuff after all.

God Fights for Us

He protects me like a strong, walled city.
I will not be defeated.

—PSALM 62:6

Here is a big question: What is God doing when you are in trouble? When your lifeboat springs a leak and you're sinking fast? When the parachute doesn't open? When your tummy is empty and so are your pockets?

I know what we are doing. Nibbling on our nails like corn on the cob. Pacing the floors. Wringing our hands.

But what does God do?

He fights for us. He steps in front of us, protects us with His presence, and takes over. "You will only need to remain calm. The Lord will fight for you" (Exodus 14:14).

His job is to fight. Our job is to trust.

Just trust. Not take over. Or question. Our job is to pray and wait.

Growing in Grace

What do you do when you worry? Bite your nails or twist your hair? Does your tummy start to ache and your head to throb? Next time, try trust—take a deep breath, say a prayer, and let God fight for you.

Don't Panic

Let us hold firmly to the hope that we have confessed.
We can trust God to do what he promised.

—HEBREWS 10:23

Have you had too many disappointments this week? One too many defeats lately and not nearly enough victories?

Read the story of the disciples on the road to Emmaus in Luke 24:13–35. The Savior they thought was dead was now walking right beside them. He went into their house and sat at their table. And then something happened in their hearts: "When Jesus talked to us on the road, it felt like a fire burning in us. It was exciting when he explained the true meaning of the Scriptures" (Luke 24:32).

Next time you're disappointed, don't give up. Just be patient and let God remind you that He's still in control. Let Him warm your heart with His Word. After all, it ain't over till it's over.

Growing in Grace

Imagine being one of those disciples on the road to Emmaus. What would it be like to lose your Savior and then suddenly find Him walking right next to you? Well . . . He is walking right next to you. He's in your house and at your table. And He will explain God's Word to you. He is God's Holy Spirit living in you.

The Cost of Lies

No one who is dishonest will live in my house.
No liars will stay around me.

—PSALM 101:7

More than once I've heard people talk about the story of Ananias and Sapphira (Acts 5:1–11) with a nervous chuckle and say, "I'm glad God doesn't still strike people dead for lying." But I'm not so sure that He doesn't. It seems to me that the punishment for lying is still death. Not death of the body, maybe, but death of: *a parent's trust*—Lies are like termites in the trunk of the family tree; *a conscience*—The real sadness of the second lie is that it's always easier to tell than the first; *a future*—Just ask the student who was flunked for cheating if that lie was really worth it.

We could also list the deaths of friendships, trust, peace, reputation, and self-respect. But perhaps the most tragic death that happens because of our lies is the death of our Christian witness. Courtrooms and judges won't listen to witnesses who lie. And neither will the world.

Growing in Grace

Why do you think people lie? Ananias and Sapphira lied to make themselves look good. Others may lie to get out of trouble or to get something they want. The problem with one lie is that it usually leads to another and another. Lies are kind of like onions—lots of layers and all of them stink!

God Loves the Truth

The Lord hates those who tell lies.
But he is pleased with those who do what they promise.

—PROVERBS 12:22

God has a strict rule about honesty.

From Genesis to Revelation, that rule is the same: God loves the truth and hates lies. In 1 Corinthians 6:9–10, Paul listed the types of people who will not be in the kingdom of heaven. The group he described is a ragged mixture of those who worship idols, get drunk, rob people, and—there it is—*lie about others.*

Such a strict rule may surprise you. *You mean my fibbing and little white lies make God as angry as drugs and drunkenness?* Yes.

Why the hard line? Why the tough stand?

For one reason: God is truth, so lying is the exact opposite of the nature of God.

Growing in Grace

Some people like to say that little white lies aren't as bad as whoppers. But think of it this way: If your pizza just had a little bit of rat poison on it instead of a whole lot, would you eat it? No! It doesn't matter how big the lie is, it still poisons your soul.

Blessed Are the Focused

Each of you received a spiritual gift. . . .
Use your gifts to serve each other.

—1 PETER 4:10

There are only so many hours in the day. Who gets them? You know what I'm talking about, don't you? "The student council needs a new treasurer. You're not afraid to speak in front of groups, you're good at organization, and you've got an A+ in math. You are perfect for the job!"

It's a tug-of-war, and you are the rope. Family life, church groups, homework, chores, sports, hobbies, friends—how do you choose who and what gets your time? Ask the One who created time how He wants you to spend your time. His answer might be something like this:

Blessed are those who see the jobs God wants them to do. Blessed are those who know that there is only one God, that He is in charge and they have stopped trying to do His job. Blessed are those who ask Him *what on earth* they are on earth to do— and they do it.

Growing in Grace

As you start this new school year, there will be lots of different activities coming your way. How do you decide what to do? Before starting something new, ask these three questions: Does it bring me closer to God? Does it bring me closer to my family? Does it make me a better person?

Fear and Faith

About midnight Paul and Silas were praying singing songs
to God. The other prisoners were listening to them.

—ACTS 16:25

Great acts of faith aren't usually born out of peace and calm. It wasn't military know-how that made Moses raise his staff on the bank of the Red Sea. He was between an army and an ocean.

It wasn't the latest medical research that convinced Naaman to dip seven times in the river. He was a very sick man without hope. It wasn't common sense that caused Paul to abandon the Jewish laws he'd followed his whole life and follow Jesus instead. He simply couldn't see any other way to go.

And it wasn't a bold bunch who prayed in a small room in Jerusalem for Peter's release from prison. It was a frightened, desperate band of backed-into-a-corner believers. It was a church with no other choice. A bunch of have-nots begging for help. And they were never stronger.

For at the beginning of every act of faith, there is often a seed of fear.

Growing in Grace

What are the things that trouble you? Maybe it's something on the news or someone you love who is hurting. You can't control it or fix it, and that scares you. Drop to your knees and pray about it. He may not show you the answer right away, but you can trust that He is working on it.

Beyond Our Imagination

I saw the hard work God has given us to do.

—ECCLESIASTES 3:10

It doesn't take a genius to know that we want more than this earth can give us. We wish for a place free of pain and hunger. Free of sickness and tears and loss. And sometimes we find ourselves asking, "Why is life so hard?"

So God gives us moments of joy. The loving hug of a parent, the comfort of a true friend, the warm sunshine on our back. These are His gifts of hope to us—like tiny slivers of light breaking through the window of heaven. God gives us these glimpses of joy to give us hope and keep us going. He is saying to us, "If you think this is good, just wait and see what I have for you in heaven."

As Paul quoted, "No one has ever imagined what God has prepared for those who love him" (1 Corinthians 2:9).

What an amazing verse! Do you see what it says? Heaven is *beyond* our imagination. Even in our most creative moments, in our wildest dreams, we cannot imagine the wonder and perfection of heaven.

Growing in Grace

Comparing our joys on earth to the joys of heaven is like comparing a flashlight to the sun. Turn on a flashlight outside at night. Yes, it will light a bit of your way. But in the morning, check out the sun. It lights up the whole way! There's just no comparison.

From the Inside Out

"I will ask the Father, and he will give you another Helper. He will give you this Helper to be with you forever. The Helper is the Spirit of truth."

—JOHN 14:16-17

Do-it-yourself is something you hear a lot these days. You can learn to build your own clubhouse, decorate your own room, bake your own birthday cake. There are a lot of things that you can do yourself. But there is no such thing as a do-it-yourself way to heaven.

To get to heaven, we need help. *Real help*. Not just happy words and a pat on the back. We need real help from the One who really loves us. Real help from the One with real power.

We need help from the One who knows our thoughts before we think them and our feelings before we feel them. We need help from the inside out. Not near us or above us. But *in* us. And the great news is that the Spirit of God will come to live inside us when we choose to follow Him.

Growing in Grace

In 2001, September 11 stopped being just another autumn day. On that day our nation knew it needed real help. So our nation prayed. This September 11, we still need help. Take time this day to pray for our nation and its leaders and that we as a country will love and follow God.

The Seed

"A grain of wheat must fall to the ground and die. Then it makes many seeds. But if it never dies, it remains only a single seed."

—JOHN 12:24

This world is all about living. Death is seen as the end of everything. But God takes a very different view of life and death. For God, death is not the end—it is the beginning. What we see as the greatest sadness, He sees as the greatest victory.

A seed must die and be buried before it can grow. So when a Christian dies, it's not just a time for sadness; it is a time to trust. Like the seed, the body is buried. And just as a buried seed sprouts new life, so our body will blossom into a new body.

The seeds of the Christians' bodies buried in the earth will blossom in heaven. Our souls and bodies will be one again, and we will be like Jesus.

Growing in Grace

To help you remember this cycle of death and rebirth, plant a walnut or an acorn this fall. Plant it in a spot in your yard, and mark it with a stick. That hard, cold thing you planted will be reborn into a leafy, green stem next spring.

Sweeter After a Rest

In six days the Lord made everything. . . .
And on the seventh day, he rested.
—EXODUS 20:11

When I was ten years old, my mother made me take piano lessons. Spending thirty minutes every afternoon on that piano bench was torture.

Some of the music, though, I learned to enjoy. I hammered the staccatos. I pounded the crescendos. But there was one instruction in the music I could never get quite right. The *rest*. That zigzag-looking sign to do nothing. What sense does that make? Why sit at the piano and pause when you can pound?

"Because," my teacher patiently explained, "music is always sweeter after a rest."

It didn't make sense to me then. But now my teacher's words ring with wisdom—divine wisdom. Music is sweeter after a rest. And life is sweeter after you rest in the Lord.

Growing in Grace

Your life can get pretty crazy. There are family things and church things, school things and sports things. Things can take over, so take time to rest in God. Just spend some time hanging out in His presence. You'll find that the world is much sweeter after you rest from it.

The Power of Your Hands

But people who do right will continue to do right.
And those whose hands are not dirty
with sin will grow stronger.

—JOB 17:9

W hat if someone made a movie about your hands? What would we see?

Everyone's movie would start much the same, with an infant's fist, then a close-up of a tiny hand wrapped around Mom's finger. Then what? Holding on to a chair as you learned to walk?

If you showed the movie to your friends, you'd be proud of some moments: your hands holding out a gift, patting a friend on the back, helping up someone who's fallen, taking food to the sick. But then there are other scenes. Hands taking instead of giving, snatching instead of offering, hitting instead of helping.

Oh, the power of our hands! Leave them uncontrolled, and they become weapons: clawing, scratching, and snatching for our own selfish wants. But control them and our hands become tools of grace and kindness—not just tools in the hands of God, but God's very own hands.

Growing in Grace

When Jesus was walking among us, He could touch the sick and the lonely, feed the poor. But now He uses your hands instead. In Matthew 25:40, Jesus said, "Anything you did for any of my people here, you also did for me." What can you do for Jesus today?

Tell the Truth

Tell each other the truth because we all
belong to each other in the same body.

—EPHESIANS 4:25

Are you in a sticky situation, wondering if you should tell the truth or not? The question to ask at times like these is, "Will God bless my lies?" Will He bless a plan built on fibs and falsehoods? Will the Lord—who loves the truth—bless this web of lies? Will God honor the schoolwork of a cheat?

No, I don't think so either.

Take a look inside your heart. Ask yourself some tough questions: *Am I being totally honest with my mom and dad? Are my words truthful? What about at school? Am I honest with my teachers? Am I a trustworthy student? An honest friend?*

Do you tell the truth . . . always? If not, start today. Don't wait until tomorrow to be truthful. The ripple of today's lies will become tomorrow's wave of fibs and next year's flood of falsehood.

Growing in Grace

Toss a stone into a pool of water. See the ripples? See how they go all the way out to touch every edge of the shore? Lies are like that. Toss one lie into the pool of your life, and its ripples will touch every part of your life. So don't toss out that first lie.

What a God!

Lord God of heaven's armies, who is like you?
Lord, you are powerful and completely to be trusted.

—PSALM 89:8

Think for a moment about who God really is and what He does for us:

He doesn't say it's okay to sin, and He doesn't change His definition of holiness.

He doesn't ignore our disobedience, and He expects us to try to be better every day.

When we sin, those sins must be punished. But—incredibly—God chooses to wipe those sins away from us and place them on His Son instead. Jesus takes the punishment for our sins.

So our sins are punished, but we are not. We are forgiven!

God does what we cannot do, so that we can be what we wouldn't even dare to dream of: *perfect before God.*

Growing in Grace

You have a lot of talents—all given to you by God. Perhaps you can sing, or paint, or throw a perfect spiral. But can you walk on water? Heal the sick person with a touch? Raise the dead and make the blind to see? No. And you can't get yourself to heaven. But God can. He's just waiting for you to ask.

The Names of God

The Lord is like a strong tower.
Those who do what is right can run to him for safety.

—PROVERBS 18:10

God has many names to show how He meets your many needs.

When you are confused about the future, go to your *Jehovah-raah*, your caring shepherd. When you are worried about the things you need, talk to *Jehovah-jireh*, the Lord who provides. Do your troubles seem too large? Seek the help of *Jehovah-shalom*, the Lord is peace. Is your body sick? Is your heart hurting? *Jehovah-rophe*, the Lord who heals you, will see you now. Do you feel like a soldier stuck behind enemy lines? Keep your eyes on *Jehovah-nissi*, the Lord is the flag that I follow.

Thinking about the names of God reminds you of the character of God. Take these names and hide them in your heart.

God is . . . the *shepherd* who guides, the *Lord* who provides, the *voice* who brings peace in the storm, the *physician* who heals the sick, and the *flag* that the soldier follows.

Growing in Grace

What are your names? Not just your first, middle, and last names, but your other names—like son or daughter, brother or sister, friend, student. Just as each of your names tells something different about who you are and what you do, so God's names tell all the different things He does for you.

A Heavy Load of Hatred

Do not be bitter or angry or mad. Never shout
angrily or say things to hurt others.

—EPHESIANS 4:31

Hatred can sneak up on you. It usually starts with something tiny, like a scratch on your brand-new bike. But then it builds. Every time you climb on your bike, that scratch is all you see. You'd only had that bike a day! You didn't see who did it, but you bet you can describe him. Big kid, wart on his chin, bully, kicks kittens for fun.

Let me say this clearly. Hatred will sour your attitude and break your back. The load of anger is simply too heavy to carry. Your knees will buckle under the strain, and your heart will break beneath the weight. The mountain of life is steep enough and hard enough to climb without a load of hatred on your back. The smartest choice—the only good choice—is for you to drop the anger.

God will never ask you to give anyone more grace than He has already given you.

Growing in Grace

Fill a backpack with four or five heavy stones. Now walk around the block or climb a hill. Easy? No! You've got a load on your back. Empty your pack. Now, that's better! Carrying around hatred and anger is just like carrying around a load of stones. So forgive . . . and take a load off.

Face-to-Face with God

May the Lord bless you from Mount Zion.
He made heaven and earth.

—PSALM 134:3

The writer of Hebrews takes us on a Discovery Channel–style tour of heaven. Listen to how he describes the mountaintop of Zion. He says when we reach the mountain we will have come to "the city of the living God, the heavenly Jerusalem. You have come to thousands of angels gathered with joy. You have come to the meeting of God's firstborn children. Their names are written in heaven. You have come to God" (Hebrews 12:22–23).

What a mountain! Won't it be great to see the angels? To finally know what they look like and who they are?

Imagine the meeting! A gathering of all God's children. No jealousy. No popular and unpopular. No in-crowd and out-crowd. We will all be perfect . . . sinless.

And imagine seeing God. Face-to-face. To finally gaze into your Father's eyes. To see Him looking at you. For all eternity.

Growing in Grace

The book of Revelation tells us some things about how heaven will look, but think for a moment about how heaven will feel. Check out Revelation 21:4: "There will be no more death, sadness, crying, or pain." No more. How amazing will that feel?

Keep Your Eyes on God

You have not seen Christ, but still you love him. You
cannot see him now, but you believe in him.

—1 PETER 1:8

Some years ago a sociologist—a person who studies how people act—went with a group of mountain climbers on an expedition. One of the things he noticed was the connection between clouds and contentment. Where there were no clouds and the climbers could see the peak of the mountain, they were full of energy and eager to help one another. But when dark, gray clouds blocked their view of the mountaintop, the climbers became bad-tempered and selfish.

The same thing happens to us. As long as our eyes are on God's majesty, there is a bounce in our step. We are happy with ourselves and happy to help others. But let our eyes focus on the dirt of this world, and we will grumble about every rock and mud puddle we have to step over. Because of this, Paul urged us to "think only about the things in heaven, not the things on earth" (Colossians 3:2).

Growing in Grace

Keep a weather journal for a week. Write down if the weather is warm or cold, sunny or cloudy. Also write down how you feel on those days. Does sunshine give you energy? Do clouds make you blue? If dark days drag you down, focus on the Son when there's no sun in the sky.

Guard the Gate

The devil is your enemy. And he goes around like a roaring lion looking for someone to eat. Refuse to give in to the devil. Stand strong in your faith.

—1 PETER 5:8–9

You wouldn't open the door to a stranger, would you? You know how dangerous that can be. But let any trashy thought knock on the door of our mind, and we let it right in! Anger shows up, and we say, "Welcome!" Revenge needs a place to stay, so we have him pull up a chair. Pity wants to have a party, so we show him the kitchen. Jealousy rings the doorbell, and we show him to the guest room. Don't we know how to say no?

Many of us don't. For most of us, watching our thoughts is, well, *unthought* of. We watch our time, our clothes, our homework, even our hair. But not our thoughts. Shouldn't we be as worried about our thoughts as we are about everything else? Jesus was. Like a trained soldier at the gate of a city, He stood watch over His mind. He guarded the gate to His heart.

If Jesus did, shouldn't we?

Growing in Grace

There's an old saying that goes, "You are what you eat." But it's just as true to say, "You are what you think." If you think thoughts of anger, revenge, pity, or jealousy—then you become angry, vengeful, pitiful, and jealous. So kick out those thoughts . . . and invite God in.

Looking Up

Lord, show us the Father. That is all we need.

—JOHN 14:8

Faith often begins with fear. Look at some of God's greatest heroes: Peter feared death and ran away. Gideon feared defeat and hid. Moses feared failure and begged God to choose someone else.

But faith begins when you are in the valley of fear and you look up to see God on the mountaintop. You see what you need—God. You see what you have—your own fears and limited abilities. And you know that you can't save yourself.

Moses had the Red Sea in front of him and an army of Egyptian enemies behind. The Israelites could swim or they could fight. But neither choice was enough to save them.

Paul was a master of the Jewish laws. But one glimpse of Jesus on the road to Damascus proved that it didn't matter how much he knew. It would never be enough.

Faith that begins with fear brings you closer to the Father. You just need to look up.

Growing in Grace

Who is your favorite hero from the Bible? Reread that person's story. What fears did your hero have to face? How did God help him or her to face them? The God who helped the heroes of the Bible is the same God who saves you. And He will help you face your fears too.

Trust God with the Future

"Don't let your hearts be troubled. Trust
in God. And trust in me."

—JOHN 14:1

Our human minds are not able to handle the thoughts of eternity in heaven. We can never understand a world without time or a place without a beginning or an end. Our minds simply don't have the hooks on which to hang those kinds of thinking caps. So God becomes like the parent who says, "Just trust Me."

Don't be troubled by when or how Jesus will return. Don't be worried about things you can't understand. Many people look for clues and hidden messages, trying to figure out exactly when Christ will come back and exactly what that day will look like. But for the Christian, the return of Christ is not a riddle to be solved or a code to be broken. It is a day to be hoped for and waited for with joy and excitement. And until that day comes, we will trust God with our future.

Growing in Grace

Take a walk through your house and count how many different items you can find that measure time and space. Things like clocks and calendars, measuring tapes and rulers. In heaven, we won't need any of these things. In heaven there will be no beginning and no end—to time or space.

In the Arms of God

"He who believes in me will have life even if he dies."
—JOHN 11:25

We don't like to say good-bye to the people we love. Whether it is saying good-bye to a friend who moves away or to a loved one who has passed away, being apart from the ones we love is hard. When death is the reason for our good-bye, it is especially tough. It is right for us to be sad and to cry, but we don't have to give up hope. Remember: They had pain here on earth, but they have no pain there in heaven. They struggled here on earth, but they have no struggles there in heaven.

You and I might wonder why God took them to heaven. But they don't. They understand. They are, at this very second, at peace and with God.

When it is cold here on earth, we can take comfort in knowing that our loved ones are safe in the warm arms of God. And when Jesus comes back, we will see them again.

Growing in Grace

Ask your parents if your family can plant a tree to honor a lost loved one. Pick a spot where you will be able to see it often. As you watch it grow, know that the God who created this tree from a tiny seed is watching over your loved one—just as you are watching over your tree.

A New Name

"I will also give him a white stone with
a new name written on it."

—REVELATION 2:17

It makes sense. Dads like giving their children special names.
Princess. Tiger. Sweetheart. Bubba. Angel. So it makes sense
that your heavenly Father would have a name for you.

And isn't it incredible to think that God has saved a name just
for you? One you don't even know? We've always thought that the
name we got when we were born is the name we will keep. Not
so. The road ahead is so bright that a fresh, new name is needed.
Your eternity is so special that no ordinary name will do.

God has one picked out just for you. There is more to your
life than you ever thought. There is more to your story than
what you have read.

And so I beg you . . . be there when God whispers your name.

Growing in Grace

Look up these verses to find some of the names God has for you:

1 John 3:1 ⎯⎯⎯⎯⎯⎯⎯⎯⎯⎯⎯⎯⎯⎯⎯⎯⎯⎯⎯⎯⎯
Romans 8:17 ⎯⎯⎯⎯⎯⎯⎯⎯⎯⎯⎯⎯⎯⎯⎯⎯⎯⎯
Ephesians 5:8 ⎯⎯⎯⎯⎯⎯⎯⎯⎯⎯⎯⎯⎯⎯⎯⎯⎯
John 21:15 ⎯⎯⎯⎯⎯⎯⎯⎯⎯⎯⎯⎯⎯⎯⎯⎯⎯⎯⎯⎯
1 Peter 2:9 ⎯⎯⎯⎯⎯⎯⎯⎯⎯⎯⎯⎯⎯⎯⎯⎯⎯⎯⎯⎯

Which name is your favorite?

A Big Change

"Rejoice and be glad. You have a great
reward waiting for you in heaven."

—MATTHEW 5:12

In the Sermon on the Mount, what Jesus promised is not some trick to give you goose bumps, or some coach's speech to pump you up. No, in Matthew 5, Jesus described God's radical remake of our hearts.

Check out how it begins: First, we see that we are in need (we're poor in spirit). Next, we repent of trying to save ourselves (we mourn). We stop trying to be boss of our lives and give control to God (we're meek). We are so grateful for God's presence that we want more of Him (we hunger and thirst). As we grow closer to God, we become more like Him. We forgive others (we're merciful). We change our way of looking at things (we're pure in heart). We love others (we're peacemakers). We suffer through unfairness (we're persecuted).

This is no small change. It's tearing down the old self and creating the new. The greater the change, the greater the joy.

Growing in Grace

Watch a home-makeover show—one where people rip out floors and tear down walls. The end of the show always has a before and an after picture. Isn't the difference amazing? But that's nothing compared to the before and after pictures of you when God finishes His heavenly makeover.

God Knows What He's Doing

Surely I talked about things I did not understand.
I spoke of things too wonderful for me to know.

—JOB 42:3

It's easy to thank God when He does what we want. But God doesn't always do what we want. Ask Job.

He lost everything, his children were killed, and his once healthy body was covered with boils and sores. Where did this misery come from? And where would help come from?

Job went straight to God and told Him his troubles. His head hurt. His body hurt. His heart hurt.

And God answered. Not with answers, but with questions. A whole ocean of questions!

After dozens of questions, Job got the point. What is it?

The point is this: God doesn't owe anyone anything. No reasons. No explanations. Nothing. If He gave them, we wouldn't be able to understand them anyway.

God is God. He knows what He is doing. And even when you don't understand, trust His heart and His love for you.

Growing in Grace

We all have questions for God. Questions like, Why? When? How? But God has some questions for you too. Can you tie up the stars in their places? Can you shout orders to the clouds? Can you pour water from the jars of heaven? Can you set a path for the thunderstorm to follow? God can. So trust Him to do what's best for you.

Ruled by Jesus

Be very careful about what you think.
Your thoughts run your life.

—PROVERBS 4:23

God wants you to "think and act like Christ Jesus" (Philippians 2:5). But how? The answer is surprisingly simple. It takes just one decision: *I will let Jesus rule my thoughts.*

Jesus is the Ruler of heaven and earth. He has the final say on everything, especially our thoughts. He has more power, for example, than your classmates. They may say you're not cool enough to hang out with them. But Jesus says you are cool enough to inherit His kingdom. And He has power over your peers.

Jesus also rules over your ideas. Suppose you have an idea to cheat on a test. But Jesus has said that stealing is wrong, and that includes stealing answers. If you have decided to let Him rule over your ideas, then the idea of cheating cannot stay in your thoughts.

To have a pure heart, we must allow Jesus to rule over all our thoughts. If we are willing to do that, He will change us to be like Him.

Growing in Grace

How many different rulers can you think of? There are presidents and prime ministers to rule over countries. Principals rule their schools. And parents rule over their children. But Jesus is Ruler of all. Choose to follow His rules above all others. Find the two greatest rules in Mark 12:29–31.

Victory over Death

Death, where is your victory?
Death, where is your power to hurt?

—1 CORINTHIANS 15:55

The joy that filled the hearts of the very first Christians was their unshakable belief that Jesus truly was the Son of God. They believed that if Jesus had been only a man, He would have stayed in the tomb. These early Christians just couldn't stay silent about the fact that the One they saw die on a cross walked again on the earth and was seen by five hundred people.

Let us ask our Father God humbly, yet boldly in the name of Jesus, to help us remember the empty tomb. Let us see the victorious Jesus: the One who defeated the tomb and defeated death. And let us also remember that we, too, will one day be given that same victory. One day, we will defeat the tomb and defeat death.

Growing in Grace

Read the Gospels' reports of the times Jesus was seen after He left the tomb. (Find these in Matthew 28:1–20, Mark 16:9–20, Luke 24:13–53, and John 20:11–29.) Count how many different people saw the risen Jesus and how many of them were willing to suffer beatings and prison to tell others what they had seen.

God, Our Father

Lord, remember your mercy and love.
You have shown them since long ago.

—PSALM 25:6

A while back, my daughter Jenna and I spent several days in the old city of Jerusalem. One afternoon we found ourselves behind an orthodox Jewish family—a father and his three small girls. One of the daughters, perhaps four or five years old, fell a few steps behind and couldn't see her father. "Abba!" she called to him. Her *abba*—her father—spotted her and immediately held out his hand.

When the light changed, he led her and her sisters across the street. In the middle of the street, he reached down and swung her up into his arms, and they went on with their journey.

Isn't that what we all need? An *abba* who will hear us when we call? Who will take our hand when we are lost? Who will guide us through the streets of life? Don't we all need an *abba* who will swing us up into his arms and carry us home? We all need a Father.

Growing in Grace

Abba means "Father." But more than that, it means "Daddy." What's the difference? Father is stiff, formal, and not much fun. Daddy is the one whose lap you curl up in, who stops to listen when you talk, and who swings you up in the air just to delight you. Abba is Daddy. Abba is God.

October

We know the love that God has for us,
and we trust that love.

—1 JOHN 4:16

A Daily Blessing

I ask the Father in his great glory to give you the power to be strong in spirit. He will give you that strength through his Spirit.

—EPHESIANS 3:16

Here is a scene that happens in Brazil thousands of times each day:

It's early morning. Time for young Marcos to leave for school. As he gathers his books and heads for the door, he stops by his father's chair. He looks into his father's face. *"Benção, Pai?"* (Blessing, Father?) Marcos asks.

The father raises his hand. *"Deus te abençoe, meu filho"* (God bless you, my son), he says.

Then Marcos heads to school, knowing he has asked for a blessing and been given one with love by his father.

We should ask the same question of our heavenly Father— *Blessing, Father?* For just like the little child wanting his father's blessing, each of us needs a daily reminder of our heavenly Father's love.

Growing in Grace

Each morning, before you leave for school or for play, ask God for His blessing. Ask Him to bless your words, your steps, your thoughts, and your actions. This quiet time together each morning will help you remember who you are and whose you are as you face the day.

Our Captain

We are many, but in Christ we are all one
body. Each one is a part of that body.

—ROMANS 12:5

When we are living our lives for God, it's like He has put us in His navy and placed us on His ship. This ship has one purpose—to carry us safely to heaven.

But this is no cruise ship. It's a battleship. We aren't called to a life of fun and games, but of service. Each of us has a different job to do. Some who have a heart for those who are drowning in sin are snatching people out of the water and pulling them onto God's boat of grace. Others are busy with the enemy, working the cannons of prayer and worship. Still others are feeding and training the crew.

Although different, we are all the same. Each of us can tell the story of our personal meeting with the Captain because each of us has met Him. We've followed Him across the gangplank of His grace and onto His boat. There is only one Captain. Though the battle is fierce, the boat is safe, for our captain is God. This ship will not sink.

Growing in Grace

Think of all the different jobs on a ship. From captain to mechanic, and from sailor to potato peeler, each person is needed. And in a church—from the preacher to the pew duster—each person is needed. Including you.

God's Greatest Dream

True love is God's love for us, not our love for God. God
sent his Son to be the way to take away our sins.

—1 JOHN 4:10

There are many things you can do for yourself. You can tie
your own shoes, pour your own milk, and ride a bike.

There are many things that you dream of doing. Things like
making the school baseball team, making the perfect layup, or
learning to play the clarinet. You may even have dreams of what
you will be when you grow up—maybe a veterinarian, an astro-
naut, a teacher, or even a preacher. These are great dreams. And
with hard work and study, you can make many of these dreams
come true.

But the greatest dream of all is one that you can't do by
yourself—no matter how hard you try. It's God's dream for you.

"God has a way to *make people right with him*" (Romans
3:21). You must believe this. God's greatest dream for you is not
to make you rich or famous or popular. God's greatest dream is
to make you right with Him.

Growing in Grace

*What are your greatest dreams? Do you want to be a scientist, a
sports star, or a prima ballerina? Dreams are wonderful. But while
you're dreaming, don't forget to ask God what His dreams for you
are. You can trust that they'll be just right—and simply amazing.*

Guarding Your Heart

If a person's thinking is controlled by his sinful self,
then there is death. But if his thinking is controlled
by the Spirit, then there is life and peace.

—ROMANS 8:6

Your heart is like a greenhouse ready to grow good fruit. And your mind is the doorway to that greenhouse, to your heart. It is in your mind that you decide which seeds are planted in your heart and which seeds are thrown away. Which thoughts are worth hanging on to and which ones need to be weeded out. The Holy Spirit is ready to help you sort out all those thoughts that try to get in. He can help you guard your heart.

The Holy Spirit stands with you in the doorway. If a thought approaches, a thought that may not be so good, do you throw open the door and let it enter? Of course not. You "capture every thought and make it give up and obey Christ" (2 Corinthians 10:5). You don't leave the door wide open and unguarded. You stand ready with handcuffs and leg irons, ready to capture any thought not good enough to enter.

Growing in Grace

Some thoughts are clearly good. Others are clearly bad. And some are kind of in between. How can you tell which are good and which are bad? Ask yourself, Would I want others to know I'm thinking this thought? Would I want Jesus to know? *If not, then toss it out!*

Out of the Boat

[Peter] shouted, "Lord, save me!"
Immediately Jesus reached out his hand and caught Peter.

—MATTHEW 14:30–31 NCV

Look at Peter. He is standing in a boat in the middle of a terrible storm. There is nothing he can do to save himself. Then he sees Jesus walking on the water. Peter knows Jesus can save him. He calls to Jesus and steps out of the boat. But the waves are crashing all around, and Peter begins to sink. He doesn't believe that he can make it all the way to Jesus. So he begs for help. He hears his Savior's voice. Jesus catches him, and he is saved.

That is faith. Faith is knowing we cannot save ourselves. It is knowing that all the good things we do won't keep us from sinking in sin. Faith is praying that Jesus will save us—and it is trusting that He really will. Paul wrote about this kind of faith: "You have been saved by grace because you believe. You did not save yourselves. It was a gift from God. You cannot brag that you are saved by the work you have done" (Ephesians 2:8–9).

Growing in Grace

Float a toy boat in a tub of water. As it sails around, think about all the things that go into making it float. Scientific things like density, mass, and displacement. Then remember the One who created all those scientific things. You can trust Him to keep you afloat no matter what troubles and storms come your way.

In the Blink of an Eye

To me the only important thing about living is
Christ. And even death would be profit for me.

—PHILIPPIANS 1:21

J ust as you want to know that your parents are safe while
you're at school, so we all want to know what happens to
those we love when they die. We want to know: *When we die, do
our souls go straight to heaven to be with God?* Can that be true?
Do we dare to believe it? According to the Bible, it *is* true and we
can believe it.

The Bible doesn't have a lot to say about the time between
a person's physical death and being raised to live with God. It
doesn't shout out its answers. It whispers them. And at the place
where all those whispers come together, we can hear God's
voice.

God tells us that, at death, the Christian joins Him in an
instant. One moment he is on earth, and the next he is face-to-
face with the Father and with those who have died earlier. And
it all happens in the blink of an eye.

Growing in Grace

*What will it be like to be face-to-face with God? To finally be able
to see Him in all His glory? And just think of all the others there
with Him! Angels, Bible heroes, lost loved ones. Who is it that you
most want to see?*

Don't Waste a Minute

Peace and mercy . . . to all of God's people.

—GALATIANS 6:16

As we get older, our vision should get better. Not the way we see here on earth or whether or not we need glasses. But our vision of heaven should get clearer. Those who have spent their lives looking for heaven get a little excited as the time draws near for them to leave this earth. They get a little skip in their step as the Holy City comes into view.

After the great artist Michelangelo died, someone found a piece of paper in his studio. On it, he had written a note to his apprentice. In the handwriting of his old age, the great artist wrote, "Draw, Antonio, draw, and do not waste time."

When you are young, time seems endless. There are so many years ahead of you. But time slips away quickly when you aren't looking. Days pass and soon turn into years. God has work for you to do here on earth—even as a child. So don't waste a minute.

Growing in Grace

Ask three different people—one your age, one your parents' age, and one your grandparents' age—what their vision of heaven is. What do they think it will be like when they get there? How are their answers different? How are they the same? Does age change people's answers?

Praises for God

Let us always offer our sacrifice to God.
This sacrifice is our praise.

—HEBREWS 13:15

Take a moment and offer these praises to God:

You are a great God.

You are holy.

Your truth never changes.

Your strength never ends.

Your discipline is fair.

You take care of our needs.

You light our path and show us the way to go.

You wash away our sins.

Your timing is perfect—never too early or too late.

You sent Your Son to save us, and at just the right time,
   He will come back again.

Your plan is perfect.

Sometimes puzzling and hard to understand.

But perfect.

Growing in Grace

Write an acrostic poem for the word "forgiven." An acrostic is a kind of poem in which each letter in a word is used to start a line of the poem. I'll get you started: **F**ather, You are holy. / **O**ver all. / **R**eaching *down to save us . . .*

A Home for Your Heart

Those who go to God Most High for safety
will be protected by God All-Powerful.

—PSALM 91:1

Chances are you've given very little thought to a home for your soul. You probably have a nice, warm house for your body to live in. Maybe even your own room. But have you thought about your soul's house? Is your soul warm and safe with God? Or is it left out in the world, where the night winds blow and the rain soaks it through? A soul left out in the world soon becomes cold.

It doesn't have to be this way. Our souls don't have to live out in the wet and cold. It's not God's plan for your soul to wander around in the world. God wants you to move out of the cold and move in . . . *with Him.* Under His roof, there is plenty of room. At His table, a plate is already set for you. In His living room, a cozy chair is waiting just for you. And He'd like you to live in His house. Why would He want to share His home with you?

Simple. He's your Father.

Growing in Grace

Take a stroll through your house. How many different things are there to make your body more comfortable? Things like heaters and air conditioners, couches and beds, blankets and pillows. You do all this for your earthly body, which is only temporary. But what are you doing for your eternal soul?

Expecting Jesus

The day the Lord comes again will be a surprise,
like a thief. The skies will disappear with a loud
noise. . . . So what kind of people should you be?

—2 PETER 3:10-11

What kind of people should we be? Great question. Peter told us, "You should live holy lives and serve God. You should wait for the day of God and look forward to its coming" (2 Peter 3:11–12).

The hope of heaven in the future, though, does not give us the right to do whatever we want today. We should be holy and wait for the Lord.

We wait on a lot things. We wait in line, in class, in the car—and we wait *expecting* our wait to end. But how are we waiting for Jesus? Are we expecting our wait for Him to end? Are we looking for Him? Too often we are content to just wait, and we forget to *expect*. We don't let the Holy Spirit change our plans. We don't let Him lead us to worship so that we might see Jesus. We are waiting, but we are not expecting.

Growing in Grace

What does "waiting for Jesus" mean? It's a lot like waiting for a vacation. You're counting down the days, but you're also busy getting ready. Packing. Making lists. Deciding which way to go. You're waiting, but you're waiting busily. Wait for Jesus busily too. Pray. Study. Teach. Get ready.

Finding Good in the Bad

Wish good for those who do bad things to you.
Wish them well and do not curse them.

—ROMANS 12:14

It would be hard to find someone worse than Judas. Some say he was a good man with a bad plan. I don't believe that. The Bible says, "Judas . . . was a thief" (John 12:6). The man was a crook. Somehow he was able to live beside Jesus, to be part of the miracles, and still be unchanged. In the end, he decided he would rather have money than a friend, so he sold Jesus for thirty pieces of silver. Judas was a rat, a cheat, and a bum. How could anyone see him any other way?

Somehow Jesus did. Only inches from the face of His betrayer, Jesus looked at Judas and said, "Friend, do the thing you came to do" (Matthew 26:50). I can't imagine what Jesus saw in Judas that was worthy of being called *friend*. But Jesus doesn't lie, and in that moment He saw something good in a very bad man.

Jesus can help us to see the good in those who hurt us too.

Growing in Grace

With some people, it's easy to see the good. But with others, it's hard to see even a glimpse of good. But it is there. Keep looking. Keep searching for the good that Jesus saw even in Judas. And keep praying that other people will find it too.

A Faithful Father

He is a faithful God who does no wrong.
He is right and fair.

—DEUTERONOMY 32:4

To know God as Lord is to know that He is Ruler and King of all the universe. To accept Him as Savior is to accept His gift of salvation that He offered through Jesus on the cross. To see Him as Father is to go a step further. A father should be the one in your life who provides for you and protects you. Earthly fathers sometimes fail at this, but God does not. See what He has done for you:

He has taken care of all your needs (Matthew 6:25–34).
He has protected you from harm (Psalm 139:5).
He has adopted you as His own child (Ephesians 1:5).
And He has given you His name (1 John 3:1).

God has proven Himself to be a faithful Father. Now it is up to us to be trusting children.

Growing in Grace

Just as your parents have responsibilities toward you, you have responsibilities to your parents. To obey. Respect. Love. Listen. You have those same responsibilities to God. After all, He is your Father.

Choose Adventure

The Lord is my light and the one who saves me.
I fear no one.

—PSALM 27:1

Jesus says our choices are clear.

On one side there is the voice of safety. It whispers worries in your ear. It tells you to stay home and stay safe. You can't lose if you don't try, right? You can't fall if you don't take a stand, right? You can't lose your balance if you never climb, right? So don't try it. Just stay home, snuggle under a blanket, and stay warm and dry.

And there is the voice of adventure—God's adventure. It whispers, *Follow Me. I've got the most amazing adventure planned for you in My kingdom. There are hearts to touch, souls to save, songs to sing, prayers to pray—and you can be part of it all.*

Don't just hide under the blankets and stay home. Choose adventure. Follow God. Make a difference. Be His light in this world!

Growing in Grace

Playing it safe means you don't open the door to strangers, don't play in traffic, and generally don't take unnecessary chances. But playing it safe doesn't mean you never take risks. You can take godly risks like being a friend to the friendless, serving the helpless, and inviting others to church.

Call It Grace

We were made right with God by His grace. And
God gave us the Spirit so that we could receive the
life that never ends. That is what we hope for.

—TITUS 3:7

You may be a good kid. You may do your chores and your homework, and you may go to sleep without feeling any guilt at all. But apart from Christ, you are not holy. And if you're not holy, how can you get to heaven?

Believe. Believe that the work has already been done for you—Jesus did the work on the cross.

Believe in the goodness of Jesus. Believe that you can never earn your way to heaven with your own goodness. Let Jesus give you His goodness instead. Believe in Him and obey His Word.

Is it really that easy? you ask. There was nothing easy about it. The cross was heavy, Jesus' blood was real, and the price was oh-so-costly! You and I could never have paid it, so Jesus paid it for us. Call it simple. Call it a gift. But don't ever call it easy.

Call it what it is. Call it *grace.*

Growing in Grace

Grace is mercy, pardon, forgiveness. It is knowing you should be punished, but you are forgiven and hugged instead. Think of a time someone gave you grace. How wonderful did that feel? How huge was your sigh of relief? As great as that was, it's nothing compared to the grace God gives you each and every day.

Your Safe Place

"God is spirit. Those who worship God
must worship in spirit and truth."

—JOHN 4:24

Don't ever think you are separated from God, with Him at the top of a great ladder and you at the bottom. God isn't up on Neptune while you are down here on earth. Because "God is Spirit" (John 4:24), He is next to you: God Himself is the roof over your head and the walls that protect you.

Moses knew this. "Lord," he prayed, "you have been our home since the beginning" (Psalm 90:1). Wow! God is your home. Home is where you can kick off your shoes and eat pickles and not worry about sitting around in your jammies.

Home is the place you know. No one has to tell you how to find your bedroom. You can know God just as well. You can learn where to run for rest, protection, and guidance. Just as your earthly house is your safe place, so God's house is your safe place of peace.

Growing in Grace

It's great to have your own room—a place to call your very own. While you may not have your own room right now, in heaven you will. Check out John 14:2: "There are many rooms in my Father's house. . . . I am going there to prepare a place for you." That's right! Jesus is preparing a room just for you!

A Treasure Map

Before the world began, there was the Word. The
Word was with God, and the Word was God.

—JOHN 1:1

The Bible has been banned, burned, made fun of, and laughed at. Scholars have called it foolish. Kings have made it illegal. A thousand times over the Bible has been declared dead, but somehow it never stays in the grave. Not only has it survived all these years, but it has also thrived. It is the single most popular book in all of history—the best-selling book in the world for years!

There is no way on earth to explain it, which is perhaps the only way to explain it. The answer for the Bible's survival is not found on earth; it is found in heaven. The Bible is God's book and God's voice. It cannot be silenced.

The purpose of the Bible is to tell the world of God's plan and His passion to save His children. That is the reason the Bible has survived for centuries. It is the treasure map that leads us to God's greatest treasure—eternal life with Him in heaven.

Growing in Grace

Hide a treasure—a candy bar or a couple of cookies. Make a treasure map with clues showing how to find it. Give it to a friend and see if he or she can find the treasure. As wonderful as it is to find your treasure, how much more wonderful will it be to find God's treasure for you?

A Heavenly Celebration

"You should be happy because your
names are written in heaven."

—LUKE 10:20

According to Jesus, the things we do here on earth matter in heaven. And they don't just *matter*. The things we do here on earth *cause* things to happen in heaven. Help someone in need, and Jesus smiles. Sing God's praises, and the angels hum along. Just let a child call out in prayer, and the Father bends to listen. And, most important, let a sinner be saved and everything stops—all of heaven celebrates.

We aren't always that happy, are we? When you hear about someone becoming a Christian, do you stop everything and celebrate? Is your good day made better or your bad day turned around? Maybe the news makes you happy—but do you celebrate?

When someone becomes a Christian, the heart of Jesus explodes with joy like fireworks on the Fourth of July. Shouldn't our hearts do the same?

Growing in Grace

What do you do when you hear someone has become a Christian? Next time, find a way to celebrate. Send a balloon, bake a cake, give a high five. If ever there were a reason for a party, this is it!

God's Smile

We do not ask these things because we are good. We ask because of your mercy.

—DANIEL 9:18

When God smiles and says we are saved, if only we'd salute Him, thank Him, and live like those who have just been given a gift from the commander in chief.

We don't usually do that, though. Instead, we keep trying to earn our way to heaven. Maybe we're afraid to admit that we really can't do it on our own. That we aren't perfect. We would rather impress God with all the great things that we do instead of telling God how great He is. We make up extra rules and try extra hard. And we think that all of our hard work will make God smile.

But it doesn't.

God's smile is not for the one who brags that he did it all on his own. God's smile is for the one who brags that God did it all for him.

Growing in Grace

What can you do to make God smile? Tell Him you need Him. Confess your sins and turn away from them. Then live like Jesus did—not as a checklist as if you are earning your way to heaven, but because you love God and want to make Him smile.

God Speaks to You

Be happy because the Lord comforts his people.
He will comfort those who suffer.

—ISAIAH 49:13

A t one time or another, we all have to deal with the death of
someone we love. God understands your hurt, and He wants
to comfort you.

If you'll celebrate a birthday without a beloved grandparent
by your side, God speaks to you. If a parent went to heaven far
too soon, God speaks to you. If you're still missing a friend who
passed away, God speaks to you.

God speaks to all who have stood or will stand in the soft
dirt near an open grave. And He gives us these words of comfort: "I want you to know what happens to a Christian when he
dies so that when it happens, you will not be full of sorrow, as
those are who have no hope. For since we believe that Jesus died
and then came back to life again, we can also believe that when
Jesus returns, God will bring back with him all the Christians
who have died" (1 Thessalonians 4:13–14 TLB).

Growing in Grace

*If someone you love has passed away, write down the things you
loved about that person. Add a photo or a drawing. When you are
missing that person, take out your list and take time to remember.
Ask God to hold your loved one close until you are together again.*

It's Called Choice

Choose life! . . . Love the Lord your God. Obey him. Stay close to him. He is your life.

—DEUTERONOMY 30:19-20

On the day God created humans, I wonder if He placed one scoop of clay upon another until the shape of a man lay lifeless on the ground.

I can imagine all the angels watching silently as God reached inside Himself, pulled out something, and placed it inside the man. It was the seed of choice. It would let the man—and all people after him—choose for themselves whether to follow God or not. No other creature in all the earth was given that choice.

God had given the man a part of Himself—that seed of choice. The God of might had created earth's mightiest. The Creator had created not just another creature but another creator. And the One who had chosen to love had created one who could love in return. Adam had a choice: to love God or turn away from Him.

And now it's your turn to choose to love God!

Growing in Grace

Choosing God is not just a one-time choice, but an everyday, several-times-a-day choice. When your feet first hit the floor in the morning, say, "I choose God." For every tough decision you face during the day, declare, "I choose God." And before you go to sleep at night, pray, "I choose God."

Do Something

Faith that does nothing is dead!

—JAMES 2:26

aith is not believing that God will do what you *want*. Faith is believing that God will do what is *right*. God is always near and always there for you. Just waiting for you to reach out to Him in prayer and praise. So let Him know. Show Him your love.

- Write a letter to Him.
- Ask for His forgiveness.
- Be baptized.
- Feed a hungry person.
- Pray.
- Teach.
- Go and tell others about Him.

Do something that shows your faith. For faith that doesn't do anything is not faith at all. *God will answer you.* He has never turned away a true and genuine show of faith. Never.

Growing in Grace

Words are only words until you do something about them. You can say you love your pet, but if you never feed it, do you? You can say you love your parents, but if you disobey them, do you? You can say you love your friends, but if don't play with them, do you? And you can say you love God, but if you never serve Him . . . do you?

A Clear View of God

Lord, even when I have trouble all around me,
you will keep me alive.

—PSALM 138:7

Let's pretend there is a window in your heart. When you look through it, you can see God. Once upon a time that window was crystal clear. You could see God just as clearly as you could see a tree or a flower.

Then, suddenly, the window cracked. First one pebble hit it, and then another, and another. Those pebbles were the problems and worries that came into your life. Now the window of your heart is a spiderweb of cracks.

And suddenly God isn't so easy to see.

It can be frightening and confusing. Why would God allow this to happen? Why can't you see Him?

When you can't see God, trust Him. Because that is when Jesus is closer than you've ever dreamed.

Growing in Grace

Look out a window. You can see clearly, right? Now breathe on it so that the glass fogs up. It's hard to see through the fog, but you know everything is still there. When the fog melts away, you'll see clearly again. It's the same with God. Sometimes we must wait for the fog (our troubles) to melt away. Then we can clearly see how God has been there the whole time.

In a Word

"I will give power to everyone who wins the victory and continues to the end to do what I want. I will give him power over the nations."

—REVELATION 2:26

Think for a minute about this question: What if the Spirit of God weren't here on earth? If you think people can be mean now, imagine what we would be like without the presence of God! If you think we are hateful to each other now, imagine the world without the Holy Spirit. If you think there is loneliness and sadness and guilt now, imagine life without the touch of Jesus.

No forgiveness. No hope. No acts of kindness. No words of love. No more food given in His name. No more songs sung to His praise. No more good deeds done in His honor. If God took away His angels, His grace, His promise of eternal life, and His servants, what would the world be like?

In a word: empty. I'd much rather have a world full of Jesus.

Growing in Grace

Imagine a world without the sun. What would happen? Darkness. Cold. Plants and animals would die. People would starve. Now think of what would happen without God. Spiritual darkness. Cold hearts. Dying souls. People starving for love. Just as the sun gives us physical light and life, God gives us spiritual light and life.

The Angels' Joy

"There is joy before the angels of God when 1 sinner changes his heart."

—LUKE 15:10

Why do Jesus and His angels rejoice over one sinner who repents? Can they see something we can't? Do they know something we don't? Yes! They know what heaven holds.

Heaven is filled with those people who let God change them. In heaven, all fighting will stop because jealousy won't exist. Gossips won't gather because there will be no secrets. Every sin is gone. Every fear is forgotten. Every worry is past.

Heaven is like pure wheat. No weeds. Pure gold. No other metals. Pure love. No selfishness. Pure hope. No fear. It's no surprise that the angels rejoice when one sinner repents. They know that one more Christian will join the wonders of heaven. They know what heaven holds.

Growing in Grace

Almost every sin boils down to one thing: selfishness. It can sneak up on you. The quickest cure for selfishness is to help someone else. When you find yourself wanting to snatch and grab, choose to share and give instead. You'll make the angels rejoice.

No Secrets from God

If anyone belongs to Christ, then he is made new. The
old things have gone; everything is made new!

—2 CORINTHIANS 5:17

Have you been there? You knew what was right. You knew
what was wrong. And you chose wrong. It's like you were
standing on the edge of the cliff, trying to make a decision, and
the ground of your goodness just crumbled under your feet. The
ledge gave way, and down you went. *Poof!*

Now what do you do? When you fall, you can forget it. You
can fib about it. Or you can face it.

We can keep no secrets from God. Confession is not telling God what we did. He already knows. Confession is simply
agreeing with God that what we did was wrong.

How can God forgive if we don't admit our guilt? Ahh,
there's that word: *guilt*. Isn't that what we want to avoid? What
we hate? But is guilt so bad? Guilt simply means that we know
right from wrong, that we hope to do better next time. Guilt is a
healthy sorrow for telling God one thing but then doing another.

Growing in Grace

*We are a lot like pumpkins. Pretty and smooth and clean on the
outside. A mess of slime and goop—sin and guilt—on the inside.
Open yourself up to God; confess your sins. He'll clean out all the
sin and guilt. And He'll carve His image on your heart.*

A Gentle Lamb

Where God's love is, there is no fear, because
God's perfect love takes away fear.

—1 JOHN 4:18

A lot of us live with a secret fear that God is angry at us. Somewhere, sometime, some Sunday school class or some television show made us believe that God is spying on us. That He's just waiting for a chance to catch us being bad so that He can punish us.

Nothing could be more wrong! God cares for us and only wants to share His love with us.

We have a heavenly Father who is filled with compassion—which means that when we hurt, He hurts. We serve a God who says that even when we're stressed out and we feel like nothing is going right, He is waiting for us. And He is ready to wrap us up in His love whether we win or lose.

God doesn't come fighting and forcing His way into anyone's heart. He comes into our hearts like a gentle lamb, not a roaring lion.

Growing in Grace

God isn't a bust-the-door-down kind of god. He is a gentleman: "I stand at the door and knock. If anyone hears my voice and opens the door, I will come in and eat with him" (Revelation 3:20). If you let Him in, heaven is your reward. Will you let Him in?

God's Faithfulness

My God will use his wonderful riches in Christ
Jesus to give you everything you need.

—PHILIPPIANS 4:19

Thankfully, God's faithfulness to us has never depended on our faithfulness to Him. He is faithful even when we aren't. He keeps His promises even when we don't keep ours. When we have lost all courage, He has not. He's made a habit of using people even when we don't think He can.

Need an example? The feeding of the five thousand. It's the only miracle—except those from Jesus' final week—that is written about in all four Gospels. Why did all four writers think it was worth telling? Maybe they wanted to show us how God doesn't give up even when His people do.

When the disciples didn't pray, Jesus prayed. When the disciples were weak, Jesus was strong. When the disciples had no faith, Jesus had faith.

God is greater than our weakness. In fact, I think it is our weakness that shows just how great God is.

Growing in Grace

God uses unlikely people. Moses—a murderer in hiding—leads God's people to the Promised Land. Gideon—a coward in a hole—is used to defeat the enemies of God's people. Then there's David and Esther and Paul. The list goes on. Think you're too weak for God to use you? Think again.

A Heart Like His

From this time on we do not think of anyone as the world does.

—2 CORINTHIANS 5:16

When we look at other people, our eyes search for so many other things—things that just aren't important. Is he rich? Is she pretty? What sports does he play? What color is her skin? Is she popular? These things don't matter to God. He sees two kinds of people: the saved and the lost.

From His point of view, every person is either:

- Entering through the narrow gate or the wide gate (Matthew 7:13–14).
- Called to heaven or headed for hell (Mark 16:15–16).

Ask God to help you look at others the way He does. To have a heart like God's is to look into the faces of the saved and be happy. They are headed for heaven. To have a heart like God's is to look into the faces of the lost and pray. For unless they turn to God, they are headed for an eternity without Him.

Growing in Grace

What do you see when you look at other people? Do you see skin color or clothes or nationality? Or do you see a beloved child of God? Pray that God will help you to see others as He sees them. And then to help them as He wants you to.

A Plate of Cookies

I have good plans for you. I don't plan to hurt you.
—JEREMIAH 29:11

One night during family devotions, I set an empty plate in front of each of my daughters. In the center of the table, I placed a collection of fruit, raw vegetables, and Oreo cookies. "Every day," I explained, "God prepares for us a plate of experiences. What kind of plate do you most enjoy?"

The answer was easy. Sarah put three cookies on her plate. Some days are like that, aren't they? Some days are "three-cookie days." But many are not. Sometimes our plate has nothing but vegetables—twenty-four hours of celery, carrots, and squash. God knows we need to build up our muscles. It may be hard to swallow, but isn't it for our own good? Most days, however, have a little bit of everything.

The next time your plate—er, day—has more "broccoli" than "Oreos," remember who made it. And if you're finding it all a little hard to swallow, talk to God about it. Jesus did.

Growing in Grace

Most days have a little bit of everything in them. A little good, a little bad. A little mad, sad, and glad. Get yourself ready for those days with a plateful of God's food—a little prayer, a little study, a little praise—and you'll be ready to face the world.

Love Is All You'll Find

We know the love that God has for us, and we trust that love.

—1 JOHN 4:16

Water must be wet. Fire must be hot. You can't take the wet out of water and still have water. You can't take the heat out of fire and still have fire.

In the same way, you can't take the love out of God and still have God. For He was and is . . . *love*.

Search deep within Him. Explore every corner of His Word. Peek into every angle. Love is all you will find. Go to the very beginning of Genesis, and you'll find it. Go to every story of every Bible hero, and you'll find it. Go all the way to the end of Revelation, and you'll see it.

Love.

No bitterness. No evil. No meanness. Just love. Perfect love. Never-ending love. Pure love. God is love.

Growing in Grace

Look at the concordance in the back of your Bible. It's the listing of words and where to find them in the Bible. How many verses have the word love *in them? On a piece of paper, draw a heart and write some of those verses in it. Be sure to add John 3:16, the greatest "love" verse of all.*

Everyone Will See Him

"After I go and prepare a place for you, I will come back. Then I will take you to be with me so that you may be where I am."

—JOHN 14:3

Someday, according to Christ, He will come back. In the blink of an eye, as fast as the lightning flashes from the east to the west, He will come back. And everyone will see Him—you will, I will. The earth will tremble, the sky will roar, and those who do not know Him will shudder in fear. But in that hour you will not be afraid, because you know Him.

And you know that He is coming to take you home.

Growing in Grace

Is there any feeling worse than being lost? Your mom was right there. You turned away for just a second, and now you can't find her anywhere. And is there any feeling better than seeing her again? Now imagine just how wonderful it will feel to see Jesus coming again!

November

"Then you will know the truth. And the truth will make you free."

—JOHN 8:32

Believe Jesus

In all these things we have full victory through
God who showed his love for us.

—ROMANS 8:37

Just as germs make our bodies sick, sin makes our souls sick. And when it comes to healing our own spiritual sickness, we don't have a chance. We might as well try to jump to the moon. We don't have what it takes to heal ourselves. Our only hope is that God will do for us what He did for the man at the pool of Bethesda—that He will step out of the temple and step into our world of hurt and helplessness. That *He* will heal us. Which is exactly what He has done.

I wish we would believe what Jesus tells us: When He says we're forgiven, let's let go of the guilt and shame. When He says we're valuable, let's believe Him. When He says He'll take care of our needs, let's stop worrying.

God is strongest when we are weakest.

Growing in Grace

Start a "thankful journal" this month. Each day, think of one thing (or more) that you are thankful for. Write it down or draw a picture of it in your journal. Then share it with your family on Thanksgiving Day.

You Are Free

"Then you will know the truth. And
the truth will make you free."

—JOHN 8:32

Think of it this way. Sin put you in a prison. Sin locked you behind the bars of guilt and shame and lies and fear. Sin did nothing but chain you to a wall of misery. Then Jesus came and paid your bail to get you out of prison. He served your time. He took your punishment and set you free. Jesus died, and when you choose to believe in Him, your old sinful self will die too. You will be made new—and free.

But the only way to be set free from the prison of sin is to pay the price. In this case, the price is death. Someone has to die—either you or a heaven-sent substitute. You cannot leave prison until there is a death. But that death happened on the cross. And when Jesus died, sin lost its hold on you. You are free.

Growing in Grace

Have you ever traded anything with a friend? "Swap you my cookie for your brownie?" The trades are always pretty even, right? Jesus is offering us a trade too. He says, "I'll take the punishment for your sin and swap it for an eternity in heaven." Pretty good trade, hmm?

Are You Listening?

"Everyone who continues asking will receive.
He who continues searching will find."

—MATTHEW 7:8

Once there was a man who dared God to speak: "Burn the bush like you did for Moses, God. And I will follow. Crumble the walls like you did for Joshua, God. And I will fight. Stop the storm like you did on the Sea of Galilee, God. And I will listen."

And so the man sat by a bush, near a wall, close to the sea, and waited for God to speak. God heard the man, so God answered. He sent fire—not for burning a bush, but a fiery passion for building a church. He tore down a wall—not of brick, but of sin. He stopped the storm—not on the sea, but in the soul.

And God waited for the man to speak. And He waited . . . and waited. But because the man was looking at bushes instead of hearts, bricks instead of people, seas instead of souls, he decided that God had done nothing.

Finally the man looked to God and asked, "Have You lost Your power?" And God looked at him and said, "Have you lost your hearing?"

Growing in Grace

Listening to God isn't something that just happens. Just like playing football or the piano, it takes practice. Try these tips as you practice: Find a quiet place. Stop talking. Read His Word. Then sit quietly and let the Spirit fill your heart with His wisdom.

Finishing the Race

Let us run the race that is before us and never give up.

—HEBREWS 12:1

The word *race* comes from the Greek word *agon*, from which we get the word *agony*. The writer of Hebrews compares the Christian's life to a race. This race is not an easy jog, but rather a demanding, hard, sometimes *agonizing* race. It takes a huge effort to finish strong.

Unfortunately, many Christians don't finish the race. Maybe you've seen some who are stopped on the side of the trail of life. They used to be running, living their lives for Christ. There was a time when they kept up. But then they became tired. They never thought the race would be this tough.

Think about Jesus and the race He ran. Jesus' best work was His final work, and His strongest step was His last step to the cross. Our Lord is the best example of One who kept going. He could have quit. But He didn't. He finished the race. By His grace, you will too.

Growing in Grace

Have you ever run in a race? It's pretty easy when you start. But then it gets harder. How do you feel halfway through? Tempted to quit? But catch one glimpse of that finish line, and you're filled with energy. How great it is to finish!

All Figured Out

I look at the heavens,
which you made with your hands. . . .
But why is man important to you?

—PSALM 8:3-4

Scientists understand how storms are created. They can map out the solar systems, measure the depths of the oceans, and send signals to faraway planets. They have studied our world, and they are learning how it works.

And, for some people, this loss of mystery has led to the loss of majesty. The more they know about the world, the less they believe in God. That's strange, don't you think? Knowing how things work shouldn't erase the wonder. It should stir up the wonder.

Yet the more some people know about our world, the less they worship God. They are more impressed with our invention of the lightbulb than with the One who created electricity. Rather than worship the Creator, they worship the creation (Romans 1:25). No wonder there is no wonder. They think they've got it all figured out.

Growing in Grace

You've probably heard about Big Bang theories and evolution. Maybe you've heard people laugh at the truth of God's creation. Don't believe something just because it's in a book or on TV. Check into apologetics—the defense of God's Word. See what scientists who are Christians have to say.

The High Cost of Getting Even

Do not try to punish others when they wrong you.
Wait for God to punish them with his anger.

—ROMANS 12:19

Have you ever watched one of those old western movies where the bounty hunter chases after the bad guy? Ever notice how the bounty hunter always travels alone? It's not hard to see why. Who wants to hang out with a guy who gets even for a living? Who wants to risk getting on his bad side?

More than once I've seen a person so angry—and so eager to get even—that he was about to explode. The whole time I was thinking, *I hope I never get on his bad list.* Grouchy folks, these bounty hunters. Best leave them alone—you never know when they might lose their temper!

If you're out to get even, you'll never rest. How can you? For one thing, your enemy may never pay up. As much as you think he owes you an apology, he may never give you one. No matter how right you are, you may never get a penny's worth of justice. And if you do, will it be enough? Best to just forgive and let God take care of the rest.

Growing in Grace

Getting even is like throwing a boomerang. You throw out the last word or the last punch, and it comes zooming right back at you. Next time, try forgiving instead. Just let it go. Give it to God. He'll take care of the justice part in His own perfect time.

God Loves You

We love because God first loved us.

—1 JOHN 4:19

God is not bound by time, so He sees all people from all times and from all places. No matter where we are, God sees each of us—from the backwoods of Virginia to the business district of London, England. No matter who we are, He sees us—from the Vikings to the astronauts, and from the cave dwellers to the kings. He sees those who live in huts and those who live in mansions. Whether we were born in Bible times or modern times, God saw each of us *before* we were ever born.

And He loves what He sees. Heart filled with emotion and overcome by pride, the Maker of the stars turns to us, one by one, and says, "You are My child. I love you dearly. I know that someday you'll disobey Me, turn your back on Me, and walk away. But I want you to know, I've already given you a way to come back."

Growing in Grace

Hold out a yardstick. Pretend each line is a moment in time. You are on one line. You can't see the next line (the future). You can only remember one or two lines behind you (the past). But God holds the whole yardstick of time. He sees all peoples and all times—all at the same time. Amazing!

Focus on the Prize

Think about Jesus. He held on patiently while sinful men were doing evil things against him. Look at Jesus' example so that you will not get tired and stop trying.

—HEBREWS 12:3

Heaven was not unknown to Jesus. He is the only person to live on earth *after* He had lived in heaven. As believers, you and I will live in heaven after our time on earth, but Jesus did just the opposite. He knew heaven *before* He came to earth. He knew what was waiting for Him when He returned. And knowing what was waiting for Him in heaven made Him able to bear the shame and suffering on earth.

"He accepted the shame of the cross as if it were nothing. He did this because of the joy that God put before him" (Hebrews 12:2).

In His last moments on the cross, Jesus focused on the joy of heaven. He kept His eyes on the prize of returning to God. By focusing on the prize, He was able not only to finish the race but also to win it.

Growing in Grace

Have you ever done something that was really hard? Perhaps you ran a race, struggled to get an A, or worked to save for something you wanted. When you were tired and wanted to call it quits, what kept you going? The prize? Remembering the prize can help you keep going.

God Is Ready to Help

He comforts us every time we have trouble, so that
we can comfort others when they have trouble.

—2 CORINTHIANS 1:4

A parent's job is to help his children when they are hurt. Think about your own parents and all that they do for you: When your feelings are hurt, do they tell you how amazing you really are? When you've been hurt, do they do whatever it takes to make you feel better? When you are afraid, do they wait with you until you feel safe?

That's what parents are supposed to do. They help their hurting children. But what if you are away from your parents, maybe at school? Or if your parents aren't the helping kind?

Then remember you have a heavenly Father who is always ready to help. When you are laughed at, hurt, or afraid, He is ready to comfort you. He will hold you until you're better, help you until you can live with the hurt, and stay with you when you're afraid of waking up and seeing the dark.

Always.

Growing in Grace

How many good things have your parents done for you just today? Be sure to give them a huge thank-you. But as much as your parents love you, God loves you a million-billion times more. You can't begin to imagine how many good things He will do for you . . . just today.

Not Guilty

Jesus said, "So I also don't judge you. You
may go now, but don't sin again."

—JOHN 8:11

If you have every wondered how God feels when you mess up,
when you sin, frame the words of John 8:11 and hang them on
your wall. Read them. Think about them. Remember them.

Or, better still, drop down on your knees. Ask God to come
and hear your prayers as you tell Him about the mistake that
you made, the wrong thing that you did. Tell Him how sorry you
are and how ashamed.

And then listen. Listen very carefully. He's saying, "I don't
judge you."

Hear His grace and forgiveness in the words of John 3:17–18,
"God did not send his Son into the world to judge the world guilty,
but to save the world through him. He who believes in God's Son
is not judged guilty."

That is God's message to you—you are not guilty.

Growing in Grace

*Cut a cross out of heavy paper. All around the edges write the words
of 1 John 1:9: "If we confess our sins, he will forgive our sins. We can
trust God. He does what is right. He will make us clean from all the
wrongs we have done." Use it as a bookmark for your Bible.*

Jesus Wore Our Coat

They have washed their robes with the blood of
the Lamb. Now they are clean and white.

—REVELATION 7:14

God has only one requirement for getting into heaven: that we be clothed with Christ. But what does that mean—*to be clothed with Christ*?

Listen to how Jesus described those who live in heaven: "Around the throne there were . . . 24 elders sitting on the 24 thrones. The elders were dressed in white, and they had golden crowns on their heads" (Revelation 4:4).

All are dressed in white. The saints. The elders. So how would you think Jesus is dressed? In white, right? No. "He is dressed in a robe dipped in blood" (Revelation 19:13).

Why is Jesus' robe not white? Why is His robe not spotless? Why is His robe dipped in blood? Paul said simply, "He changed places with us" (Galatians 3:13).

Jesus wore our coat of sin to the cross.

Growing in Grace

Who would you like to change places with? A sports star or famous singer? A Hollywood actor or actress? The president or a princess? What about the prisoner on death row—the one sentenced to die for his crimes? No? But that's just what Jesus did for you and for me.

Keeping Secrets

If you hide your sins, you will not succeed.

—PROVERBS 28:13

Some secrets can be fun—like a secret surprise birthday party for someone you love.

Some secrets can be dangerous—like hiding the fact that someone is being bullied or hurt.

But some things we think are secrets—like sin—aren't really secrets at all.

Some people think they can hide their sins. And they may be able to hide them from other people. Mom may never know that word you said. Dad may never know who really broke the window. Your teacher may never find out who cheated on the test. But those sins aren't really secret. Because the One who matters most knows.

God sees your secret sins—and He is hoping that you won't keep them secret anymore.

Growing in Grace

You may be wondering why you need to confess—or tell God—your sins if He already knows all about them. The reason is because we need to admit that we were wrong. God can't make us right again until we tell Him we were wrong. Is there anything you need to tell God today?

Saying "Thank You"

Thank the Lord because he is good.
His love continues forever.

—PSALM 106:1

Worship is what happens when you are aware that the gift you've been given is far greater than anything you can give.

Worship is like the traveler who is lost in the desert. The one thing he wants more than anything is the one thing he can't seem to find—water. So when he does finally find that pool of water, he just can't help but shout out his thankfulness.

Worship is the thank-you that just can't be quiet.

Sometimes people try to make a science out of worship, with rules for our songs and for our prayers. But worship isn't supposed to be about rules—it's supposed to be so much more.

Worship is the heart's thank-you . . . offered by the one who is saved to the Savior, by the one who is healed to the Healer, and by the one who is delivered to the Deliverer.

Growing in Grace

There are many ways to worship God. Try a different way today. Paint a picture of praise. Sing a song of salvation. Write a poem of His promises. Say thank You in a whole new way.

A Place for the Tired

*Do not lose the courage that you had in
the past. It has a great reward.*

—HEBREWS 10:35

The reed. It's a slender and tall stalk of river grass. Yet it's
so fragile, so easily bruised. What once stood so proud and
strong can easily be knocked over at the edge of the water.

Sometimes we can be like bruised reeds. Maybe we stood so
tall and so proud once, thinking life was just right. Then something happened. We were bruised by mean words, someone's
anger, or a friend's betrayal.

The bruised reed. This world knows what to do with us when
we're no longer standing up tall. This world wants to break us so
that we can never stand up tall again.

But the Bible tells us that God won't do that. He has a special
place for people who are bruised and tired. And God will help us
stand up tall again.

Growing in Grace

*Imagine the way a mother bird shelters her babies. She tucks them
up under her wing, warm and safe from all harm. That is just what
God wants to do for you when you are hurting. "He will protect you
like a bird spreading its wings over its young" (Psalm 91:4).*

Fix Your Eyes on Jesus

I pray that you will have greater understanding in your heart.
Then you will know the hope that God has chosen to give us.

—EPHESIANS 1:18

What does it mean to be just like Jesus?

The world has never known a heart as pure as Jesus', a person as perfect. He always listened closely to His Father so that He never missed a heavenly whisper. His mercy was so great He never missed a chance to forgive. No lie came from His lips; no sin clouded His eyes. He helped when others turned away. He kept going when others quit.

Jesus is the perfect example for how every person should live. God urges you to keep your eyes upon Jesus. Focus your heart on Him, and make Him the center of your life.

Growing in Grace

Jesus has given you the greatest of all gifts. What is the greatest gift you can give to Him? It's to make Him the center of your life. That means that before every choice, you ask, "Is this what Jesus would want me to do?" And before every word, "Is this what Jesus would want me to say?"

God Knows the Answers

If any of you needs wisdom, you should ask God for it.

—JAMES 1:5

Maybe you have questions about God, about who He is and what He does. You're not alone. Many of God's people had questions, worries, and doubts too.

Thomas doubted that Jesus had really risen from the dead. So did Jesus turn him away?

Moses worried about talking to Pharaoh and about leading the Israelites. Did God tell him to just forget it and go back home to Midian?

Job lost everything—his family, his herds, his health. But did God turn away from him?

After Paul became a believer, he was arrested and beaten. Did God leave him?

No. God never turns away someone with a sincere heart. Tough questions don't stump God. He wants to hear our questions. God never turns away the honest searcher. Go to God with your questions. You may not find all the answers, but in finding God, you know the One who does.

Growing in Grace

What are some of the questions you can't wait to ask God? Questions like, What happened to the dinosaurs? How far does space really go? What was the parting of the Red Sea really like? Just imagine getting to sit with God and listen to His answers.

Dare to Be Different

Now we do not live following our sinful selves, but we live following the Spirit.

—ROMANS 8:4

Some people are not who they should be. Instead of giving friendship and encouragement to those around them, they treat them unkindly. They laugh at others and make fun of them. Sometimes they pretend that others just aren't important enough for them to even notice. We call them bullies. God calls them lost.

So what do you do? What do you do when the bullies are the popular kids everyone else wants to be like? Do you dare to be different? Do you dare to be the person God made you to be? Or do you just go along with the crowd and be like them?

It's your choice, but you don't have to make it alone. Jesus Himself said, "You can be sure that I will be with you always" (Matthew 28:20). *Always.* When the bullies laugh, when the in-crowd puts you in the out-crowd, Jesus will be there with you.

Growing in Grace

If you or someone you know is being picked on or bullied, what can you do? First, pray and ask God to bring people into your life to help you. Then talk to a trusted grown-up—a parent, someone from church, or a teacher. God uses His people to answer your prayers.

It's Your Choice

"If anyone wants to follow me, he must say "no"
to the things he wants. He must be willing to
die on a cross, and he must follow me."

—MARK 8:34

Imagine this: On one side of you stands the crowd. *On the other side of you is Jesus.*

The crowd is yelling, teasing, and criticizing Jesus. They want you to do the same. *On the other side stands Jesus. His face is bruised and swollen. His eye is black. But He is ready to keep His promise to save you.*

The crowd wants you to join them. They promise you all the fun and flash and fortune of this world. *Jesus wants you to join Him. He promises to save you from this world and take you home to His.*

The crowd tells you that if you want to fit in, you must follow them. *Jesus says, "If you follow Me, you will stand out. But I will stand up for you."*

The crowd promises to please you. *Jesus promises to save you.*

God looks at you and asks, "Which will you choose—the crowd or Jesus?"

Growing in Grace

What does it mean to choose Jesus? It means Sunday is a day to pray, not play. It means fitting in isn't nearly as important as following Him. It means loving your neighbor even when your neighbor isn't lovable. Choosing Jesus means bringing a bit of heaven down to earth.

Look Up

If we are not faithful,
he will still be faithful,
because he cannot be false to himself.

—2 TIMOTHY 2:13

God gives us His blessings because *He* is so great—not because we are so great.

Why is that important to know? So you won't lose hope. Look around you. Doesn't it sometimes seem like there isn't enough food to feed all the hungry people? Like there aren't enough doctors to take care of all the sick? Like there aren't enough people to tell the world about Jesus?

So what do we do? Throw up our hands and walk away? Tell the world we can't help them?

No! We don't give up. We look up—to God. We trust Him. We believe Him when He says He will use our hands to do His work. Galatians 6:9 says, "We must not become tired of doing good. We will receive our harvest of eternal life [heaven] at the right time. We must not give up!"

Growing in Grace

Showing God's love doesn't have to be expensive or difficult. Ask your parents to help you buy packages of hand warmers. With their help, give them to people out in the cold—the crossing guard at your school, the mail carrier, or the homeless person on the corner.

Turn to Jesus

If we live, we are living for the Lord. . . . So
living or dying, we belong to the Lord.

—ROMANS 14:8

Do you ever feel like you're all alone? Like no one else could possibly understand how you're feeling? Do you wish there was someone you could turn to for encouragement, for hope, for courage? There is. Jesus.

Turn to Jesus and His love. When you feel like your friends have all left you. When you know you've messed up and you're not sure how to make it right. Turn to Jesus. Ask Him to take away your confusion and guilt. Ask Him to show you the right thing to do. And trust Him to always love you and help you through the hard times.

Jesus wants you to turn to Him. He wants to be the most important person in your life, the greatest love you'll ever know. He wants you to love Him so much that there's no room in your heart and in your life for sin. Ask Him to come and live in your heart. He won't say no.

Growing in Grace

Zacchaeus climbed a tree to see Jesus. Four friends ripped open a roof to see Jesus. What will you do to see Jesus? Will you choose church over a ball game? Bible class over a movie? Prayer time over play time? Choose Jesus, and I promise you'll be glad you did.

A Diligent Search

Anyone who comes to God must believe that he is real
and that he rewards those who truly want to find him.

—HEBREWS 11:6

The different Bible translations can help us better understand God's Word. The New International Version of the Bible writes Hebrews 11:6 this way: "God . . . rewards those who earnestly seek him." But the New King James Version® says, "He is a rewarder of those who *diligently* seek Him."

Diligently—what a great word! It's a big word that means "never give up, keep going no matter what." Be *diligent* in your search for Jesus. Stop searching the Internet and search for Jesus. Don't just read this book about Jesus. Read dozens of them, starting with His book, the Bible.

Don't be satisfied with a once-a-week Sunday school lesson. Be like the heroes of the Bible and *diligently* search for Jesus each day. Worship Him as the wise men did. Do as Matthew did: invite Jesus into your house. Be like Zacchaeus: climb a tree. Do whatever it takes to see Jesus.

Growing in Grace

There are lots of books to read about Jesus. Children's Bible storybooks are a great place to start. There are even Bible translations just for kids, like the International Children's Bible®. Also check out the Chronicles of Narnia series by C. S. Lewis for Christian action and adventure.

When God Says No

"He who comes to me will never be hungry. He who believes in me will never be thirsty."

—JOHN 6:35

Sometimes the one thing you want is the one thing you can't have. Maybe it's that you want your best friend to stay and not move to another town. Or you want your grandmother's sickness to go away.

So you pray and wait.

No answer.

You pray and wait some more.

Still no answer.

What if God says no? What if God says, "not right now," or even just plain no? If God says no, what will you do? If God says, "I've given you My grace, and that is enough," will you be content?

Content. That's the word. Content means being at peace even if God gives you nothing more than what He already has given—His love, His mercy, and His grace.

Growing in Grace

What do you do when your parents say no? Throw a fit? Or trust that they know what is best? Paul said, "I have learned the secret of being happy at any time in everything that happens" (Philippians 4:12). That means being happy even when your parents—and God—say no.

Your Best for God

In Christ Jesus, God made us new people so that we would do good works. God had planned in advance those good works for us. He had planned for us to live our lives doing them.

—EPHESIANS 2:10

Some people will do anything to be in first place—even if it means using their words or actions to push others into last place. For people like that, doing their best is all about being number one.

Don't get me wrong. God wants you to do your best. This world needs people who try hard. People who take pride in their work. God wants you to use the gifts and talents that He has given you in a way that pleases—and praises—Him. If you're an A+ student, use your gifts to help others learn. If you're a great third baseman, show others how to be a good sport by the way you win *and* lose. If you're a fabulous artist, use your art to remind people of the beauty of God all around them.

Just remember . . . use your words, gifts, and talents to honor God, not to get honor and glory for yourself.

Growing in Grace

Words are some of the most powerful tools—or weapons—we have. Just a few right words can make someone's day. And just a few wrong words can ruin a life. When you open your mouth to speak, be sure you are building up and not tearing down.

Jesus' Family

"My true brother and sister and mother are
those who do the things God wants."

—MARK 3:35

It may surprise you to know that Jesus had brothers and sisters. But He did. Mark wrote this about Jesus' family: "His mother is Mary. He is the brother of James, Joseph, Judas, and Simon. And his sisters are here with us" (Mark 6:3).

And it may also surprise you to know that Jesus' family was less than perfect. They were human, after all. Mark even told us that Jesus' family didn't always understand Him and why He was preaching. Once, they even tried to stop His preaching and take Him home because "people were saying that Jesus was out of his mind" (Mark 3:21).

How do you think Jesus treated His family when they didn't agree with Him or understand Him? The same way He treated all people. With kindness and patience, with love and respect. And that's just how He wants you to treat your family—even when they don't understand you and you don't understand them.

Growing in Grace

What does God say about dealing with difficult people? Check out these verses: Don't hold a grudge (Proverbs 10:12). Just let it go (19:11). But most of all, love them anyway and pray for them (Matthew 5:44).

Heavenly Rewards

"When the master comes and finds the servant doing his work, the servant will be very happy."

—MATTHEW 24:46

The stadium is packed today. Everyone has come to see *him* play. As soon as he walks into the stadium, the fans are on their feet. He steps up to the plate, bat in hand. The crowd roars. He swings, and the ball soars into the air and into the stands. Home run! The fans are still on their feet long after he crosses home plate.

Not everyone can be a home run king. For every million kids who dream of it, only one makes it. Most of us don't hit the big ball, don't get the parade, don't wear the gold medal, don't give the president's speech. And that's okay. We know that in this world, only a few people win crowns.

In heaven, though, it's a whole different story. Heavenly rewards are not limited to a chosen few, but "to all those who have waited with love for him to come again" (2 Timothy 4:8). That's so much better than any crown on earth!

Growing in Grace

Use your talents—in sports, in music, in art—to earn jewels in your heavenly crown. Share your talent with younger children, helping them to learn a new sport or hobby. As you teach, show them the same love, patience, joy, and kindness that God shows you.

The Bridge

I said, "I will confess my sins to the Lord."
And you forgave my guilt.

—PSALM 32:5

Once there were a couple of farmers who couldn't get along with each other. A wide, deep ditch separated their two farms, but as a sign of their hatred for each other, each farmer built a fence on his side of the ditch to keep the other out.

In time, however, the daughter of one farmer met the son of the other, and the couple fell in love. They were determined not to be kept apart by the foolishness of their fathers. So they tore down the fence and used the wood to build a bridge across the ditch.

That's just what confession does. When you tell God your sins, you tear down the fence that separates you from Him. Confession, then, becomes the bridge over which you can walk back into God's arms.

Growing in Grace

What would happen if there weren't any bridges? There would be no crossing over rivers or lakes or canyons. You simply wouldn't be able to get where you wanted to go. And if it weren't for Jesus—the bridge between our sin and God—we wouldn't be able to get to where we want to go. Heaven.

Jesus Knows Us by Name

The Lord is my shepherd.
I have everything I need.

—PSALM 23:1

Sheep aren't smart. They have a habit of wandering into running creeks for water. Then their wool soaks up the water, gets heavy, and causes them to drown. They need a shepherd to lead them to "calm water" (Psalm 23:2).

Sheep cannot protect themselves. They have no claws, no horns, no fangs. They are helpless. Sheep need a shepherd with a "rod and . . . walking stick" to protect them (Psalm 23:4). Sheep have no sense of direction. They need someone to lead them "on paths that are right" (Psalm 23:3).

We need a shepherd too. Because we, too, have a habit of getting stuck in troubles we should have avoided. Because we cannot defend ourselves against the evil lion—the devil—who prowls around seeking some lost soul to devour. And because we sometimes lose our way in life. We need a Shepherd to care for us, to protect us, and to guide us. And we have one—Jesus! He knows each of His sheep by name. He knows *your* name.

Growing in Grace

Sometimes it's easy to forget that the Bible is a personal message for each of us. To help you remember, read Psalm 23. In every place that says I or me or my, put your name. And remember that this is God's personal message to you.

Nothing Less Than Jesus

"I have obeyed my Father's commands, and I remain in his love. In the same way, if you obey my commands, you will remain in my love."

—JOHN 15:10

God rewards those of us who *truly* seek Him. Not just those who know every memory verse but those who let His verses change their lives. Not just those who lead the prayers but those who trust God to answer their prayers. And not just those who sing every note perfectly but those who sing praises to Him with all their heart.

The heavenly reward goes to those who truly look for Jesus. And what is the heavenly reward? Nothing less than being like Jesus. "And as the Spirit of the Lord works within us, we become more and more like him" (2 Corinthians 3:18 TLB).

Can you think of a greater gift than to be like Jesus? Jesus had no guilt; God wants to wash away yours. Jesus had kindness for the sick and courage for the challenges. God wants you to have the same. He wants you to be just like Jesus.

Growing in Grace

God wants you to be just like Jesus. What does that mean? The answer is in Galatians 5:22–23. Those who are filled with God's Spirit show "love, joy, peace, patience, kindness, goodness, faithfulness, gentleness, self-control"—the fruits of the Spirit. Which of these can be seen in you?

Let Him

Praise the Lord, day by day.
God our Savior helps us.

—PSALM 68:19

Sometimes it's hard to leave the past in the past. You messed up. You failed. You did that thing you said you would never do again. You flunked. Maybe it was a test or your parents' trust. Yes, you've told God you're sorry. You know that He has forgiven you and forgotten all about it. But still you can't seem to let it go. You keep remembering the mistake.

Hear this: Even if you've messed up, even if you've failed, even if everyone else has turned their back on you, Jesus will never turn away from you. He wants to take all your worries away—whether you're worried about past mistakes or something that might happen in the future.

But only you can let go of your worries. No one else can do it for you. Only you can give all your worries to the One who cares for you (1 Peter 5:7). Say a prayer today and ask God to take your worries away . . . and then let Him!

Growing in Grace

Worrying is like saying you don't really trust God to take care of you. You're just not sure He's up to the task. But the Bible says, "Give all your worries to him, because he cares for you" (1 Peter 5:7). Give your worries to God—and don't snatch them back again. He will do what's right for you.

The Love of God

I pray that you . . . will have the power to understand the greatness of Christ's love. I pray that you can understand how wide and how long and how high and how deep that love is.

—EPHESIANS 3:18

There is no way our human minds can understand the love of God. How can He love *all* the people in the world? How can He forgive us when we keep messing up again and again?

For thousands of years, people have thought about and wondered about the love of our Father. How could Jesus love us enough to step down from the power and glory of heaven and be born as a baby to poor parents huddled in a stable? How could God love us enough to send His Son to die on the cross to save us?

How can you explain such love? What can you say to that kind of love? The only thing you can say is, "Lord, thank You, and I love You too."

Growing in Grace

Some of the most wonderful things in this world are things we cannot fully explain—love, forgiveness, hope, dreams. But we don't have to understand them to enjoy them. What are some things you don't understand but still enjoy?

December

The ways of God are without fault.
The Lord's words are pure.

—PSALM 18:30

The Winner's Circle

*The Lord will give a reward to everyone,
slave or free, for doing good.*

—EPHESIANS 6:8

There is a lot that we don't know about heaven, but this we do know: the day Jesus comes back will be a day of reward. Those who were nobodies on earth will be somebodies in heaven. Those who never heard people cheer for them will hear the cheers of the angels. Those who missed the blessing of a father on earth will hear the blessing of their Father in heaven.

Those who were put down on earth will be lifted up in heaven. The forgotten will be remembered, the ignored will be welcomed, and the faithful will be honored.

In heaven, the winner's circle isn't just for the rich and famous. It's for a heaven full of God's children who "will receive the crown of life that God has promised to those who love him" (James 1:12 NIV).

Growing in Grace

Start a different kind of Christmas countdown. Give a gift to someone else each day. It doesn't even have to cost a thing. A kind word. A helping hand. A friendly smile and a warm hug. Give others a glimpse of what the winner's circle will be like in heaven.

God Is for You

*The Lord will be happy with you.
You will rest in his love.
He will sing and be joyful about you.*

—ZEPHANIAH 3:17

Let's pretend that life is like a big race. Look at the sidelines—that's God cheering you on. Look past the finish line—that's God clapping. Listen for Him in the bleachers, shouting your name. Too tired to finish? He'll carry you. Too hopeless to keep going? He'll pick you up. God is *for* you.

God is for *you.* If He had a calendar, your birthday would be circled. If He drove a car, your name would be on His bumper sticker. If there's a tree in heaven, He's carved your name in it.

"Can a woman forget the baby she nurses? Can she feel no kindness for the child she gave birth to?" God asks in Isaiah 49:15. Can you imagine your mom feeding you and then asking, "What is that kid's name?" No. Mothers don't do that. They stroke your hair, touch your face, sing your name over and over. Do mothers forget? No way. But "even if she could forget . . . I will not forget you," God promises (Isaiah 49:15).

Growing in Grace

Do something today to show your mom how much you love her. Thank her for all she does for you. Offer to help with the dishes. Take out the trash. Write her a note. If she asks why, tell her it's just because you love the way she loves you.

What Do You Expect?

The ways of God are without fault.

—PSALM 18:30

I like the story about the fellow who went to the pet store to buy a singing parakeet. The man lived alone, and his house was too quiet. The store owner said he had just the bird for him, so the man bought it.

The next day the man came home from work to a house full of music. He went to feed the bird and saw for the first time that it had only one leg. He felt cheated that he'd been sold a one-legged bird, so he called the store and complained.

"What do you want," the store owner asked, "a bird that can sing or a bird that can dance?"

Good question. God always answers our prayers. But sometimes it's not the answer we expect—like the man's one-legged bird. And we're disappointed. When that happens, we have to ask ourselves: *What do we really want?* Remember, God only wants the very best for you. So if His answer is not what you expect, maybe you need to *change* what you expect.

Growing in Grace

Disappointments can be as bitter as lemons. Ask a grown-up to help you make homemade lemonade. Sample the lemon first. Sour, hmmm? Then taste the lemonade. Much better! When you add the sweetness of God (sugar) to your disappointments (lemons), they can turn out to be blessings (lemonade).

Cut Off from God

When someone sins, he earns what sin pays—death. But God gives us a free gift—life forever in Christ Jesus our Lord.

—ROMANS 6:23

Sin does to a soul what scissors do to a flower. A cut stem separates a flower from its source of life. At first, the flower is pretty, still colorful and strong. But when you watch that flower over several days, the leaves start to wilt and the petals fall off. No matter what you do, the flower will never live again. Put it in water. Poke the stem in dirt. Cover it with plant food. Do whatever you want, but the flower is dead.

Imagine that your soul is like that flower. When you sin, it's like slowly cutting your soul off from God, and your soul starts to wither and die. The result of sin is not a bad day or a bad mood, but a dead soul. The signs are easy to spot—lying lips and cursing mouths, feet that run to do evil and eyes that don't see God.

But unlike the flower, the soul can be healed—through Jesus. And all you have to do is ask.

Growing in Grace

Take a look at a freshly cut Christmas tree. It's been cut off from its roots, but it still looks wonderful. It's even all dressed up with lights. But watch that tree over time. Its needles begin to fall off, and soon it's all brown and brittle—just like us when we're cut off from God.

What God Thinks

Lord, you have done such great things!
How deep are your thoughts!

—PSALM 92:5

God's thoughts are not our thoughts. They are not anything like ours. Our thoughts aren't even in the same neighborhood.

We're thinking, *I want to play and have fun.* He's thinking, *I want you to know My Son.* We dream of raising our high scores. He dreams of raising us up to heaven. We do everything to avoid hard times. God uses hard times to make our faith stronger. We say, "I want to have it all." God says, "My Son gave it all."

We love earthly things that rust and break. God loves heavenly things that last forever. We are overjoyed by our victories. He is overjoyed by our confessions.

We look at the Nike star player with the million-dollar smile and say, "I want to be like him." God points to His Son—who suffered the cross to save you—and says, "I want you to be like Him."

Growing in Grace

There are so many chances to be like Jesus every day, but especially during the holidays. Help an elderly neighbor decorate her tree. Sweep the snow off the church's sidewalk. Give someone the gift of your time and love.

The Perfect Family

I will be your father, and you will be my sons and daughters, says the Lord All-Powerful.

—2 CORINTHIANS 6:18

Each of us would love for our family to be the perfect family. But even Jesus didn't have that. Look at what He said about His family: "My true brother and sister and mother are those who do the things God wants" (Mark 3:35).

When Jesus' brothers didn't share His beliefs, He didn't try to force them (John 7:1–9). He knew that His spiritual family could provide Him with what His own family didn't.

Maybe you don't have the perfect family. Or maybe your family is usually pretty great, but you need a little extra encouragement. Where do you go? God has an answer for that—your church family. They are your brothers and sisters in Christ. Turn to them when you need a little extra care and encouragement, when you need a hug or someone to simply listen.

Let God's family give you what you need. That's why God gave them to you. And remember, even if your family isn't the dream family, don't lose heart. God can change families.

Growing in Grace

Build a gingerbread house from scratch or from a kit. You can make that house just the way you want it. As you work, pray that God will bless your house and your family. Pray that He will make your home just the way He wants it.

No Worries in Heaven

He will wipe away every tear from their eyes. There
will be no more death, sadness, crying, or pain.

—REVELATION 21:4

You probably don't think much about death. But what do you do to avoid death? Probably a lot. You take vitamins, get your shots, look both ways before crossing the street, and avoid playing in traffic. Why? Because you are worried about staying alive. That won't be a worry in heaven, because you'll live forever.

In fact, you won't be worrying at all. Some of us worry about getting hurt. We won't worry in heaven, because in heaven we'll feel no pain. Some of us worry about getting sick. We won't worry in heaven, because in heaven we'll be healthy forever.

On earth we are made of dust. Our physical bodies grow old and wear out. But in heaven our bodies will be different. They will never grow old or wear out. Jesus promises that if we will believe in Him, if we will "be faithful," then He will give us "the crown of life" (Revelation 2:10).

Growing in Grace

The holidays can be a time of sadness for some people, especially those who've lost a loved one. Adopt a shut-in from your church this Christmas. Bake some cookies and take them with you when you go for a visit. The gift of your time can be the very best gift of all to someone who is lonely.

Let God Decide

When a good man prays, great things happen.

—JAMES 5:16

When we pray, we are telling God that we need Him. We are admitting that without Him, we know we would never make it to heaven. It is only by His mercy that we are lifted up and saved. Prayer reminds us of *who God is* (the One in charge) and *who we are* (the one He loves enough to help).

I believe there's great power in prayer. I believe that God heals the sick and wounded and that He can raise the dead. But I don't believe we tell God what to do and when to do it.

God knows that sometimes we don't even know what we should pray for. When we trust our prayers to Him, we trust Him to do what is right for us—even if it's not what we asked for. We let God decide what is best.

Growing in Grace

Sometimes we don't know how to explain what we're feeling. It's okay. God has a plan for that: "The Spirit himself speaks to God for us, even begs God for us. The Spirit speaks to God with deep feelings that words cannot explain" (Romans 8:26). Just open your heart to God, and let the Holy Spirit speak.

Can We Really Complain?

I have learned to be satisfied with the things I
have and with everything that happens.

—PHILIPPIANS 4:11

Ask yourself this question: What if the only gift God ever gave you was His grace—His forgiveness so that you can be saved and go to heaven? Would you be happy?

Maybe you've begged God to help you pass a test. Or find your lost pet. Or even heal someone you love. What if His answer is, "No. My grace is enough. Saving you is enough"? Would you be happy?

You see, from heaven's point of view, grace *is* enough. If the only thing God did was save us, could we really complain? If He only gave us eternal life, would we dare grumble about a hurting body? If He only gave us all the riches of heaven, would we dare whine about being poor on earth?

If you have eyes to read these words and hands to hold this book, God has already given you a mountain of grace. But because He loves you so much, He doesn't just give you grace. He answers your prayers too.

Growing in Grace

Even when we have nothing, we are so richly blessed with the love of God. Share some of your earthly blessings with those in need. Encourage your family or Sunday school class to adopt a family who's struggling. Bring in gifts and groceries. Secretly deliver them with a note that says, "A gift from God."

God's Holy City

"The bride belongs only to the bridegroom."
—JOHN 3:29

John's descriptions of the future in Revelation can take your breath away. His description of the final battle is graphic. Good clashes with evil. The holy and sacred battle the sinful. The pages are filled with the shrieks of dragons and smolder with the fires of blazing pits. But in the middle of the battlefield there is the most beautiful sight. John described it in chapter 21: "I saw the holy city coming down out of heaven from God. This holy city is the new Jerusalem. It was prepared like a bride dressed for her husband" (v. 2).

In this final mountaintop scene, God pulled back the curtain and let John peek into heaven. God gave him a glimpse of his future reward. And when John sat down to write about what he saw, he compared heaven to the most beautiful image earth has to offer. The holy city, John said, is like "a bride dressed for her husband."

There are many beautiful things on this earth, but we will never see anything as beautiful as God's heaven.

Growing in Grace

How does your family get ready for the holidays? Do you put up lights? Trim the tree? Bake and decorate? Everything needs to be just right for your guests. Just imagine: God does the same for you as He prepares your heavenly home. He's getting everything just right for you.

Just Pray

If one of you is having troubles, he should pray. If
one of you is happy, he should sing praises.

—JAMES 5:13

Do you want to know how to be better at praying? Pray. Don't
get ready to pray. Just pray. Don't worry about prayer. Just
pray. Sunday school lessons about prayer are great, but to really
get better at prayer, you have to—you guessed it—*pray*.

Whether you sit or stand, say them in your mind or with a
shout—whether you are inside, outside, or even upside down
isn't really important for your personal prayers. Do whatever
works for you. But don't think about it too much. Don't be so
worried about how your prayers should look and sound that you
never get around to praying. Better to pray awkwardly than not
at all.

God hears every prayer and blesses every person who prays.
And the more you pray, the easier it will become. Soon it will be
just like talking to an old friend—the very best Friend of all.

Growing in Grace

*What makes you want to pray? Is it nature? The people around
you? A lighted Christmas star? Write in a journal the things that
make you want to pray and what you pray for. Every week or so,
look back through what you've written and see how God has shown
Himself in your life.*

God Isn't Hard to Find

Surely goodness and mercy shall follow me
all the days of my life;
and I will dwell in the house of the LORD forever.

—PSALM 23:6 NKJV

As a child, it's fun to play hide-and-seek. But that is a game that God never plays. You see, God never hides; He always seeks.

God started seeking His children right there in Genesis. He was there in the garden, looking for Adam and Eve. They were hiding in the bushes, ashamed and afraid. Did God wait for them to come to Him? No, His words rang out through the garden. "Where are you?" God asked (Genesis 3:9).

Now, God knew where Adam and Eve were hidden, but He wanted them to know that He was searching for them. That He hadn't left them all alone. And He wanted them to come out and find Him. All through the Bible God calls out to His children, hoping that they will come out and find Him.

He's calling to you too. He's not hard to find. He's only a word away. Pray that He will help you find Him today.

Growing in Grace

Where are you? Are you hard for God to find? Are you hoping He won't see what you're doing? Are you hoping He won't hear what you're laughing about with your friends? If you are hoping that God doesn't know what you're up to, maybe you need to change what you're up to.

His Children

Some people did accept him. They believed in him. To them he gave the right to become children of God.

—JOHN 1:12

My family and I once lived in Brazil. While we were there, we met several American families who had come there to adopt children. The families would spend days, sometimes weeks, struggling with a different language and a strange city. There were endless forms to fill out, dozens of people to meet with, and lots of money to be paid—all with the hope of taking a child home to the United States.

Hasn't God done the same for us? As Jesus, God came into our world, faced down the temple rulers, and paid the largest, most unimaginable price to adopt us. We have every legal right given to His children. We are just waiting for Him to return. We are, as Paul said, "waiting for God to finish making us his own children" (Romans 8:23).

Growing in Grace

When a child is adopted into a family, he is given certain rights. He is given the family name. He has a right to be taken care of. He will inherit the family's home. When you are adopted by God, He gives you certain rights too. He gives you His name, He takes care of you, and you will inherit His home.

Every Child Has a Name

"I am the good shepherd. I know my sheep, as the
Father knows me. And my sheep know me."

—JOHN 10:14

When a shepherd looks at his sheep, he doesn't just see a large flock. The shepherd knows each of his sheep. Each one is special, unique. And he calls them by name.

When we see a crowd of people, we see just that—a crowd. We see people, not *each person*, but people. A herd of humans. A flock of faces. That's what we see.

But not so with Jesus, the Good Shepherd. He knows each of His sheep. Each face is special to Him. Each face is different. Each face has a story. Each face is a child. And each child has a name.

The Shepherd knows His sheep. He knows each one by name. The Shepherd knows you. He knows your name. And He will never forget it.

Growing in Grace

It's eleven days until Christmas. Each day, pick a different person to pray for. Someone you've never prayed for before. It's okay if you don't know each person's needs. God does. He's their Shepherd too.

Choose to Forgive

The Lord hates what evil people do.
But he loves those who do what is right.

—PROVERBS 15:9

Maybe you were hurt a long time ago. A parent blamed you when it wasn't your fault. A teacher ignored you. A friend betrayed you. And you are angry.

Or maybe you were hurt just last week. The friend who owes you money just bought a new skateboard. Or you're the only one not invited to the party. And you are hurt.

Part of you is broken inside, and the other part is mad. Part of you wants to cry, and part of you wants to fight. It's like there's a fire burning in your heart. It's the fire of anger.

And you have to decide: *Do I put the fire out or heat it up? Do I get over it or get even? Do I let my hurts heal, or do I let hurt turn into hate?*

Revenge is bad. But what it does to you is even worse. When you choose not to forgive, anger is all you'll have left.

Growing in Grace

Is there someone you're holding a grudge against? Make him or her a Christmas card. As you create, ask God to help you forgive that person. And as you drop the card in the mailbox, let all your anger drop away with it.

Words of Promise

God will give a son to us. . . .
His name will be Wonderful Counselor,
Powerful God . . . Prince of Peace.

—ISAIAH 9:6

I love Christmas cards. They are like promises printed on paper. Tiny bits of truth that appear in my mailbox. Line after line declares the reason we celebrate a birth that happened more than two thousand years ago.

Jesus became like us, so we could become like Him.
Angels still sing, and the star still calls to us.
He loves each one of us like there is only one of us to love.

Christmas cards are cheerful little reminders that say, "For God loved the world so much that he gave his only Son . . . so that whoever believes in him may not be lost, but have eternal life" (John 3:16).

Growing in Grace

Start a collection of Christmas cards this year. How many different promises can you find on the cards? Be sure to pray for each person who sends you a card. And when you send off your own cards, seal them with a prayer for that family.

Because of What You Need

"God did not send his Son into the world to judge the world guilty, but to save the world through him."

—JOHN 3:17

Can you imagine parents who want to adopt a child saying, "We'd like to adopt Johnny, but first we want to know a few things. Does he have a house to live in? Does he have money for college? Does he have a ride to school every morning and clothes to wear every day? Can he cook his own meals and wash his own clothes?"

No adoption agency would listen to such talk. The agent would hold up her hand and say, "Wait a minute. You don't understand. You don't adopt Johnny because of what he has. You adopt him because of what he needs. He needs a home."

The same is true with God. He doesn't give you His name because of your great sense of humor or your talents or your money. He doesn't adopt you because of what you have. He adopts you because of what you need—Him.

Growing in Grace

Ask three people—one your age, one your parents' age, one your grandparents' age—about the greatest gifts they've ever been given. How are their gifts different? The same? Does it make you look at the gifts you've been given differently? Or the gifts you want to give?

Room for God?

"Here I am! I stand at the door and knock."

—REVELATION 3:20

Some of the saddest words on earth are "We don't have room for you."

Jesus knew the sound of those words. He was still in Mary's tummy when the innkeeper said, "We don't have room for You."

And when He was hung on the cross, the message was much the same: "We don't have room for You in this world."

Even today Jesus is treated the same way. He goes from person to person, from heart to heart, knocking and asking if He can come in.

Every so often, He is welcomed. Someone throws open the door of his or her heart and invites Him to stay. And to that person Jesus gives this great promise: "There are many rooms in my Father's house. . . . I am going there to prepare a place for you" (John 14:2). What a wonderful promise He gives us! We make room for Him in our hearts, and He makes room for us in His house.

Growing in Grace

Make room for someone who is left out—at the lunch table, at recess, or in your circle of friends. You might just be making a new friend. And you'll definitely be making Jesus smile.

Down on Your Knees

God is against the proud,
but he gives grace to the humble.

—JAMES 4:6

The city of Bethlehem, where Jesus was born, still exists today. If you visit the city, you can actually visit a small church there that marks the spot where some people believe Jesus was born. In the church is a high altar, and behind the altar is a cave, a little cavern lit by silver lamps.

You can go into the main building and admire the ancient church. You can also go into the quiet cave where a star set into the floor recognizes the birth of the King. There is just one thing, however. You have to stoop. The door is so low you can't go in standing up.

The same is true of Jesus. You can stand up tall to see the world, but to really see the Savior, you have to get down on your knees in prayer.

Growing in Grace

Today when you pray, try praying on your knees. It will change the way you look at everything. Praying on your knees helps your heart to be humble. From your knees you can see how big God's creation is and big God must be. And from your knees, you can see how great God is that He would stoop down to listen to your prayers.

God's Gift

Every good action and every perfect gift is
from God. These good gifts come down from
the Creator of the sun, moon, and stars.

—JAMES 1:17

The truth cannot be avoided: saving ourselves simply does not work. There is no way to get ourselves to heaven.

But Paul told us that God has made a way for us to get to heaven. He gives it to us as a gift. That's right. A gift. Salvation— being with God in heaven forever—is His gift to us. For "every perfect gift is from God." And salvation is God's greatest, most perfect gift of all. We just have to accept it.

Write this down and remember it: Salvation is given by God, powered by God, and created by God. It's not something that we can earn. It's not something that God owes us because of the good things we have done. Salvation is God's gift to us.

Growing in Grace

As you give gifts to others this season, think of the gifts God gives to you. Gifts that can't be bought or wrapped. Gifts like love, mercy, forgiveness, hope—and the greatest of gifts, salvation. What gifts does God ask in return? For you to love Him and obey Him.

An Extra-Ordinary Night

Today your Savior was born in David's
town. He is Christ, the Lord.

—LUKE 2:11

The night that Jesus was born was an ordinary night with ordinary sheep and ordinary shepherds. And if it were not for a God who loves to stick an *extra* on the front of *ordinary*, the night would have passed just like any other. The sheep would have been forgotten, and the shepherds would have slept the night away.

But God loves to add His "extra" to the most ordinary of things.

So on that night, the black sky exploded with brightness. One minute the shepherds were sound asleep; the next they were rubbing their eyes and staring into the face of an angel.

The night was no longer ordinary.

The angel came in the night because that is when lights are best seen and most needed. God shows Himself to us in our darkest times and in the most ordinary of things for the same reason. Because that is when He is most needed and best seen. He's easy to find—just look for the "extra" in the ordinary.

Growing in Grace

God is easy to find this time of year. See Him in twinkling lights and hear Him in the "Hallelujah Chorus." But God is also in the ordinary, the everyday. He's in the perfection of each snowflake and the whistling winter wind. When you learn to see God in the ordinary, no day is ever truly ordinary again.

The Gift of Grace

Whoever finds me finds life.
And the Lord will be pleased with him.

—PROVERBS 8:35

Have you ever traded for something? Maybe watched your mom and dad trade for a car? It usually goes something like this: *If you give me this, then I'll give you that.*

Other religions are that way. They are barter systems—which simply means people trade their way to heaven. Their god says to them, *If you do this for me, then I'll do this for you.* Their god saves them based on what they do (works), what they feel (emotions), or how much they know (knowledge).

Christianity isn't like that at all. We don't bargain with God. We don't have anything to bargain with. Yes, we should go to church, pray, read our Bible, and help others. But no matter how good we are, our goodness is never good enough to trade for His grace. His grace doesn't depend on what we do, what we feel, or what we know. His grace depends on Him.

Grace is His gift.

Growing in Grace

Christianity is in the spotlight this time of year. Use the holidays as a chance to show other people who Jesus is and why He came. Show them your joy and love—with what you do, not just what you say. Because when you live with the joy of Jesus, people notice.

God's Great Gifts

Thanks be to God for his gift that is too wonderful to explain.

—2 CORINTHIANS 9:15

Why did God do it? Did He have to give the birds a song and the mountains a peak? Was He forced to put stripes on the zebra and the hump on the camel? Why did He make creation so amazing? Why did He go to such trouble to give us such gifts?

Why do you? You do the same thing. You hunch over a craft and bend over a drawing. There's glue on your fingers and glitter in your hair. But this isn't just any old gift. This is the extra-special gift for the extra-special person. Why do you do it? You do it so your mom's eyes will shine. You do it so your dad's jaw will drop. You do it to hear those words of disbelief: "You did this for me?"

That's why you do it. And that is why God did it. Next time you see a beautiful sunrise, just imagine God saying, "Do you like it? I did it just for you."

Growing in Grace

Make a gift for someone you love. Paint a picture. Make a necklace of beads. Decorate a cookie. Give it with a smile and a hug. It will be treasured—not just because of what it is, but because it was made with love.

Jesus' Family Tree

Joseph was the husband of Mary, and Mary was
the mother of Jesus. Jesus is called the Christ.

—MATTHEW 1:16

You may be surprised to see some of the people in Jesus' family tree: Jacob the cheat, David the murderer, Rahab the pagan. It seems like Jesus' not-so-great-grandparents made some big mistakes. But God still promised to use them to send His Son.

Why did God use these people? He didn't have to. He could have just laid the Savior on a doorstep. Would have been simpler that way. And why does God tell us their stories in the Bible?

Simple. He wants us to know that when His people mess up and the world goes wild, God stays calm.

Want proof? Read the last name in Jesus' family tree. In spite of all the mixed-up mess-ups of His ancestors, the last name on the list is the one He promised—Jesus.

No more names are listed after Jesus' name. No more are needed. It's as if God is telling us, "See, I did it. I sent a Savior for you. I sent My perfect Son to save My imperfect people. Just as I promised."

Growing in Grace

Christmas Day is almost here. With all the excitement of family and friends, food and gifts, don't forget to say thank You. Thank God for giving us the very best gift of all—His Son—each and every day of the year.

God Became a Man

He gave up his place with God and made himself nothing.
He was born to be a man and became like a servant.

—PHILIPPIANS 2:7

On a starry night, more than two thousand years ago, Jesus was born. It all happened in a most amazing moment . . . a moment like no other.

The Holy One became a human. He stepped out of the majesty of heaven and into the arms of a humble peasant girl.

The All-Powerful One, in an instant, became flesh and blood. The One who was larger than the universe became the tiniest of infants. And He who created the world with a word chose to depend upon a young girl named Mary for His human life.

God had come down from heaven. God had come near to His people . . . to show us the way back home to heaven.

Growing in Grace

Take some time today to read Luke 1:26–38 and Luke 2:1–20, the story of how Jesus came to earth. Then read John 3:1–21, the story of why Jesus came to earth. This is what Christmas is all about.

The Strength of God's Love

Christ died for us while we were still sinners. In this way God shows his great love for us.

—ROMANS 5:8

When you read about Jesus' life on earth, it's as if He is saying, "Can anything make Me stop loving you? Watch Me speak your language, sleep on your earth, and feel your hurts. Look at Me! The Maker of all that you see. Watch Me sneeze, and cough, and blow My nose. You wonder if I understand how you feel? See the toddler at Mary's table; that's God spilling His milk. Look into the dancing eyes of that kid playing with His friends in Nazareth; that's God walking to school.

"Do you want to know how much I love you? I love you enough to leave heaven. To be a toddler and stub My toe as I learn to walk. To smash My thumb in the carpenter's shop. I love you enough to be insulted by the very people I created. To be betrayed by My friends. To die on the cross for you. That's how much I love you."

Growing in Grace

What are the strongest things you can think of? Steel? Concrete? Superman? Dynamite? They are nothing compared to the strength of God—nothing! "I am sure that nothing can separate us from the love God has for us" (Romans 8:38).

True Joy

*You changed my sorrow into dancing . . .
and clothed me in happiness.*

—PSALM 30:11

Have you ever wanted to do something so badly that you just knew you would be happy forever if you could do it? Maybe you wanted to make the team, get a part in the play, or take a special vacation. Finally, you got to do it. And it was great! . . . For a while. Why didn't your happiness last forever?

Why? Because the happiness and joys of this world don't last forever. Because they aren't true joy. *True joy*—the kind that lasts forever, through good times and bad—comes only from God.

True joy doesn't come from getting to do things; it comes from admitting that there are some things you can't do—like forgive your own sins or save yourself.

It's kind of funny. In this world, admitting that you *can't* do something doesn't usually lead to joy. Confessing mistakes isn't ordinarily followed by total forgiveness. But then again, God is not known for being ordinary. And the joy that He wants to give you? It isn't ordinary either.

Growing in Grace

As the new year approaches, many people start making goals. Things like exercise more, eat better, or make better grades. Think about your spiritual goals for the year. Make one of them to find a little bit of God's joy in every day.

The Snowflake

He called you to share in his glory in Christ.
That glory will continue forever.

—1 PETER 5:10

It can be hard to believe that the perfect and holy God can forgive every mistake we make. The lies we tell, the times of gossip and jealousy, the angry words. Sometimes we get so caught up in thinking about how *bad* we have been, that we forget how *good* God is.

Of all the wonders of God's creation, I think the snowflake is one of the best. Think about it. Is there anything purer or cleaner than a snowflake that's come straight down from the heavens?

Now listen to God's promises in Psalm 51:7: "Take away my sin, and I will be clean. Wash me, and I will be whiter than snow."

That's right. God promises to wash away all your sins and to make you as pure and clean as that snowflake that's come straight down from heaven. Forgiveness is His gift to you—you just have to accept it.

And the more you accept God's forgiveness, the more likely you are to forgive others.

Growing in Grace

Have you ever gotten your foot stuck in the mud? Even when you pull it out, the mud still sticks to you. You need help getting clean again. Sin is lot like that mud. Even when you stop sinning, the yuck still sticks to you. Ask God to forgive you—and He will make you clean again.

God Is Faithful

They all continued praying together. Some women,
including Mary the mother of Jesus, and Jesus'
brothers were also there with the apostles.

—ACTS 1:14

Friends are the people we go to for encouragement and a listening ear. But sometimes even our friends can hurt us. Maybe a friend has said something hurtful. Maybe a friend has betrayed you. Or maybe a friend has recently moved away.

A troubled friendship can leave you feeling empty and hurt inside. Jesus understands. After all, Judas was His friend, and Judas betrayed Him. Peter was His friend, and Peter said he didn't even know Him. John was His friend, and he ran away when Jesus was arrested.

Friends aren't always faithful, but God is. So the next time a troubled friendship leaves you hurt, ask God to comfort you. Ask Him to fill that emptiness with His peace. And then pray for your friend—God can touch the heart of your friend too.

Growing in Grace

Some people are hard to get along with. Although you can't change what others do, make sure you aren't part of the problem. "Show mercy to others; be kind, humble, gentle, and patient. Do not be angry with each other, but forgive each other. If someone does wrong to you, then forgive him" (Colossians 3:12–13).

Our Job

"All I have is yours, and all you have is mine. And my glory is shown through these men."

—JOHN 17:10

God wants to change your face. No, not the color of your eyes, or the shape of your nose, or whether or not you have dimples.

God wants to add His glory to your face—just like He did for Moses. When Moses came down the mountain with the Ten Commandments, his face "was shining because he had talked with the Lord" (Exodus 34:29).

Let me be very clear. This change is *God's* job, not *yours*. Your job is not to stick some fake, frozen smile on your face. Your job is simply to stand before God with a prepared and willing heart and then let God change your face.

And He does. He wipes away the tears. He mops away the sweat. He softens your worried brow. He touches your cheeks. He changes your face as you worship Him. God makes you shine.

Growing in Grace

Our job is to stand before God with a prepared and willing heart. How do we do prepare our hearts? By reading God's Word. Try to read it every day. There are even guides for reading through the whole Bible in a year. Or read a proverb or a psalm each day. January 1 is a great time to start!

Wishful Words

*"I leave you peace. My peace I give you. I do
not give it to you as the world does. So don't let
your hearts be troubled. Don't be afraid."*

—JOHN 14:27

Jesus has a message just for you. It is whispered in every word
of the New Testament:

If only you knew that I came to help and not judge. If
only you knew that tomorrow will be better than today.
If only you knew the gift that I bring you: eternal life. If
only you knew I want you safely home with Me.
If only you knew.

What wishful, wistful words to come from the lips of God.
How kind that He would let us hear them. How important it is
that we stop to hear them. If only we knew to trust God. Trust
that He is in our corner. Trust that God wants what is best for us.

If only we could learn to trust Him. Won't you trust Him?

Growing in Grace

*The things of this world end. Holidays end, years end, even lives
end. But God never ends. His love, His faithfulness, His promises,
His mercy, grace, and forgiveness never end. Believe Him and His
Word. Make that your number one goal this coming year—to trust
God completely.*

Reading the Bible

The Bible is *the* most important book you will ever read. It is God's plan for your life. In the Bible, God tells you how to love Him and how to love others. He tells you what is right and what is wrong. And most important of all, He tells you how to get to heaven. Because the Bible is so important, it's a good idea to read something from it every day.

Try one of these reading plans to help you get started. Put a check next to each one as you read it. *30 Days with Jesus* walks you through the life of Jesus, telling of the things He did and taught while He was here on earth. *90 Days Through the Bible* gives you all the major happenings of the Old and New Testaments, beginning with the Creation in Genesis and going all the way through to Revelation.

30 Days with Jesus

1. John 1:1–51   _____
2. Luke 2:1–52   _____
3. Mark 1:1–11   _____
4. Luke 4:1–44   _____
5. John 3:1–36   _____
6. Luke 5:1–39   _____
7. John 4:1–54   _____
8. Luke 6:1–49   _____

9. Luke 7:1–50   ——
10. Luke 8:1–56   ——
11. Mark 8:1–38   ——
12. Luke 10:1–42   ——
13. Matthew 5:1–48   ——
14. Matthew 6:1–34   ——
15. Matthew 7:1–29   ——
16. Luke 14:1–35   ——
17. Luke 15:1–32   ——
18. Luke 16:1–31   ——
19. John 8:1–59   ——
20. Luke 17:1–37   ——
21. Luke 18:1–43   ——
22. John 9:1–41   ——
23. Luke 19:1–48   ——
24. Luke 20:1–47   ——
25. John 10:1–42   ——
26. John 11:1–57   ——
27. Mark 13:1–37   ——
28. Luke 22:1–71   ——
29. Matthew 27:1–66   ——
30. Luke 24:1–53   ——

90 Days Through the Bible

1. Genesis 1:1–2:3   ——
2. Genesis 3:1–24   ——
3. Genesis 6:9–7:24   ——

For all the times you've
felt different, left out, and alone . . .

God has a message of hope for you.

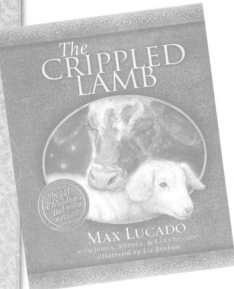

Crafted by master story-
teller Max Lucado with
his three daughters, *The
Crippled Lamb* tells the story
of a little lamb who is different and left behind.
But one starry night, he
learns a lesson that is true
for us all: "Don't be sad . . .
God has a special place for
those who feel left out."

Available at bookstores everywhere or
online at www.thomasnelson.com